# The Kids'
# World Almanac®
# of History

**Also by Deborah G. Felder**
The Kids' World Almanac® of Animals and Pets

# The Kids' World Almanac® of History

**DEBORAH G. FELDER**
**Illustrated by John Lane**

**WORLD ALMANAC**
AN IMPRINT OF PHAROS BOOKS · A SCRIPPS HOWARD COMPANY
NEW YORK

First published in 1991.

Library of Congress Cataloging-in-Publication Data
Felder, Deborah G.
The kids' World Amanac of history / Deborah G. Felder.
      p.       cm.
Includes index.
Summary: A survey of history, focusing on such aspects as explorers, inventions
and discoveries, disasters, people, and the arts.
ISBN 0-88687-496-3 : $14.95. — ISBN 0-88687-495-5 (pbk.) : $6.95
    1. History—Juvenile literature.    [1. History.]    I. Title.
D10.F38  1991                                                  91-3708
900—dc20                                                          CIP
                                                                  AC

Pharos Books are available at special discounts on bulk
purchases for sales promotions, premiums, fundraising or educational
use. For details, contact the
Special Sales Department,
Pharos Books,
200 Park Avenue, New York, NY 10166.

Printed in the United States of America

Pharos Books
A Scripps Howard Company
200 Park Avenue
New York, NY 10166
10 9 8 7 6 5 4 3 2 1

Interior design: Typography Too, Annapolis, Maryland

## Dedication

For my father, a true history buff;
for Lisa Novak, a true friend;
and for you, the readers,
who make history every day.

# Contents

# Acknowledgements

My thanks to Hana Lane, John Lane, Robin Langley Sommer, Sue Iacuzzi, and the librarians of the Russell Library in Middletown, Connecticut, for their invaluable help, creative input, and patience during the various stages of this book.

# CHAPTER 1

# Explorers

. . . . . . . . . . . . . . . . . . . . . . . . . . . . . . . . . . . . . . . . . . .

Who were the first people to set foot in America? How did the
Pacific Ocean get its name? Why did an entire American colony of
over 100 people simply vanish? What great moment in space
exploration took place in July 1969? As you explore this chapter,
you'll discover the answers to these questions, plus fascinating
facts on the greatest explorers and explorations in history.

# Who *Really* Discovered America?

As you probably know, it's often said that Italian explorer Christopher Columbus discovered America. He was definitely a very important explorer, but people had explored and settled the Americas *before* 1492, the year Columbus sailed on the first of his four voyages to the New World. The time in history before Columbus arrived in America is known as the pre-Columbian era.

## The First Discoverers and Settlers of America

| | |
|---|---|
| Between 18,000 and 14,000 B.C. | It's believed that the first Americans walked across a land bridge (an isthmus later broken by the Bering Strait) from Siberia to Alaska. They spread through North, Central, and South America. But evidence found at Puebla, New Mexico, in 1967 suggests that people arrived in America even earlier—35,000 to 40,000 years ago. The first Americans were hunters who used flint weapons and tools. |
| 8000 B.C. | Carbon-14 dating tests have shown that people were living near what is now Front Royal, Virginia; Kanawha, West Virginia; and Dutchess Quarry, New York. |
| 7000 to 600 B.C. | Farming cultures were founded in Mexico, and crops such as corn and squash were developed. |
| 1500 B.C. to A.D. 1535 | The great Indian civilizations of Mexico and Central and South America flourished. They included the Olmecs, Zapotecs, Mayans, and the Incas of South America. These civilizations were conquered and destroyed by the Spanish conquistadors (conquerors) in the 1500s. |

c. 200 B.C. to
A.D. 400

The Hopewell Culture flourished. This was the most notable ancient American Indian (Native American) culture. Most of these Indians lived in what is now southern Ohio, but there were also related groups in Michigan, Wisconsin, Indiana, Illinois, Iowa, Kansas, Pennsylvania, and New York. The name comes from the Hopewell Farm in Hamilton County, Ohio, where the first site, a group of burial mounds, was explored. The people of the Hopewell Culture were farmers, hunter-gatherers, and fishers.

# 9 Pre-Columbian Explorers of the Americas

**HSI AND HO, Chinese Astronomers—c. 2640 B.C.**
Hsi and Ho were ordered by Emperor Huang Ti to make astronomical observations in the land of Fu Sang—the lands to the east of China. Hsi and Ho sailed across the Pacific Ocean to the Bering Strait and down the North American Pacific coastline. They stayed with the "Yao people," ancestors of the Pueblo Indians, who lived near the Grand Canyon. Hsi and Ho also visited what is now Mexico and Guatemala before returning to China. A Chinese geographical text and a chronicle mention the journey of Hsi and Ho.

**HUI SHUN, Chinese Buddhist Priest—A.D. 458**
Some scholars claim that Hui Shun of China sailed to Alaska and journeyed on foot down the North American Pacific coastline to

PRE ~ COLUMBIAN

SIBERIA

ALASKA

MIGRATION ROUTE OF FIRST AMERICANS

C A N A D A

UNITED STATES

BAFFIN BAY

HUDSON BAY

HOPEWELL AREA

MAYANS

ZAPOTECS

INCAS

SOUTH

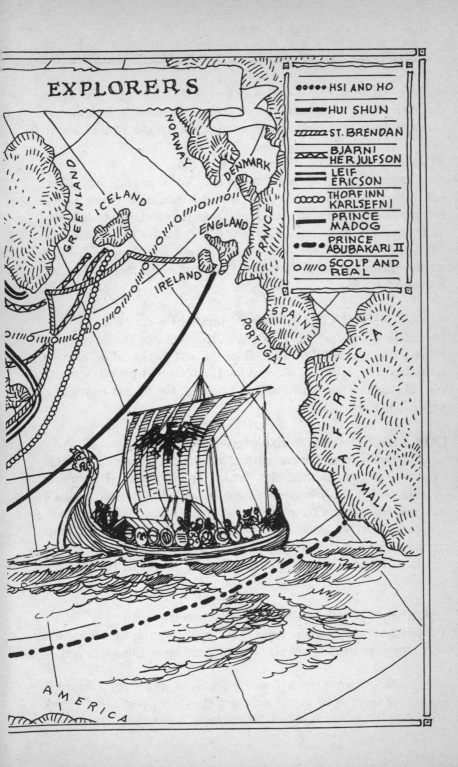

EXPLORERS

HSI AND HO
HUI SHUN
ST. BRENDAN
BJARNI HERJULFSON
LEIF ERICSON
THORFINN KARLSEFNI
PRINCE MADOG
PRINCE ABUBAKARI II
SCOLP AND REAL

GREENLAND
ICELAND
NORWAY
DENMARK
ENGLAND
IRELAND
FRANCE
SPAIN
PORTUGAL
AFRICA
MALI
AMERICA

Mexico. There he taught and preached Buddhism to the Indians of the region. It's also said that he named Guatemala in honor of Gautama Buddha (an Indian philosopher, the founder of Buddhism).

## ST. BRENDAN, Irish Priest—c. A.D. 550

St. Brendan is said to have sailed west in a curragh (a leather-hulled boat still used in Ireland) with 17 monks. In seven years, they traveled to Iceland, Greenland, and Newfoundland, and may even have reached Grand Cayman Island in the Caribbean Sea. *The Voyage of Saint Brendan the Abbot* and *The Book of Lismore* are two manuscripts of the Middle Ages that tell the story of St. Brendan's travels.

## BJARNI HERJULFSON, Norse Merchant—A.D. 986

Two Icelandic sagas* of the Middle Ages say that Herjulfson was blown off course while sailing from Iceland to Greenland to visit his father. He sighted a forested land, which was probably northern Labrador or southern Baffin Island, but he did not consider it worth exploring.

## LEIF ERICSON, Norse Explorer—1003

Ericson sailed from Greenland to North America with a 35-man crew. It's thought that he first landed at Baffin Island, opposite Greenland. He also landed at a place he called "Vinland," which was probably northern Newfoundland. Some scholars think "Vinland" may have been Virginia, Nova Scotia, or New England, but most scholars agree that Leif Ericson did land somewhere in North America. When he returned to Greenland in 1004, he received the honorary name "Leif the Lucky."

## THORFINN KARLSEFNI, Norse Explorer—1010

According to two Icelandic sagas, Thorfinn Karlsefni, Leif Ericson's brother-in-law, tried to set up the first permanent European settle-

* *Icelandic sagas were written in the 12th and 13th centuries. They were records of the historic or legendary people and events of the heroic age of Norway and Iceland.*

ment in Vinland. A son, Snorri, was born to Thorfinn and his wife in Vinland. Snorri was the first European child to be born in America. Thorfinn traveled to Long Island, the Hudson River, and may have reached the Chesapeake Bay. In 1014, the settlers sailed back to Greenland, because of Indian attacks.

## PRINCE MADOG AB OWAIN GWYNEDD,
### Welsh Prince—1170 and 1190

A respected Welsh historian of the Middle Ages and two noted seventeenth-century historians claim that Prince Madog of Wales sailed across the Atlantic in 1170. He landed somewhere in the Americas and built a settlement. The site of the settlement may have been in what is now Florida; Mobile, Alabama; or the West Indies. Madog left 120 men in the new colony and sailed back to Wales. When he returned to the settlement in 1190, he discovered that most of his men had been killed, probably by Indians. Madog died in the New World soon after his return.

## ABUBAKARI II, King of Mali—1311

King Abubakari was a Muslim from the West African country of Mali. Arab historical and geographical documents of the Middle Ages and Malian oral epics say that he sailed across the Atlantic to Northeastern South America. He and his crew landed in Panama in Central America, and they may have traveled south, settling in the Inca Empire of South America.

## JOHANNES SCOLP, Danish Sea Captain
### and JOAO VAZ CORTE REAL, Portuguese Nobleman—1476

This expedition to North America was set up by King Alfonso of Portugal and King Christian I of Denmark. They wanted Scolp and Real to find a sea route to China. The Danish-Portuguese fleet sailed across the Atlantic to Labrador and explored Hudson Bay, the Gulf of St. Lawrence, and the St. Lawrence River. They couldn't find a sea passage to Asia and sailed back to Denmark. No one in Denmark or Portugal paid much attention to the discoveries of Scolp and Real.

# Explorers' Hall of Fame

| EXPLORER NATIONALITY | YEAR AND MAJOR DISCOVERY/EXPLORATION |
|---|---|
| **John Cabot** Italian Employed by England | **1497:** North American coast, Cape Breton Island, Newfoundland. |
| **Vasco da Gama** Portuguese | **1497–1499:** Da Gama rounded the Cape of Good Hope, continued up the west coast of Africa, and sailed across the Indian Ocean to India. His voyage opened up a route to the wealth of the East. |
| **Amerigo Vespucci** Italian | **1499:** Discovered the mouths of the Amazon River. |
| **Vasco Nuñez de Balboa** Spanish | **1513:** Marched across the Isthmus of Panama and discovered the ocean later called the Pacific. |
| **Juan Ponce de León** Spanish | **1513:** Explored the Florida coast to Key West. Legend has it that he was seeking a spring with waters having the power to restore youth—the so-called Fountain of Youth. De León had also sailed with Columbus on the Admiral's second voyage in 1493. |
| **Hernando Cortés** Spanish | **1519:** Explored Mexico. He arrived at Tenochtitlan (now Mexico City), the capital of the Aztec empire, in November. He took the Aztec ruler, Montezuma, hostage, and tried to govern the empire through him. Eventually, the Aztecs rebelled, fought the Spanish, and lost their fight and their empire. |
| **Ferdinand Magellan** Spanish | **1520–1521:** Explored the Rio de la Plata (Silver River) between Argentina and Uruguay and discovered the present-day Straits of |

| EXPLORER NATIONALITY | YEAR AND MAJOR DISCOVERY/EXPLORATION |
|---|---|
| | Magellan and Tierra del Fuego at the tip of South America. Despite the terrible hardships of the journey and the mutiny of some of his officers, Magellan rounded the continent. He reached the Marianas and the Philippines, where he was killed during a fight between two groups of natives. |
| **Giovanni da Verrazano** Italian Employed by France | **1532:** Explored the North American coast, probably from North Carolina to Maine, and possibly New York Bay. |
| **Francisco Pizarro** Spanish | **1532:** Explored Peru. Pizarro was seeking the fabled wealth of the Incas. He climbed the Andes Mountains to Cajamarca. There he seized Atahualpa, ruler of the Incas with his half-brother, Huascar. Pizarro demanded and received a huge ransom for Atahualpa and then had him and Huascar killed. |
| **Jacques Cartier** French | **1534:** Canada, the Gulf of St. Lawrence, Magdelan Islands, Prince Edward Island (first called Isle Saint-Jean). Like other explorers, Cartier searched for and failed to find the Northwest Passage said to cut through North America to Asia. |
| **Alvar Nuñez Cabeza de Vaca** Spanish | **1536:** Texas coast and interior, probably New Mexico and Arizona, and possibly California. Cabeza de Vaca and his men were the first non-Native Americans to see buffalo. |
| **Hernando de Soto** Spanish | **1539–1541:** De Soto and his crew were on a treasure hunt for gold, silver, and jewels. They landed on the Florida coast, probably near Tampa Bay. They traveled through the Carolinas and Georgia to Tennessee and then |

| EXPLORER NATIONALITY | YEAR AND MAJOR DISCOVERY/EXPLORATION |
|---|---|

south to Alabama. Heading northwest, they were probably the first non-Native Americans to see and cross the Mississippi River. The group continued up the Arkansas River and into Oklahoma, but found no treasure. Back on the banks of the Mississippi, De Soto died, and was buried in the river.

**Francisco Vásquez de Coronado**
Spanish

**1540–1541:** The southwestern U.S.; the Colorado River. Coronado heard stories of the great wealth of the Seven Cities of Cibola (also known as El Dorado) in New Mexico and of Quivara, a kingdom farther to the east. Coronado never found riches among the Indian pueblos, but he and his lieutenants visited and sometimes waged needless warfare with the Indians of the region. One of Coronado's lieutenants, Garcia Lopez de Carderas, discovered the Grand Canyon.

**Martin Frobisher**
English

**1576:** Frobisher's Bay in Canada. Frobisher was seeking the Northwest Passage. Licensed by Queen Elizabeth I and backed by a group of merchant adventurers, he sailed to South Baffin Island. He brought back some black ore thought to contain gold and an Eskimo to prove he had actually reached Cathay (China). The ore didn't contain gold, and nobody thought that Frobisher's discovery was very important. But Frobisher became a celebrity after he commanded a ship in Sir Francis Drake's 1585 expedition to the West Indies. He was also knighted for helping his country defeat the Spanish Armada (naval fleet) in 1588.

**Sir Francis Drake**
English

**1577–1580:** Drake sailed from England with five ships to raid Spanish territories on the

| EXPLORER NATIONALITY | YEAR AND MAJOR DISCOVERY/EXPLORATION |
|---|---|

Pacific coast of the New World (England and Spain were enemies.) Drake's ship, the *Golden Hind*, was the only one to reach the west coast of South America. Drake captured a rich Spanish treasure ship and used its charts to sail farther up the coast, possibly as far as present-day Washington. He was looking for a sea passage to the Atlantic, but he couldn't find one. He did cross the Pacific and visit the Moluccas, the Celebes, and Java. He rounded the Cape of Good Hope and sailed home to England, where he was knighted by Queen Elizabeth I for his exploits.

**Sir Walter Raleigh** **1595:** The Orinoco River and Guiana in South English America. Raleigh was looking for El Dorado, the mythical city of gold and other riches. Raleigh and his men did bring home some specimen ores that contained gold, but El Dorado remained a myth.

| EXPLORER NATIONALITY | YEAR AND MAJOR DISCOVERY/EXPLORATION |
|---|---|
| Samuel de Champlain French | **1603–1609:** Champlain explored the St. Lawrence River in Canada and the New England coast from Maine to Martha's Vineyard. He made the first detailed charts of the coast. He set up a colony at the site of Quebec, which became the capital of New France. In 1609, Champlain accompanied a war party of Huron Indians against the Iroquois and discovered the lake in New York/Vermont that bears his name. |
| Captain John Smith English | **1607:** Explored the territory around the Jamestown settlement of Virginia. Smith was supposedly captured by Chief Powhatan and was about to have his head smashed when Powhatan's daughter, Pocahontas, threw herself on him. Powhatan spared Smith's life. Pocahontas later married a Jamestown settler named John Rolfe and moved to England. |
| Henry Hudson English | **1609–1611:** Hudson was first hired by an English company to find the Northwest Passage from the Atlantic to China, but he was unsuccessful. Then the Dutch East India Company hired him to find it. Hudson, sailing his ship the *Half-Moon*, became the first European explorer to sail up the river later named for him. In 1610, the English financed another expedition to find the Northwest Passage. Hudson entered Hudson Strait between Greenland and Labrador and reached Hudson Bay. He and his crew were forced by ice to winter there. The next summer, his starved and diseased crew mutinied and set Hudson, his son, and seven other men adrift in a small boat without food or water. Hudson and his companions were never seen again. |

| EXPLORER NATIONALITY | YEAR AND MAJOR DISCOVERY/EXPLORATION |
|---|---|
| **Father Jacques Marquette and Louis Joliet** French | **1673:** Governor Frontenac of New France (Canada) sent Father Marquette, a missionary, and Joliet, an explorer, to find a great south-running river (the Mississippi) rumored to be in what is now Wisconsin and Illinois. They reached the upper Mississippi by sailing through the St. Lawrence waterway to the Wisconsin River. The two sailed down the Mississippi beyond the mouth of the Arkansas River, decided that the Mississippi emptied into the Gulf of Mexico, and sailed north again. Marquette and Joliet proved it was possible to sail from the St. Lawrence River all the way south to the Gulf of Mexico. |
| **Robert Cavelier, Sieur de La Salle** French | **1682:** La Salle sailed from the upper Mississippi to the Gulf of Mexico. He took possession of the whole valley for France and called the region Louisiana. |
| **Vitus Bering** Danish Employed by Russia | **1728–1741:** Tsar Peter I of Russia chose Bering to explore northeastern Siberia. Bering sailed north through the strait later named for him. The discovery of the strait proved Asia and America were separate continents. In 1741, on another expedition, Bering sighted Mount St. Elias in Alaska. His lieutenant, Aleksey Chirikov, discovered the Alaskan coast. |
| **Alexander Mackenzie** Canadian | **1789–1793:** Mackenzie, a fur trader, sailed from his headquarters at Fort Chipewyan on Lake Athabaska in Alberta to Great Slave Lake and up a then-unknown river (now the Mackenzie River) to the Beaufort Sea. But he hadn't found a route to the Pacific. In 1793, he set off on another expedition. He and his party sailed up the Peace River and |

| EXPLORER<br>NATIONALITY | YEAR AND<br>MAJOR DISCOVERY/EXPLORATION |
|---|---|
| | the Parsnip River in British Columbia, crossed the Continental Divide, discovered and followed the Fraser River, and headed overland over the Coast Ranges toward the coast. They descended the Bella Coula River in a borrowed dugout to its mouth in a tidal inlet of the Pacific. Mackenzie had completed the first overland journey across North America north of Mexico. |
| **Meriwether Lewis and William Clark** <br>American | **1803–1806:** In 1803, the U.S. bought a large block of American land for $15 million from France—the Louisiana Purchase. President Thomas Jefferson sent Lewis, who was his private secretary, a former soldier, and a fellow Virginian, and Clark, also a Virginian soldier, to explore this vast territory. Lewis and Clark and their party set out from St. Louis and reached present-day South Dakota in 1804. In the spring of 1805, they set out for the West. Their guides and interpreters were a French-Canadian trapper and his Native-American wife, Sacajawea. They crossed the Rockies in Montana and finally reached the Pacific coast in Oregon (outside the purchased territory). Splitting up into two parties for the return, they met at Fort Union and reached St. Louis in September 1806. Despite the hardships of traveling over rough, uncharted terrain, run-ins with rattlesnakes and grizzlies, and skirmishes with Native Americans, the expedition suffered only one casualty—a man who died from an attack of appendicitis. Lewis and Clark's journals, their reports of the Indians they had met and traded with, and the specimens they brought |

| EXPLORER<br>NATIONALITY | YEAR AND<br>MAJOR DISCOVERY/EXPLORATION |
|---|---|
| | back were of great value. The Lewis and Clark expedition paved the way for future American westward expansion. |
| **Ernest Shackelton**<br>British | **1908–1909:** Although many earlier explorers had reached Antarctica, Shackelton pioneered the way to the South Pole by discovering a route that led across the polar plateau. He came within 100 miles of the South Pole. |
| **Robert Peary**<br>American | **1909:** Since 1891, Peary had explored Greenland and the Arctic regions on several expeditions. In 1909, he became the first explorer to reach the North Pole. |
| **Roald Amundsen**<br>Norwegian | **1911:** Amundsen had sailed the famed Northwest Passage through Arctic waters and ice in 1903–1906 and later planned an expedition to the North Pole. When he heard that Peary had beaten him to it, Amundsen decided to try for the South Pole. On December 14, 1911, he and four others became the first people to reach the pole. |
| **Robert Falcon Scott**<br>British | **1912:** Scott and four companions started their search for the South Pole in 1910. When they reached it on January 18, 1912, they found Amundsen's tent and realized the Norwegian explorer had gotten there first. Scott and his men suffered from illness, lack of food, blizzards, and frostbite as they tried to retreat. All five explorers died. |
| **Richard E. Byrd and Floyd Bennett**<br>American | **1926:** Byrd and Bennett flew from Spitzbergen, Norway, across the North Pole—the first aviators to do this. In 1929, Byrd and three others became the first to fly over the South Pole. |

# Christopher Columbus—
# The Superstar Explorer

**Born:** 1451, Genoa, Italy

**Died:** 1506, Valladolid, Spain

**Name in Italian:** Cristoforo Columbo

**Name in Spanish:** Cristóbal Colón

**First Jobs:** Weaver (his father was a weaver and shopkeeper), seaman on the Mediterranean, chartmaker (like his younger brother, Bartholomew), sugar buyer in the Portuguese islands off Africa. It was during this last job that Columbus met ships' navigators and pilots who believed in the existence of islands farther west across the Atlantic. At the age of 31 or 32, Columbus became a master mariner in the Portuguese Merchant service.

**First Voyage, 1492–1493:** It took Columbus eight years to convince King Ferdinand and Queen Isabella of Spain to finance an expedition to the New World. Columbus, three small ships (the *Niña*, the *Pinta*, and the *Santa Maria*, captained by Columbus), and 88 men finally set sail on August 3, 1492. They landed on San Salvador (now part of the Bahamas) October 12. Columbus also discovered Cuba and Hispaniola (now Haiti-Dominican Republic). He set up a colony on Hispaniola.

**Second Voyage, 1493–1496:** Columbus sailed back to Spain on the *Niña*. The Spanish rulers were impressed with his discoveries and honored his contract, which made him "admiral of the ocean sea," and governor general of all new lands he had discovered or would discover. Columbus sailed back to the New World in September or October 1493, with 17 ships and 1,500 men. He also carried long-horned cattle on this voyage. He discovered Dominica, the Leeward Islands, Puerto Rico, and Jamaica, and explored the southern coast of Cuba. He set up a second colony on Hispaniola, since the first had been destroyed by Indians. However, the new colonists were more interested in looking for gold than in organizing a colony. When Columbus tried to enforce strict discipline, some of the colonists rebelled. They seized ships and sailed back to Spain to complain about Columbus's governorship.

**Third Voyage, 1498–1500:** The novelty of the New World was wearing off in Spain, and there were reports of bad conditions in the Hispaniola colony. Columbus's fleet was knocked down to six ships, and he was forced by the Spanish rulers to take convicts as colonists to the islands. Columbus left Spain May 30, 1498, and sailed farther south. At the island of Trinidad (off the coast of present-day Venezuela) he spotted the South American continent on August 15, 1498, and mistook it for an island. He called it Isla Sancta (Holy Island). He entered the Gulf of Pasia and landed, for the first time, on a continent. Then he sailed into the mouth of the Orinoco River, but instead of exploring farther, decided to hurry back to Hispaniola to administer his colony.

In 1500, because there were reports of terrible conditions in the colony, an independent governor, sent by Ferdinand and Isabella, arrived in Hispaniola. He sent Columbus back to Spain in chains.

**Fourth Voyage, 1502:** Back in Spain, Columbus was immediately released from his chains. But he wasn't the celebrity he had been—by this time, other European explorers had sailed to the New World and discovered more of the northeast South American coastline. Columbus's misrule of the Hispaniola Colony didn't help his reputation either. Eager to reestablish his reputation with a fourth expedition, he hoped to sail farther west, past the islands he'd discovered, and find Asia (Europeans had been looking for new trade routes to the East since about 1400). Columbus managed to get four ships and 150 men together and, in 1502, he set sail again. He discovered St. Lucia, Honduras, Costa Rica, and Panama. Columbus tried to get back to Hispaniola, but was marooned on Jamaica for a year. After he was rescued, he was forced to abandon his hopes of reaching Asia. He returned to Spain and died in 1506, his exploits almost forgotten.

**Why Columbus Was an Important Explorer:** Although people had explored America before Columbus, their discoveries were converted into saga, legends, and local history and never acted upon by navigators. Columbus's voyages and discoveries paved the way for other European explorers, conquerors, and settlers and marked a new epoch in American history. Columbus was a remarkable navigator and a person of vision and determination. This combination of skill and persistence in pursuing his dream made him special.

# The Mystery of the Lost Colony of Roanoke

**Where:** Roanoke Island, North Carolina

**When:** 1590 (some sources say 1591)

**The Mystery:** In 1587, Sir Walter Raleigh sent a group of men, women, and children from England to colonize Roanoke Island (a first colony, sent in 1585, had returned to England in 1586). The colony was led by Governor John White and included White's wife, daughter, and granddaughter. (White's granddaughter was Virginia Dare, the first non-Native-American child born in the New World). Added supplies were needed to survive the bitter winter ahead, so White returned to England. But because England was at war with Spain, White couldn't sail back to Roanoke until 1590. When White stepped ashore, all he found was some rusted debris and the word CROATOAN carved into the bark of a tree near the gate of the fort. The letters CRO had been carved into another tree stripped of its bark. The entire colony of over 100 people had totally vanished.

**What Happened to Them?** No one has ever been sure, but experts have come up with several theories. The settlers might have been killed by the Croatoan Indians, but there were no signs of violence. They may have moved to nearby Croatoan Island, where Cape Hatteras is located, or joined the Croatoan or Hatteras Indians. One theory has it that the colony migrated north toward Virginia and settled among peaceable Indians. In 1937–40, about 40 stone tablets, supposedly inscribed with the history of the lost colony, were discovered. The stones tell of the death of many colonists (including Virginia Dare) from disease and Indian attacks and the migration of others to as far away as present-day Atlanta, Georgia. The stones may or may not be a hoax. So the lost colony of Roanoke still remains one of the greatest disappearing acts and mysteries in history.

# Explorers of Africa

### HENRY THE NAVIGATOR (1394–1460), Prince of Portugal— The Patron of Exploration
After Henry helped Portugal conquer Ceuta, on the northern tip of Morocco in North Africa, he became very interested in exploring the continent. He set up a base for explorations in Sagre, Portugal

(1416), and later added a naval arsenal, an observatory, and a school of geography and navigation there. The nearby port of Lagos was used as a harbor for his ships.

Henry's navigators explored the Madeira Islands (1418–1420), and, little by little, the west coast of Africa. These explorations intensified after Henry's captains returned with gold and slaves. From 1444 to 1446, between 30 and 40 ships sailed for the west coast under the prince's authority. His captains discovered the Senegal River (1444), rounded Cape Verde (1444), and reached a point near present-day Sierra Leone. It's said that Henry became concerned by the abuses of the slave trade and forbade the kidnapping of Africans.

Henry's contributions to the art of navigation and the progress of exploration helped Portugal establish its colonial empire and became an important world power in the 1500s.

## RICHARD BURTON (1821–1890)—Explorer in Disguise

Burton was an English explorer, writer, and linguist. He started working for the East India Company in 1842 in India and learned the Persian, Afghan, Hindustani, and Arabic languages. In 1853, wearing various disguises, he journeyed to the holy cities of Mecca and Medina in Arabia. In 1854, he and fellow English explorer John Speke explored Somaliland; Burton continued on alone to Harar, Ethiopia, disguised as an Arab merchant. In Harar, Burton met with the local ruler. From 1857 to 1859, Burton and Speke traveled together to East Central Africa to find the source of the Nile; instead, they discovered Lake Tanganyika. Burton later visited Utah in the U.S., and explored the Bight of Biafra (a bight is a curve in a coastline which forms a large open bay) and Dahomey in Benin, and the Gold Coast. He explored Santos in Brazil and became the British consul at Damascus in Syria and at Trieste, where he died.

## JOHN SPEKE (1827–1864)—Discoverer of Lake Victoria

Speke joined fellow English explorer Richard Burton in expeditions to Somaliland and East Central Africa. Together they discovered Lake Tanganyika in 1858. Then Speke continued on alone and discovered Victoria Nyanza (Lake Victoria, named by Speke for

Queen Victoria) on the Uganda-Tanzania-Kenya border, which he believed to be the source of the Nile River. In 1862, Speke returned to the lake and proved that the Nile originates from the north end of Lake Victoria.

## HEINRICH BARTH (1821–1865)—Traveler to Timbuktu

This German explorer first traveled through the eastern Mediterranean countries (then called the Levant) and North Africa (1845–1847). He entered the service of the British government and joined an expedition to Western Sudan in 1849. He visited the Fulani and Hausa peoples, discovered the upper Benue River, explored the Chad region, then headed through northern Nigeria. Barth was interested in the Islamic culture of western Africa, so he made his way to Timbuktu, where he stayed for eight months. (Timbuktu, in present-day Mali, was a center of commerce and Islamic study. Moslem rulers there had imported Egyptians in the 1200s and 1300s to make Timbuktu a center of trade and learning.)

## DAVID LIVINGSTONE (1813–1873)—Scottish Missionary

From 1841 to 1852, Livingstone was a medical missionary for the London Missionary School in present-day Botswana. While there, he crossed the Kalahari Desert and reached Lake Ngami (1849). In 1851, he discovered the Zambezi River. Livingstone continued his exploration of Africa in the hope of abolishing the slave trade by opening up missionary stations. He followed the Zambezi River and discovered Victoria Falls, then reached the east coast at Quelimane, Portuguese East Africa, in 1856. From 1857 to 1863, Livingstone explored the Zambezi region, then returned to England. He returned to Africa in 1866 to seek the source of the Nile and discovered Lakes Mweru and Bangweula. In 1871, he reached the Lualaba tributary of the Zaire River.

Livingstone became sick and returned to Ujiji on Lake Tanganyika. He was found there by Henry Morton Stanley, a journalist for the *New York Herald*. Stanley had been sent to Africa to do a story on Livingstone. When Stanley finally came face to face with the explorer, he said the now-famous words, "Dr. Livingstone, I presume?" Stanley couldn't persuade the ailing explorer to leave Africa; instead, he accompanied Livingstone on an expedition to the north end of Lake Tanganyika (1871–1872). In 1873, Livingstone died in the village of Chief Chitambo. The explorer's body was carried to the coast by his African followers; it was then sent to England and buried in London's Westminster Abbey.

# Explorers of Asia

### GIOVANNI DE PIANO CARPINI (c. 1180–1252)— First visitor to the Mongol Empire

In 1245, this Italian Franciscan monk was sent by Pope Innocent IV to the Court of the Mongols in China. (The powerful Mongol empire was made up of Mongol tribes which had been unified by Genghis Khan.) Carpini and Friar Benedict of Poland started their journey in Lyons, France, and traveled to the Volga River in Russia, where they found the camp of a Mongol prince. They then traveled across central Asia to the imperial court at Karakorum, where Carpini and Benedict witnessed the installation of Genghis Khan's grandson, Kublai, as the great Khan of the Mongols. Carpini returned to Lyons in 1247 and wrote about his journey. This work, called *Liber Tartarorum*, is a complete and important account of Mongol manners, history, policy, and military tactics. It was the first travel/cultural history book to appear in Europe.

### MARCO POLO (1254?–1324?)—A Favorite of Kublai Khan

In 1271, Marco Polo and two Catholic missionaries traveled with Marco's father, Niccolo, and his uncle, Maffeo, from Venice to

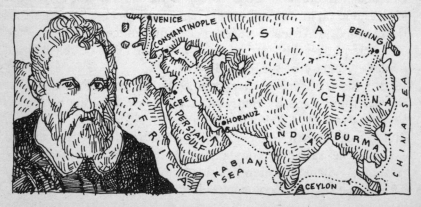

Kublai Khan's court at Kaifeng in Cathay (the Tartar or Mongolian name for China). The missionaries soon abandoned the expedition, which reached Cambuluc (present-day Beijing) in 1275. Marco became a favorite of Kublai Khan, who sent him on many business trips for the empire in Central and North China and in the states of Southeast Asia, including India. For three years, he allegedly ruled the Chinese city of Yanchow.

In 1295, the Polos returned to Venice. Marco joined the Venetian forces fighting Genoa and in 1296 was taken prisoner. During his time as a prisoner, Marco dictated an account of his travels to a fellow prisoner and scribe from Pisa named Rusticiano. *The Travels of Marco Polo* told the wonders Marco had seen in Asia, including paper currency, asbestos, coal, firecrackers, fruit-flavored ices, and noodles.

# Explorer of Australia, New Zealand, and the South Pacific

**CAPTAIN JAMES COOK (1728–1779)—**
**English Discoverer of Hawaii**
In 1768, Cook sailed off on an expedition to chart the transit of the planet Venus. On this trip, he circumnavigated the globe and explored the coast of New Zealand and the east coast of Australia. From 1772 to 1775, Cook commanded a two-ship expedition to the South Pacific. He disproved the theory that there was a huge southern continent, explored the Antarctic Ocean and the New Hebrides, and discovered New Caledonia. In 1776, Cook sailed for the South Pacific again and in 1778 discovered the Hawaiian Islands, which he called the Sandwich Islands, after the Earl of Sandwich. He then searched the northwest coast of North America for a passage to the Atlantic, but failed to find one. On his return voyage, he was killed by Hawaiians at Kealakekua Bay.

Cook's navigator during his first visit to Hawaii was William Bligh, later to become famous as the captain of HMS *Bounty*, scene of the well-known mutiny of 1789.

# Space Exploration
## Highlights in the History of Space Exploration

**1543**  Polish astronomer Nicholas Copernicus published *De revolutionibus orbium Coelestium (On the Revolutions of Celestial Spheres)*, which stated that the earth rotates on its axis and, with all the other planets, revolves around the sun. Before this, people thought that the sun and the planets revolved around the earth.

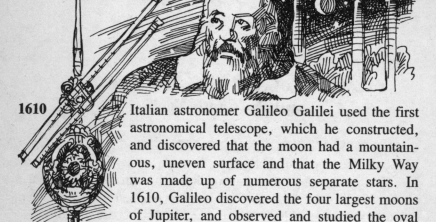

**1610**  Italian astronomer Galileo Galilei used the first astronomical telescope, which he constructed, and discovered that the moon had a mountainous, uneven surface and that the Milky Way was made up of numerous separate stars. In 1610, Galileo discovered the four largest moons of Jupiter, and observed and studied the oval shape of Saturn, the phases of Venus, and spots on the sun.

**1675**  The first observatory, the Royal Greenwich Observatory, was established at Greenwich, England, by Charles II. It was moved to Hurstmonceaux Castle in Sussex in 1948.

**1781**  English astronomer William Herschel discovered a new planet, Uranus.

**1846**  Neptune was discovered by English astronomer John Couch Adams. Soon after, a French astronomer, Urbain Jean Joseph Leverrier, also discovered the planet. He was given sole credit for the discovery, since Adams's sighting had not been published. But later the two men were honored equally for their discovery.

**1926**   American scientist Robert H. Goddard launched the first liquid-fuel rocket and showed that rockets could be used to carry scientific apparatus into the upper atmosphere.

**1930**   American astronomer Clyde Tombaugh of the Lowell Observatory at Flagstaff, Arizona, discovered the planet Pluto.

**Post-World War II**   American and Soviet scientists worked on the development of powerful rockets.

**1957**   On October 4, the first artificial satellite, *Sputnik I*, was launched into space by the Soviet Union.

**1958**   On January 31, artificial satellite *Explorer 1*, was launched into space by the U.S.

**1959**   In September, *Luna 2*, launched by the Soviet Union, made a hard landing on the moon. In November, *Luna 3* took pictures of the moon's far side as it flew by.

**1961**   Soviet cosmonaut Yuri Gagarin became the first man in space.

**1963**   Soviet cosmonaut Valentina V. Tereshkova, aboard *Vostok 6*, became the first woman in space.

**1968**   American astronauts Frank Borman, James A. Lovell Jr., and William A. Anders, aboard *Apollo-Saturn 8*, made the first flight to the moon. They didn't land, but views of the lunar surface were televised to the earth.

**1969**   American astronauts Neil A. Armstrong, Edwin "Buzz" Aldrin Jr., and Michael Collins, aboard *Apollo-Saturn 11*, became the first humans to land on the moon. They stayed for 21 hours, 36 minutes, 21 seconds and collected 48.5 pounds of soil and rock samples.

**1971**     On November 13, the unmanned U.S. space probe *Mariner 9* became the first to orbit Mars. It sent back over 7,000 photos of the planet.

**1972**     *Pioneer 10*, an unmanned U.S. probe, was launched on March 3. It contained a special plaque so designed that if extraterrestrial beings in a remote solar system should find it, they could calculate the location of Earth in our solar system. It also contained an illustration of male and female humans. *Pioneer* passed Jupiter in 1973 and sent back close-up pictures of the planet. On June 14, 1983, it exited the solar system.

**1973**     The first American manned orbiting space station, *Skylab 2*, was launched.

**1975**     *Viking 1* was launched on August 20. It landed on Mars July 29, 1976. This unmanned probe did scientific research and sent photos of the surface back to earth.

**1981**     The first U.S. Space Shuttle, *Columbia*, was launched.

**1983**     The first U.S. woman astronaut, Sally Ride, was launched into space aboard the first *Challenger* Space Shuttle.

**1990**     The Hubble Telescope was launched from Cape Canaveral, Florida, on April 25. It is hoped that over the next 15 years, the telescope will show five to ten trillion objects in space, including stars at birth, galaxies in their infancy, planets of other stars, and age and size of the universe, and possibly, the fate of the universe.

# CHAPTER 2

# Inventions and Discoveries

This chapter features facts on history's major inventions and discoveries. But you'll also get the inside story behind the invention of such everyday household and personal items and appliances as dishwashers, toasters, toothbrushes, and band-aids. There's also a lineup of looney inventions that will probably *never* be used in anyone's household!

# Inventors' Hall of Fame

| INVENTOR/<br>NATIONALITY | YEARS/<br>INVENTION(S) |
|---|---|
| **Arkwright,<br>Richard**<br>English | **1732–1762:** Water-frame machine for spinning cotton. Arkwright and his partner, Josiah Strutt, set up huge cotton mills using these machines and helped to start the factory system. |
| **Babbage,<br>Charles**<br>English | **1792–1871:** The analytical (calculating) machine, a forerunner of modern computers. |
| **Baird,<br>John Logie**<br>Scottish | **1888–1946:** The first practical television; transatlantic television; color television; the noctovisor, an instrument that used infrared light to make objects visible in the dark or through fog. |
| **Bell,<br>Alexander Graham**<br>American | **1847–1922:** Telephone. On March 10, 1876, Bell, a former teacher of the deaf, uttered the first words transmitted through a telephone apparatus, ''Watson, come here; I want you.'' |
| **Braille,<br>Louis**<br>French | **1809–1852:** The Braille raised-dot system of printing and writing for the blind. Louis Braille, blind since the age of 3, formulated his system at the age of 15. |
| **Daguerre,<br>Louis**<br>French | **1789–1851:** The Daguerrotype, a photograph produced on a silver-coated copper plate and developed with mercury; the diorama. |
| **Daimler,<br>Gottlieb**<br>German | **1834–1900:** Gasoline-powered automobile, 1889. Daimler's improvements to the internal combustion engine contributed a great deal to the development of the auto industry. Daimler also invented the motorcycle. |

| INVENTOR/ NATIONALITY | YEARS/ INVENTION(S) |
| --- | --- |
| **Eastman, George** American | **1854–1932:** Roll film and the Kodak camera (1888); color photography (1928). |
| **Edison, Thomas Alva** American | **1847–1931:** The superstar inventor. Edison invented the transmitter and receiver for the automatic telegraph, the phonograph, light bulb, light sockets, safety fuses, underground power conductors, founded the first electric light power plant in the world at Pearl Street in New York City (1881–1882), built and operated an experimental electric railroad (1880), built an iron and nickel storage battery, developed the kinetoscope (a forerunner of movies), and showed how moving pictures and sound could work together. As a kid, Edison had been a terrible student, and no one—except his mother—thought he would amount to much as an adult. |
| **Franklin, Benjamin** American | **1706–1790:** The Franklin stove; bifocal glasses; a glass harmonica; the lightning rod. |
| **Fulton, Robert** American | **1765–1815:** Fulton was a gunsmith and painter as well as an inventor. He is best known for inventing the first commercially successful steamboat, the *Clermont*, launched in 1807. |
| **Gutenberg, Johann** German | **c. 1397–1468:** Printer believed to be the first European inventor of movable type (similar printing had been done earlier in China and Korea). Because of movable type, more books could be printed; earlier books had been handwritten—a long, slow process. |

| INVENTOR/ NATIONALITY | YEARS/ INVENTION(S) |
|---|---|
| **Huygens, Christiaan** Dutch | **1629–1695:** The pendulum clock. Huygens got the idea from Galileo's theory of the pendulum. |
| **Laennec, Dr. Rene** France | **1781–1826:** The stethoscope. He described this instrument and the symptoms he found while listening through it in a book on the subject. |
| **Langley, Samuel Pierpont** American | **1834–1906:** Experimental power-driven model aircraft with a light engine (1896) which proved that flight was mechanically possible. He built another flying machine which he tried, unsuccessfully, to launch over the Potomac River in 1903. Langley was laughed at for his attempts. In 1914, the airplane was rebuilt with a higher-powered engine, and it was flown. Langley, an astronomer and physics professor, had received only a high-school education. He had continued his studies on his own at Boston libraries. |

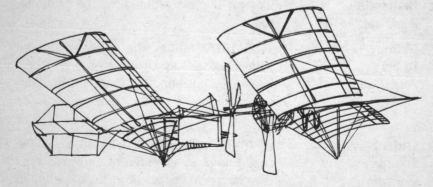

| **Marconi, Guglielmo** Italian | **1874–1937:** The wireless telegraph (1895). Marconi, a physicist, was experimenting with homemade apparatus and sent longwave signals over a distance of more than a |

| INVENTOR/ NATIONALITY | YEARS/ INVENTION(S) |
|---|---|
| | mile. He received the 1909 Nobel Prize in physics for his work in wireless telegraphy. |
| McCormick, Cyrus American | **1809–1884:** The reaper. The invention of this harvesting machine meant that farmers no longer had to harvest their grain by hand. Actually, McCormick's father had started work at his blacksmith shop on the reaper, but had given it up. |
| Montgolfier, Joseph and Jacques French | **1740–1810, 1745–1799:** The first practical hot-air balloon. On June 5, 1783, the Montgolfier brothers sent up a large linen bag inflated with hot air. The flight covered more than a mile and lasted 10 minutes. Later that year, a manned Montgolfier balloon sailed over Paris. |
| Morse, Samuel American | **1791–1872:** The magnetic telegraph; Morse code. Morse demonstrated his telegraph to Congress in 1844 by transmitting the now-famous message, "What hath God wrought?" over a wire from Washington, D.C., to Baltimore. Inventors in Europe had worked on the telegraph before Morse and there had been earlier codes very similar to his, but he has always received credit for the invention of both. |
| Nobel, Alfred Swedish | **1833–1896:** Dynamite. Nobel, a chemist working in his father's small weapons factory, was looking for a safer, more easily controlled explosive. He put together nitroglycerine and a substance called kieselguhrdiatomite and called it dynamite. He also invented an explosive gelatin more powerful than dynamite. Nobel began to feel uneasy about the potential wartime |

| INVENTOR/ NATIONALITY | YEARS/ INVENTION(S) |
|---|---|
| | uses of these deadly weapons. He left a fund in his will for Nobel Prizes to be given to outstanding people for their work in physics, chemistry, medicine, literature— and for their efforts in promoting international peace. |
| **Otis, Elisha Graves** American | **1811–1861:** The first automatic-elevator safety brake (1852) and the first passenger elevator (1857). Otis's inventions made it possible for skyscrapers to be built. |
| **Sholes, Christopher** American | **1819–1890:** In 1867, Sholes and his associates, Samuel Soule and Carlos Glidden, invented the first practical commercial typewriter. It was manufactured by Philo Remington and put on the market in 1874. This typewriter had only capital letters. Early typewriter users included writers Mark Twain and Henry James, and Dr. Sigmund Freud, the founder of psychoanalysis. |
| **Sikorsky, Igor** American | **1889–1972:** The helicopter. |
| **Trevithick, Robert** English | **1771–1833:** In 1800, Trevithick invented a high-powered steam engine. His steam carriage debuted on Christmas Eve, 1801, and his steam locomotive was the first, used in Wales on a railway in 1804. Trevithick also developed steam engines for use in mines and invented a steam threshing machine. |
| **Watt, James** Scottish | **1736–1819:** The steam piston engine, 1769. Watt improved on Thomas Newcomen's steam engine of 1705. These were the first steam engines. Watt also made up the |

| INVENTOR/ NATIONALITY | YEARS/ INVENTION(S) |
|---|---|
| | word *horsepower,* and the watt, a unit of electrical power, was named for him. |
| **Whitney, Eli** American | **1765–1825:** The cotton gin, 1793. This machine separated cotton fiber from the seeds of the plant, so that cotton could be processed more quickly. |
| **Wright, Orville Wright, Wilbur** American | **1871–1948, 1867–1912:** Motorized airplane. The Wrights used their bicycle shop and factory to build their planes. On December 17, 1903, at Kitty Hawk, North Carolina, they made the first flights in a power-driven airplane. The first flight, made by Orville, lasted 12 seconds, and the fourth, made by Wilbur, covered 852 feet in 59 seconds. |
| **Zworkyin, Vladimir Kosma** American | **1889–1982:** Modern TV picture tube; icono-scope, the forerunner of today's TV camera. |

# Inventions Closer To Home

## AIR CONDITIONING

The term "air conditioning" was reportedly coined by physicist Stuart W. Cramer, who studied humidity control in textile mills. This control of the moisture content in textiles had been known as "conditioning the air." Cramer created a popular expression by turning this phrase into the compound noun, air conditioning.

The air conditioner was invented by engineer Willis Carrier in 1911. Carrier used a conventional steam heater modified so that it would accept cold water and circulate cold air. His air conditioner also decreased humidity.

The first air-conditioned movie theatre opened in Chicago in 1919. By 1930, over 300 U.S. theaters were advertising "cool air" in huge letter on their marquees. The first air-conditioned department store was New York's Abraham and Straus (1919).

## BLENDER

This popular kitchen mixing machine was invented by Stephen J. Poplawski of Racine, Michigan, in 1922. Poplawski designed the machine so that he could easily mix his favorite drink—malted milkshakes.

## BROWN PAPER GROCERY BAG

Charles Stillwell, a former Civil War soldier, invented this simple item we can't do without. In 1883, Stillwell came up with a machine to produce paper bags. Earlier bags had been pasted together by hand, and their V-shaped bottoms kept them from standing on their own. They also couldn't be folded easily or stacked conveniently. Stillwell's bag was flat-bottomed, and its sides were pleated. He called it the S.O.S.—"Self-Opening Sack."

## CAN OPENER

The first patented can opener was invented by Ezra J. Warner of Waterbury, Connecticut, in 1858. It had a large, curved blade that had to be driven into the top of a can, then worked around the inside of the rim. The U.S. military used Warner's can opener during the Civil War.

The modern, hand-operated can opener with the cutting wheel that rolls around the can's rim was invented by William W. Lyman in 1870.

## IRON

The ancient Greeks used a heated bar that looked like a rolling pin to press pleats into garments and remove creases. The Romans used a flat metal mallet that hammered out wrinkles. Ironing was done by slaves in Roman times. The Vikings of the tenth century came up with an iron that looked like an upside-down mushroom and was rocked back and forth on damp clothes. Pleats were the hot fashion in Viking times: in fact, that was how you could tell how well-to-do someone was. Peasants didn't have the time or the servants to iron pleats into their clothes.

In the 1400s, rich Europeans used "hot box" irons, which had compartments for heated coals or a hot brick. Less wealthy families used flat irons—a piece of metal with a handle that was heated from time to time over the fire. But soot from the fire frequently got onto the clothes. Families in the 1800s used gas-heated irons, which sometimes leaked, exploded, or caused fires. In 1882, inventor Henry W. Weely received a patent for his invention—the electric iron. But his iron heated up slowly and few households had electricity at that time. The electric iron was perfected by a meter reader named Earl Richardson in 1905, and in 1926, electric steam irons came on the scene.

## CLOTHES WASHERS AND DRYERS

It's not clear who actually invented washing machines. Everyone had to wash clothes, so people were probably always looking for ways to make their chore easier. On sea voyages, men washed clothes by placing them in a cloth bag with a rope attached, throwing the bag overboard, and letting their laundry toss and turn in the sea for several hours.

Early popular washing machines were tubs in which a device called a "dolly" was placed. The dolly resembled a stool, had legs, and was used to pummel clothes and squeeze water from them. In the early 1800s, people in Western Europe used wooden boxes as washers. They were operated by a hand-held crank, which tumbled the box around and agitated the clothes. Around 1915, electric, motor-driven washers appeared in England and the U.S. Automatic washers similar to those we have today arrived in 1939.

Dryers were the brainchild of a French inventor, M. Pochon. In 1800, he came up with the "ventilator," a circular metal drum pierced with holes. Hand-wrung clothes were placed into the ventilator, which was hand-cranked and rotated over an open fire.

## DISHWASHER

In 1886, Josephine Cochrane, a wealthy woman who lived in Shelbyville, Illinois, patented her design for a dishwashing machine. This labor-saving device had individual wire compartments for plates, saucers, and cups, and the compartments fastened around the circumference of a wheel that stood in a large copper boiler. A motor turned the wheel and allowed hot soapy water to squirt up from the boiler's bottom onto the dinnerware. Mrs. Cochrane's dishwasher won the highest award at the Chicago World's Fair in 1893.

## GASLIGHT

Natural gas is, well, natural, and is found under the ground. The Chinese burned natural gas 3,000 years ago to evaporate brine and produce salt. Early fire-worshipping tribes built temples around natural gas jets, lighting them to produce eternal flames.

In the 1600s Belgian chemist Jan Baptista van Helmont first manufactured coal gas. His work later inspired French chemist Antoine Lavoisier to think about lighting the streets of Paris with coal gas. He had constructed a lamp in the 1780s, but before his scheme could be carried out, the French Revolution occurred, and he was guillotined.

In 1813, the first gas company was established in London and home gas lamps began to appear. By 1860, clean, efficient, inexpensive gas was lighting homes, factories, and streets.

## KITCHEN RANGE

Early ranges were set up in brick nooks by a large open fireplace and had heated tops. British inventor John Silothrope patented a large metal cooking range in 1630. It was fired by coal, which would soon replace wood as the favored family fuel. But the slower-heating, free-standing cooking range took awhile to become popular. In 1802. British iron founder George Bodley came up with a cast-iron, even-heating, coal-powered, closed-top kitchen range that contained a flue. This was the standard range model in kitchens until the 1900s. German inventor Fredrick Albert Winson was the first to develop the gas-powered range (1802). Gas was a cleaner fuel than coal, but until the 1830s, gas ranges leaked fumes and sometimes exploded. Electric stoves appeared in 1890, but their thermostats were crude and electricity was very expensive at the time. Most homes didn't have it.

## LAWN MOWER

If it hadn't been for English textile-plant foreman Edwin Budding, families might still be mowing lawns with scythes (crescent-shaped blades with handles). In 1830, Budding adapted the new rotary shearing machine into a 19-inch roller mower. It had rotating cutters that operated against fixed ones. Large, horse-drawn versions of this mower appeared in the 1860s, and hand-pushed rotary mowers became popular in the 1880s. The gasoline-powered mower was developed by Edwin George, a U.S. Army colonel, in 1919. He installed the gasoline motor from his washing machine into a hand-pushed, roller-blade mower.

## MATCHES

In 1826, an English apothecary (pharmacy) owner, John Walker, was stirring up some chemicals in his laboratory with a stick. He saw that a drop of a chemical mixture of antimony sulfide, potassium chlorate, gum, and starch had stuck to the end of the stick. He scraped the stick against the stone floor to remove the drop, and the drop burst into flame. He later made some three-inch-long sticks tipped with this mixture and ignited them for friends by pulling them between a sheet of coarse paper. Samuel Jones, who had observed one of Walker's demonstrations, set up a match-manufacturing business. He called his matches "Lucifers."

The Lucifer Match became popular with Londoners, but the French found its chemical smell unpleasant. In 1830, Charles Sauria, a French chemist, came up with matches that used primarily phosphorus. This removed the smell and made matches burn longer. But phosphorus was poisonous, and many match-factory workers developed a bone-poisoning disease called "phossy jaw."

In 1911, the Diamond Match Company developed a nonpoisonous match.

The matchbook was invented in 1892 by American attorney Joshua Pusey. But he placed the striking surface on the *inside* cover of the matchbook, which sometimes caused all 50 matches to ignite. The Diamond Match Company bought Pusey's patent in 1895 and moved the striking surface to the *outside* of the matchbook.

## MICROWAVE OVEN

Microwave ovens work by the use of electromagnetic energy, which agitates the water molecules in food and produces enough heat to cook the food quickly. The electronic tube (called a magnetron) that produces microwave energy was invented by English scientists John Randall and Dr. H.A. Boot in 1940. It was used in Britain's radar defenses during World War II.

In 1946, Raytheon Company engineer Dr. Percy Spencer discovered that the magnetron could cook foods. A few years later, Raytheon brought out the Radar Range which, because of its large size and tangle of tubes, wiring, and cooking fans, was used mainly by restaurants. In 1952, the Tappan Company produced a more compact microwave oven for family use.

## NYLON

Jackets, bags, tents, socks, and underwear are just some of the things made from this popular synthetic fabric. Nylon thread was invented in 1934 by a research chemist named Wallace Hume Carothers, who was working for the Du Pont Company. Carothers invented the thread by squeezing a chemical solution through a hypodermic needle. Originally known as Polymer 66, nylon was first used for stockings and toothbrush bristles.

## PINS

Around 3000 B.C., the Sumerians, an ancient civilization in the southern part of Mesopotamia (the area between the Tigris and Euphrates Rivers, around present-day Iraq), fashioned straight pins of iron and bone. The ancient Greeks used straight pins made of ivory and bronze to adorn hair and clothing.

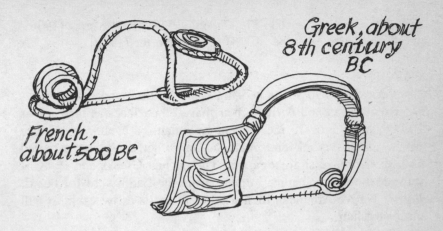

Greek, about
8th century
BC

French,
about 500 BC

U-shaped pins, the ancestors of today's safety pins, originated in Central Europe about 1000 B.C.. This pin was made of bronze and had its point cradled away in a curved iron. Greek and Roman women of the sixth century B.C. used a fibula—a pin with a coiled middle that produced tension and provided the fastener with a springlike opening action. The safety pin, with the point completely covered by a metal sheath, was invented in three hours in 1825 by New Yorker Walter Hunt. In 1832, Hunt also invented a sewing machine that could sew a straight seam, but only for a few inches.

## PLASTIC
The first plastic material was Celluloid, a chemical mixture of nitrocellulose and camphor. Celluloid was developed around 1850 by Alexander Parkes, an English natural science professor. At the time, Celluloid was considered a useless novelty, and Parkes sold the patent for it to John Westey Hyatt, an Albany, New York, printer. Hyatt first used Celluloid to make billiard balls. By 1890, there were Celluloid collars, cuffs, shirtfronts, combs, hand mirrors, jewelry, and kids' toys. The camera's inventor, George Eastman, introduced Celluloid photographic film, and Thomas Edison thought that Celluloid could be used to make motion-picture film.

As plastics became more sophisticated, other polymers (synthetic chemical compounds) were spun off from them, including cellophane (1912), acetate (1927), vinyl (1928), plexiglas (1930), acrylicsa (1936), styrene (1938), and polyester (1940).

## RAZOR

Cave drawings and sharpened flints and shells found at gravesites show that Asian and African men shaved their faces as far back as 20,000 years ago. To the ancient Egyptians, a clean-shaven face was a status symbol, and pharaohs and other nobles were buried with their bronze straight razors. The ancient Greeks and Romans shaved; the word "barber" comes from the Latin word for beard, *Barba*. Native-American men used clam shells as tweezers to pull out beard hair.

The safety razor was invented in 1762 by a French barber, Jean Jacques Perret. It had a metal guard on one edge of the blade. The T-shaped razor made its debut in the 1880s in the U.S. Disposable blades were the brainchild of traveling salesman-inventor King Gillette in 1895. Gillette developed his idea with the help of Professor William Nickerson of the Massachusetts Institute of Technology, who had invented a push-button system for elevators. In 1903, the first razors with disposable blades went on sale. Gillette's invention eventually made him a multimillionaire.

The electric razor was invented in 1931 by Jacob Schick and contained a small electric motor. The electric shaver was slow to catch on, but eventually it became popular.

## SEWING MACHINE

In 1830, a French tailor, Barthelmy Thimmonier, invented a machine that could sew 200 single-thread stitches a minute. The French government hired Thimmonier to sew military uniforms on his 80 sewing machines. But other tailors felt threatened by this new machine, and an angry mob of them stormed Thimmonier's factory and nearly killed him. Thimmonier fled to a small town, where he died in poverty.

In 1832, Walter Hunt, inventor of the safety pin, constructed a sewing machine, but never patented his invention. In 1846, after five years of work, Boston machinist Elias Howe constructed and patented a sewing machine that could sew 250 firm stitches a minute. The needle on Howe's machine was curved and moved horizontally. Howe also constructed the first machine that could sew leather. In 1851, another Boston machinist, Isaac Singer, invented a sewing machine that, unlike Howe's, could stitch continuously and had a straight needle that moved up and down. It also had a lever that held the fabric in place and a foot-operated treadle (Howe's had a hand-driven wheel).

## TOASTER
In the 1800s, the first device for toasting bread was manufactured in the U.S. It was a "cage" made of tin and wire that sat on the opening in a coal stove and held four slices of bread tilted toward the center. One side of the bread was toasted by the rising heat from the fire; then the pieces of bread were turned over. Electric toasters made of wire appeared in the early 1900s. In 1919, Minnesota mechanic Charles Strite constructed the first pop-up toaster, which he sold to the Childs restaurant chain. The Toastmaster was the first pop-up toaster manufactured for the home. It took some years of technical fine-tuning, however, before pop-up toasters produced toast that was browned evenly on both sides.

## TOOTHBRUSH
The ancient Egyptians used "chew sticks"—pencil-sized twigs with one frayed end—to clean their teeth. Many African tribes still use chew sticks as toothbrushes, and in some parts of the U.S., especially in the rural South, chew sticks are known as "twig brushes."

The first bristle toothbrush originated in China around 1498. The Chinese used bristles hand-plucked from the backs of hogs living in cold climates (the cold weather causes hogs to grow firmer bristles). European traders brought these bristle toothbrushes home with them. In 1770, Joseph Addis, imprisoned in England's Newgate Prison for provoking a riot, saved a small bone from the meat he had been served. He bored tiny holes in the bone, then got some hard bristles with the help of his prison guard. He cut the bristles down, tied them into tufts, put glue on the ends, and wedged them into the holes in the bone. When Addis was released from prison, he manufactured his prison-made toothbrush. It was an instant success.

## UMBRELLA
Umbrellas were used in Mesopotamia and in ancient Egypt, Greece, and Rome as sunshades. The word "umbrella" comes frcm the Latin word *umbra*, meaning "shade." In many present-day African societies, an umbrella bearer walks behind the tribe's chief to shield his head from the sun.

Roman women waterproofed their paper umbrellas—or parasols—by oiling them. Until the 1700s, umbrellas were thought of as accessories for women. In 1750, Jonas Hanway of England decided to prove that umbrellas were for both men and women, and for 30 years he never left his house, rain or shine, without one. Finally, men began to get the message that umbrellas were very practical accessories, and they became popular. In fact, for awhile they were called "Hanways."

## VACUUM CLEANER
In 1899, John Thurman of St. Louis, Missouri, patented his "pneumatic carpet renovator," a motor-driven, carpet-vacuuming machine.

*vaccuming about 1870*

In 1901, English inventor H. Cecil Booth came up with a filtering bag made of tightly woven cloth that would trap dust better and cause air to be suctioned up inside the machine. Booth's first commercial vacuum cleaner was about the size of a present-day refrigerator. It contained a pump, a dust-collection chamber, and a power unit, and it had to be moved along on a dolly. Two people were needed to operate it: one to steer the dolly and another to work the long, flexible hose. One of Booth's first cleaning assignments was to vacuum the carpet at Westminster Abbey for the coronation of Edward VII. The church's cleaning staff was amazed at the amount of age-old dust Booth's machine vacuumed up.

## VELCRO

Velcro was the brainchild of Swiss mountaineer Georges de Mestral. While on an Alpine hiking trip in 1948, de Mestral became annoyed by the burrs that constantly clung to his pants and socks. Then he realized that he might be able to use this "clinging" principle to create a new kind of fastener.

The only expert who thought that de Mestral's idea was possible was a weaver at a textile factory in Lyons, France. Using a tiny loom, he created two strips of cotton fabric, one with tiny hooks, and the other with smaller eyes. This "locking tape" stuck together until it was pulled apart. By the 1950s, nylon was used for this tape instead of cotton. De Mestral called the new product "Velcro," from the French words for "velvet," *vel,* and "hook," *crochet.*

Today Velcro has many uses as a zipperlike fastener: securing gear and spacesuits in the zero-gravity environment of space, fastening clothing and diapers here on earth, and sealing chambers of artificial hearts.

## WHEEL

This important object first came into use during the Bronze Age (about 3500 B.C.), when people began to use oxen and horses to pull carts. Some sources say that the Europeans introduced it to Native Americans during the age of exploration. But no one is sure who actually *invented* the wheel.

## ZIPPER

In 1893, Chicago mechanical engineer Whitcomb Judson invented two chains with hooks and eyes that could be fastened together by pulling a slider up between them. Judson intended his invention to take the place of boot lacings and buttons on high-button shoes. He patented his device as a "clasp locker or unlocker for shoes."

In 1913, engineer Gideon Sundback invented a smaller, lighter, and more reliable fastener that became more popular than Judson's. In 1923, B.F. Goodrich came out with rubber galoshes that used the new "hookless fasteners." It's said that the name "zipper" came from the *zip* sound the fasteners made.

# 7 Patented Inventions
# That Haven't Made It—
# and Probably Never Will

● The eyeglass frame with adjustable rearview mirrors—so that you can see yourself coming and going.

● A fluid-operated zipper.

● A carry-all hat that contains a compartment for carrying small items.

● The baby-patting machine. This machine is supposed to put a baby to sleep by the use of a mechanical hand that pats the baby's backside from time to time.

● The electronic snore depressor. Every time this machine detects a snore, it electrically shocks the snorer.

● A better mousetrap. The mouse trips a sensor that causes a chamber to lift up and dump the rodent into a plastic bag, causing suffocation.

● A shampoo called "Skunked" that can wash skunk spray out of fur, hair, and clothing.

# Some Major Scientific Discoveries and Inventions

| DISCOVERY | YEAR | DISCOVERER | NATIONALITY |
|---|---|---|---|
| Anesthesia (ether) | 1842 | Crawford W. Long | American |
| Artificial heart | 1982 | Robert Jarvik | American |
| Bacteria | 1676 | Anton van Leeuwenhoek | Dutch |
| Blood circulation | 1628 | William Harvey | English |
| Calculus | 1670 | Isaac Newton | English |
| Classification of plants and animals | 1735 | Karl Linnaeus | Swedish |
| Computerized tomography (CAT Scan) | 1973 | Alan Macleod Cormack, Godfrey N. Hounsfield | British |
| Cyclotron | 1930 | Ernest O. Lawrence | American |
| DNA (deoxyribo-nucleic acid) | 1951 | Frances Crick, James Watson, Maurice Wilkins | English American English |
| Electron | 1897 | Joseph J. Thompson | English |
| Falling bodies, law of | 1590 | Galileo Galilei | Italian |
| Fahrenheit temperature scale and mercury thermometer | 1714 | Gabriel Fahrenheit | German |
| Fire | c. 12,000 B.C. | Unknown | Unknown |
| Geometry | c.300 B.C. | Euclid | Greek |

| DISCOVERY | YEAR | DISCOVERER | NATIONALITY |
|---|---|---|---|
| Gravitation, law of | 1687 | Isaac Newton | English |
| Heredity, laws of | 1865 | Gregor Mendel | Austrian |
| Holograph | 1948 | Dennis Gabor | British |
| Human heart transplant | 1967 | Dr. Christiaan Barnard | South African |
| Insulin | 1922 | Fredrick Banting, Charles Best, J.J.R. Macleod | Canadian Scottish |
| Intelligence testing | 1905 | Alfred Binet, Theodore Simon | French |
| Isotopes, theory of | 1912 | Frederick Soddy | English |
| Laser, first working model | 1960 | T.H. Maiman | American |
| Light, speed of | 1675 | Olaus Roemer | Danish |
| Light, wave theory | 1690 | Christiaan Huygens | Dutch |

| Motion, laws of | 1687 | Isaac Newton | English |
|---|---|---|---|
| Neutron | 1932 | James Chadwick | English |

| DISCOVERY | YEAR | DISCOVERER | NATIONALITY |
|---|---|---|---|
| Nuclear fission | 1939 | Otto Hahn and other physicists | German |
| Nuclear reactor | 1942 | Enrico Fermi and other physicists | American |
| Oxygen | 1774 | Joseph Priestley | English |
| Ozone | 1840 | Christian Schönbein | German |
| Penicillin | 1929 | Alexander Fleming | Scottish |
| Periodic table of elements | 1869 | Dmitri Mendeleev | Russian |
| Planetary motion, laws | 1609 | Johannes Kepler | German |
| Quantum theory | 1900 | Max Planck | German |
| Radar | 1904 | Christian Hulsmeyer | German |
| Radar, first practical | 1934–1935 | Robert Watson-Watt | English |
| Radioactivity | 1896 | Henri Becquerel | French |

Albert Einstein

| | | | |
|---|---|---|---|
| Radium | 1898 | Pierre and Marie Curie | French |
| Relativity theory | 1905 | Albert Einstein | German |

| DISCOVERY | YEAR | DISCOVERER | NATIONALITY |
|---|---|---|---|
| Robotics | 1962 | The Rand Corp., IBM | American |
| Test-tube baby | 1978 | Patrick Steptoe, Robert G. Edwards | British |
| Vaccines | | | |
| measles | 1954 | John Enders, Thomas Peebles | American |
| polio | 1953 | Jonas Salk | American |
| polio, oral | 1955 | Albert Sabin | American |
| rabies | 1885 | Louis Pasteur | French |
| smallpox | 1796 | Edward Jenner | English |
| Xerography (photocopying) | 1938 | Chester Carlson | American |
| X-ray | 1895 | Wilhelm Roentgen | German |

# The Origins of 6 Popular Medical Aids

• **Alka-Seltzer,** the well-known fizzing pain and indigestion reliever, was developed by Miles Laboratories and debuted in 1931. Its original ingredients were aspirin and baking soda. In the mid-1970s, Miles brought out the Alka-2 Antacid tablet, which was aspirin free. (Aspirin irritates the stomachs of many people.)

• **Aspirin,** acetylsalicylic acid, is probably the most popular pain reliever in the world. Before aspirin was developed, people used salicin, an extract from the bark of the willow tree and the meadowsweet plant. In 1853, a German chemist, Felix Hoffman, who worked at the Farbenfabriken Bayer drug firm, mixed a batch of synthetic salicin. He hoped it would help ease the pain of his father's rheumatoid arthritis. It worked, and Bayer decided to market the new pain-killer. They took the "a" from *acetyl,* and "spir" from *Spiraea* (part of the Latin name for the meadowsweet plant), and "in" (a popular suffix for medications), and called the new medicine "aspirin." In 1899, aspirin was marketed as a loose powder; tablets appeared in 1915.

● **Band-aids** were the brainchild of Johnson & Johnson employee Earle Dickson, who created them around 1920 for his accident-prone wife. He took a small wad of sterile cotton and gauze and placed it in the center of an adhesive strip. Two pieces of crinoline were placed over the bandage's sticky parts and could be stripped off.

● The first person to come up with an idea for **contact lenses** was the 16th-century Italian painter, sculptor, architect, and engineer Leonardo da Vinci. He suggested that the eye could be placed against a short, water-filled tube sealed at the end with a flat lens. The water came in contact with the eyeball and refracted light rays as a curved lens does. French opticians in the 1680s experimented with smooth gelatin that was placed over the eyeball. A small fitted glass lens was fitted over the layer of gelatin. In 1877, Swiss physician Dr. A.E. Fich developed a hard, thick, glass contact lens, which wasn't very comfortable. Plexiglas lenses that covered the entire eyeball appeared in 1936, and in the mid-1940s, American opticians produced the first lens that covered only the cornea.

● Two glass blowers from Pisa, Italy, are said to have separately invented **eyeglasses** in the 1280s. One was Alessandro Spina; the other was Salvino Armato. Armato impaired his eyesight while doing light-refraction experiments. He is thought to have devised thick, curved correcting lenses to improve his sight.

● Before eyeglasses were introduced into China around 1430, Chinese judges wore smoke-colored quartz lenses over their eyes to conceal their expressions in court. These were the first **sunglasses**. They later tinted vision-correcting eyeglasses for the same reason.

In the 1930s, the U.S. Army Air Corps commissioned Bausch & Lomb, an optical firm, to produce glasses that would protect pilots from high-altitude glare. Bausch & Lomb came up with glasses tinted a dark green and soon marketed them to the public as Ray-Ban aviator sunglasses.

# Highlights in the History of Computers

**1833**   English mathematician and inventor Charles Babbage invented the analytical (calculating) machine, a forerunner of modern computers.

**1852**   Lady Augusta Ada Lovelace of England, who worked with Babbage, became the first programmer. She is credited with telling a machine what to do by using punch cards to program algebraic patterns. The U.S. Department of Defense uses a programming language called ADA in Lady Augusta's honor.

**1930**   American engineer and physicist Vannevar Bush built the differential analyzer, one of the earliest computers.

**1943**   The computer Mark I was built at Harvard University. It was huge—over 50 feet long, 10 feet tall, and weighed five tons. It had been built with parts of calculators and adding machines, and it contained 500 miles of wires. Mark I was able to multiply a 25-digit number in seconds.

**1946**   ENIAC (Electronic Numeral Integrator and Computer) was built at the University of Pennsylvania. It was about the size of a school gym and weighed 30 tons. ENIAC was the first electronic computer, and it contained 18,000 electron tubes, 70,000 transistors, and 6,000 switches. The U.S. Army used ENIAC to determine the paths of bullets and bombs.

**1950**   EDVAC, the first computer to use binary arithmetic and store programs, was built at the University of Pennsylvania. It could be programmed like today's computers.

**1951**   UNIVAC I, the first computer to process letters as well as numbers, was built in the U.S. It was also the first computer to be mass produced.

The first computer-animated movies were made at MIT (Massachusetts Institute of Technology).

**1962**     The IBM company developed the IBM 704, a computer that was programmed to play checkers.

**1970**     An all-computer art show took place at New York City's Jewish Museum. The show featured software.

**1974**     The first PC, or personal computer, was developed by the Intel Corporation of California. It had an 8-bit computer on a chip and was called the 8080.

**1976**     CRAY I, the first commercial supercomputer, was developed in the U.S. Named for Seymour Cray of Cray Research, this computer is one of the most powerful in the world today. It can make 200 million calculations per second. The U.S. government has used Cray I to make top-secret weapons research calculations, and the U.S. National Weather Bureau uses the computer to make weather forecasts. The more powerful CRAY 2 computer came out in the 1980s.

**1988**     In November, a computer "virus" spread through many university, military, and corporate computers. A set of instructions was designed to copy itself and spread from computer to computer through networks of shared discs. The virus filled up the memory capacity of computers linked to the 60,000-member Internet network. The computers ran out of memory and became inoperable. However, no information was destroyed. The virus was designed by Cornell University graduate student Robert Morris Jr, who claimed his intention was to test the security of computer systems.

# CHAPTER 3

# War and Peace

· · · · · · · · · · · · · · · · · · · · · · · · · · · · · · · · · · · · ·

Wars have been fought since the beginning of recorded history. People wage war for a variety of reasons: to keep or gain power, territory, or wealth; to spread religious or political ideas; or for independence. Below are some famous wars of the past—why they began and how they ended. There are also descriptions of different types of soldiers, a rundown of military leaders who conquered the most territory, a roundup of superspies, and a lineup of notable citizens of the world who worked for peace and won the Nobel Peace Prize for their efforts.

# Famous Wars in History

**PERSIAN WARS**
**When:** 500 B.C.–449 B.C.
**Opponents:** The Persian Empire vs. the Greek city-states.*
**Who won:** The Greeks
**Why did they fight?:** The Persian Empire, ruled by Darius I, included all of Western Asia and Egypt, but there were a few Greek city-states on the coast of Asia Minor (present-day western Turkey). These city-states rebelled against Darius's tyrannical rule. Athens, Eretria, and the Ionian cities fought the Persians, but were beaten. Darius decided to punish Athens and Eretria and to add Greece to his vast empire. The Persians invaded Greece several times with huge armies and navies, but they were eventually defeated by the Greeks. The Greek victory ended the danger of Persian invasions of Europe and strengthened Greece's position as a developing commercial and naval power.
**Major battles:** Marathon (490 B.C.), in which 10,000 Greek infantrymen (foot soldiers) defeated 20,000 Persian infantrymen, cavalry (horse soldiers), and archers: Thermopylae (480 B.C.), led and won by Darius's son, Xerxes, to avenge the Persian defeat at Marathon; Salamis (480 B.C.), one of the last battles, in which the Persian fleet was destroyed by a Greek force.

**PELOPONNESIAN WAR**
**When:** 431 B.C.–404 B.C.
**Opponents:** Athens vs. Sparta.
**Who won:** Sparta
**Why did they fight?:** These two Greek city-states had been longstanding rivals. The Athenian empire was made up of allied Greek states known as the Delian League (the league's treasury was kept in the Temple of Apollo at Delos). Athens was a naval empire which ruled the Aegean Sea, the shores of southeast Macedonia, Gallipoli and Byzantium (in present-day Turkey),

---

*City-states were communities whose governments controlled the lives of citizens in the city and in the surrounding countryside.*

and many colonies on the shores of the Black Sea. Sparta was a land empire. Its center was the Peloponnesus peninsula, and its chief allies were the cities of Corinth and Thebes. Athens was a democracy, where the people shared in the rulership of the state; Sparta was an oligarchy, ruled by a board of five Ephors, or overseers, elected each year by the drawing of lots. The war began after Athens fought Corinth for the island of Corcyra and the city of Potidaea. Sparta and Athens battled each other until 404 B.C., when Athens surrendered. The Athenian empire was destroyed, and Sparta became the main power in Greece for about 30 years.

## PUNIC WARS (from the Latin *Punicus*, a Carthaginian)
**When:** 264 B.C.–146 B.C.
**Opponents:** Rome vs. Carthage
**Who won:** Rome
**Why did they fight?:** Carthage, a city on the northern shore of Africa, was beginning to control northwest Africa and the islands and commerce of the western Mediterranean. Rome had conquered most of Italy and wanted to expand its empire and break Carthage's hold on the Mediterranean. There were three Punic Wars. The first lasted from 264 B.C. to 241 B.C., and was eventually won by the Romans. Carthage had to pay Rome compensation for the war and give up Sicily. The Second Punic War began in 218 B.C. after the Carthaginian general Hannibal conquered the Spanish city of Sagantum, a Roman ally. Rome declared war on Carthage and won in 201 B.C. Rome owed its success to its stubborn will, excellent military organization, superior economic resources, and its generals. The Third Punic War, 149 B.C.–146 B.C., resulted in the total destruction of Carthage by the Romans. Rome accused Carthage of breaking the peace treaty by keeping King Masinissa of Numidia, a Roman ally, away from the city. Rome declared war and blockaded Carthage, but the city refused to surrender. Roman general Scipio Africanus Minor conquered the city house by house and sold the surviving inhabitants into slavery. Then the city was razed and its site plowed up.

**Cultural fact:** The word "Punic" refers not only to a citizen of Carthage, but to the Phoenician dialect of that city. Carthage had been established by traders from Phoenicia, an ancient nation of the eastern Mediterranean. The Phoenicians were famed as traders and sailors, and they developed an alphabet that was eventually adapted by the Greeks and Romans into the alphabet used for writing English.

## THE CRUSADES
**When:** Between the 11th and 13th centuries.
**Opponents:** European Christians vs. the Moslems of the Holy Land.
**Who won:** The Moslems
**Why did they fight?:** There were nine crusades in all, fought by European kings and warriors who wanted to regain control of the land in which Jesus had lived. The crusaders conquered Jerusalem in 1099, but they were driven out by 1291. The Children's Crusade, led by a French peasant boy, Stephen of Cloyes, set out from Marseilles in 1212. Some sources say that the children were sold into slavery by unscrupulous ship captains. Another group of children traveled from Germany to Italy, where most of them died from disease and hunger. The great Moslem leader during the crusades was the sultan and warrior Saladin. During the third crusade, a famous battle took place around 1189 between Saladin's army and the army of Richard I of England. In 1192, Richard negotiated a treaty with Saladin that gave Christians the right to visit holy places in Jerusalem.

*After the Crusades:* The word "crusade" came to mean any holy mission, especially expeditions sanctioned by the Pope against "heretics" and "heathens," basically non-Christians. The crusades also brought Europe into closer contact with new ways of living and thinking and gave Europeans an expanded knowledge of geography. Venice and other Mediterranean cities became important ports for trading. And the idea of chilvary, a code of behavior among knights, was developed. The code of chivalry stressed bravery, military skills, generosity in victory, piety (religious loyalty), and courtesy toward women.

## HUNDRED YEARS' WAR
**When:** 1337–1453
**Opponents:** England vs. France
**Who won:** The English invaders won several decisive battles, but the French finally drove them out.
**Why did they fight?:** In 1152, Eleanor, the daughter of the French Duke of Aquitaine, married the English King Henry II. The English got the province of Aquitaine (also called Guienne) in southwest France as part of the marriage settlement. Over the years, the French retook parts of Aquitaine. The English kings resented having to recognize the French kings as their feudal lords. King Edward III of England decided to fight for complete sovereignty over Aquitaine. He also wanted to control Flanders (a country that was part of present-day Belgium and France), an important market for English wool and a source of cloth, and he resented France's support of Scotland against England. In 1337, Edward gave himself the title King of France, and in 1339, English forces invaded France.

The Hundred Years' War was fought in France, and the country suffered great misery. Farmlands were destroyed, the population was greatly reduced by war, and bandits terrorized the countryside. The terrible disease of bubonic plague, also called the Black Death, swept through the entire continent. Civil wars in France added to the chaos.

*About the war:* A number of major battles were fought during the long course of the war. Crécy (August 26, 1346) was won by Edward's armies. The French forces outnumbered the English and used crossbows, but the English used a new weapon—the longbow. The six-foot high longbow could shoot ten to twelve three-foot-long arrows a minute over a range of 300 yards. The

smaller crossbow could fire only two arrows a minute. The English also won the Battle of Poitiers in 1356, captured King John II of France, and held him hostage in England. As a result of the Treaty of Brétigny, the English got a large ransom for John, the northern French city of Calais, and practically all of Aquitaine. But the French broke the treaty and renewed the fighting. By 1373, they had won back most of the territory given to the English. In 1415, the English won a decisive battle at Agincourt in Normandy. King Henry V of England personally commanded his outnumbered forces and inspired his knights, longbowmen, and foot soldiers to victory. By 1429, the English and their French allies, the nobles of Burgundy, controlled almost all of France north of the Loire River. But the Burgundian nobles reallied themselves with the French King Charles VII, and by 1453, French forces had taken back all the territory the English had conquered, except Calais. By this time, English nobles were undergoing a power struggle for the throne of England, and the country made no more attempts to conquer France.

## THE FRENCH AND INDIAN WAR
**When:** 1754–1763
**Opponents:** Great Britain vs. France
**Who won:** Great Britain
**Why did they fight?:** The British and French had been engaged in a struggle for colonial North America since 1689. The French and Indian War was the last of a series of four wars. Indian tribes in the region allied themselves with either the French or the British and warred with each other. The decisive battle of this war was fought at Quebec, the stronghold of New France, in 1759. On the Plains of Abraham, British forces led by General James Wolfe defeated the army of French General Louis Joseph de Montcalm. Four days later, Quebec surrendered. Both generals died in the battle. In 1760, the city of Montreal fell to the British. The Treaty of Paris in 1763 ended French control of Canada. Great Britain was firmly in control of the American colonies and Canada, and colonists began to think of themselves as Americans rather than British.

**AMERICAN REVOLUTION—also called the War of Independence and the Revolutionary War**
**When:** 1775–1783
**Opponents:** The thirteen American colonies vs. Great Britain
**Who won:** The Americans
**Why did they fight?:** The colonies wanted independence from Great Britain to develop their own political and economic institutions. The British tightened political control on the colonies and made them pay for their own defense and return tax revenue to Britain. Taxes were levied on molasses and sugar in 1764, and the Stamp Act was passed by Parliament in 1765. The act required the payment of a tax to Britain on a variety of papers and documents, including newspapers. Special stamps had to be attached to the papers and documents proving that the tax had been paid. Colonial leaders such as Samuel Adams and Patrick Henry spoke out against the Stamp Act, and societies like the Sons of Liberty were formed. The Stamp Act Congress was called to protest the fact that colonists were taxed but did not have the right to be represented directly in the British legislature. The cry went up: "No taxation without representation!" The Stamp Act was repealed in 1766, but the colonists were ready to revolt, especially after Parliament passed the Townshend Acts in 1767. The four acts levied taxes on such imports as glass, paint, paper, and tea. The British repeated the Townshend Acts, but kept the tea tax and gave the British East India Company the sole right to sell tea directly to the colonies, undercutting American merchants. In 1773, a group of colonists dressed as American Indians boarded the company's ship in Boston Harbor and dumped hundreds of chests of tea overboard. The British tried to punish the colonists for this Boston Tea Party by closing the port of Boston, but this move only strengthened the colonists' will to revolt.

*The Declaration of Independence:* This famous document, largely written by Thomas Jefferson, was ordered and approved by the Continental Congress, an assembly of delegates from the thirteen colonies, and adopted on July 4, 1776. It declared the colonies separate from Great Britain, offered reasons for the separation, and laid out the principles for which the Revolutionary War was being fought. Signers included John Adams, Benjamin Franklin, John Hancock, and Thomas Jefferson.

*Major battles of the revolution:* The fighting began in 1775 with the Battle of Lexington and Concord in Massachusetts. British troops skirmished with colonial Minutemen (armed civilians, called Minutemen because they were ready to fight alongside regular soldiers at a moment's notice). Several Americans were killed, and the colonists withdrew. Paul Revere, a silversmith and patriot, made his famous midnight ride before this battle, alerting the Americans to the British advance toward them. The Battle of Bunker Hill in Boston in 1775 was won by the British. They drove the Americans out of their fort at Breed's Hill to Bunker Hill after the Americans had run out of gunpowder. Before retreating, the Americans killed a number of British troops. In 1775, George Washington was made commander-in-chief of the continental army. He and his men won early victories at Trenton and Princeton, and he led the American troops to victory in the last great battle of the war at Yorktown, Virginia. There, the British general, Lord Charles Cornwallis, surrendered to Washington.

The Americans were helped in their struggle by French ships and troops, including the French nobleman and general Marquis de Lafayette. They were also aided by Polish military commander Casimir Pulaski and Prussian army officer Baron Friedrich von Steuben.

## THE NAPOLEONIC WARS
**When:** 1803–1815

**Opponents:** France vs. Great Britain, Italy, Spain, Austria, Prussia, Holland, Russia

**Who won:** France, under the leadership of Corsican-born general, then first consul, and later emperor, Napoleon Bonaparte, conquered and occupied the countries mentioned above, except for Great Britain and Russia. The armies of the allied powers of Prussia, Sweden, Great Britain, Austria, and Russia defeated Napoleon, first at the Battle of the Nations at Leipzig, Germany, in 1813, and then at Waterloo, Belgium, in 1815.

**Why did he fight?:** Napoleon was a brilliant military strategist and an inspiring commander. He staged a coup d'etat (an overthrow of the government) in 1799 and had himself crowned emperor by the Pope in 1804. (Actually, he took the crown from the Pope and placed it on his own head.) Napoleon developed a code of laws, the *Code Napoléon* (also called the Napoleonic Code), which served as a model for the legal codes of other countries. But he wanted to establish an empire throughout Europe. He tried to invade England, but his invasion fleet of 1803–1805 was repeatedly struck by storms. In 1812, after his conquests of Italy, Spain, Austria, Prussia, and Holland, Napoleon invaded Russia. The invasion turned out to be a big mistake for Napoleon and marked the beginning of his downfall. Napoleon and his 500,000-strong Grand Army, fought the Battle of Borodino in 1812, in which both sides suffered heavy losses. Napoleon entered Moscow on September 14 and found only a few thousand civilians there—the rest of the citizens had evacuated the city. Fires broke out all over Moscow the next day, possibly set by French looters at first and then spread by Russian incendiaries. The city was almost totally destroyed, and Napoleon and his army were forced to retreat. They marched back across Europe through the snow and bitter cold. Soldiers starved and froze to death during the retreat.

After his defeat at Leipzig by the allies, Napoleon surrendered and was exiled to the island of Elba in the Mediterranean. He gathered a small army together and marched into Paris in 1815. There, he began his "rule" of the Hundred Days. In June, his army was crushed at Waterloo by British forces led by the Duke of Wellington. Napoleon was exiled to the island of St. Helena in the South Atlantic, where he died in 1821.

## WAR OF 1812

**When:** 1812–1815

**Opponents:** The United States vs. Great Britain

**Who won:** The United States

**Why did they fight?:** The U.S. felt that the British were violating American shipping rights by such practices as the impressment of American seamen (the British seized sailors from their ships and forced them into naval service on British ships). The Americans mounted an unsuccessful attack on Canada; the British retaliated by marching on Washington, D.C., and burning the White House. The Battle of Lake Erie was fought between the British and American navies; the U.S. Navy, commanded by Oliver Hazard Perry, won. The greatest victory for the U.S. came at the Battle of New Orleans, in which future president Andrew Jackson was the commanding officer. However, the battle was fought two days after the peace treaty ending the war had been signed. The armies hadn't received this vital piece of information.

**CIVIL WAR—also known as the War Between the States and the War for Southern Independence**
**When:** 1861–1865
**Opponents:** The northern U.S. states (the Union) vs. the southern U.S. states (the Confederacy).
**Who won:** The northern states
**Why did they fight?:** Historians have been arguing about the basic causes of the Civil War for years, but most agree that it grew out of deep-seated differences in the social structure and economy of the North and South. The South was largely agricultural, and its economy and way of life was based on slavery, the terrible practice of buying and selling black Africans as unpaid plantation workers. The South had grown wealthy from the use of slave labor and the manufacture of such agricultural staples as cotton. They believed in states' rights, including the right to secede (separate) from the Union. The North was agricultural, but it was also expanding industrially. Machines were beginning to replace people. The North never had

the huge pool of slave labor that the South had and their economy wasn't dependent on slavery. Political differences between the North and South came to a head over the issue of westward expansion. The question was: should slavery be permitted in the new states and territories or be confined to the South?

*The Road to War:* The division between North and South grew after the Missouri Compromise of 1820 and the Compromise of 1850, both of which set up slave states, free states, and territories that could decide the issue for themselves. The Compromises failed to satisfy leaders on either side of the slavery issue. The only good things to come out of the Compromise of 1850 were California's admittance to the Union as the 31st state and the banning of slavery in the District of Columbia. However, the Fugitive Slave Law, which punished runaway slaves, became harsher. The Supreme Court made the Dred Scott decision in 1857, ruling that a slave did not become free when taken into a free state, Congress could not bar slavery from a territory, and blacks could not be citizens. But abolitionists— people in the North who wanted to ban slavery—were becoming more vocal. Abolitionist John Brown and his "army" attacked proslavery forces at Osawatomie, Kansas, in 1856 and seized the U.S. Armory at Harpers Ferry, Virginia, in 1859. Brown was captured by U.S. Marines and hanged. In 1860, Abraham Lincoln was elected president of the U.S. The South was afraid the new president would enforce abolition. Soon after the election, South Carolina seceded from the Union, followed by eleven other Southern states in 1861. These states set up their own government, the Confederate States of America, and chose Jefferson Davis as president. On April 12, Confederate forces fired on the Union's Fort Sumter in Charleston, South Carolina and captured the fort on April 14. The Civil War had officially begun.

# Some Major Battles and Events of The Civil War

**1861**    On July 21, Confederate forces defeated Union troops at the first Battle of Bull Run, in Virginia. A year later, the South won another victory at the Second Battle of Bull Run.

**1863**    On January 1, President Lincoln issued the Emancipation Proclamation, which freed "all slaves in areas still in rebellion."

Union forces won a major victory at Gettysburg, Pennsylvania, July 1–4. By July 4, the entire Mississippi River was in Union hands.

On November 19, Lincoln gave the Gettysburg Address, which expressed the hope that the nation would emerge freer and more united after the war.

**1864**    Union general William Tecumseh Sherman marched through Georgia. He captured and burned Atlanta on September 1; on December 22, he took Savannah.

**1865**    Confederate general Robert E. Lee surrendered 27,800 troops to Union general Ulysses S. Grant at Appomattox Court House, Virginia, April 9. On April 18, General J.E. Johnston surrendered 31,200 troops to Sherman at Durham Station, North Carolina. The last Confederate troops surrendered May 26.

On April 14, Abraham Lincoln was fatally shot in Ford's Theatre, Washington, D.C., by Confederate patriot John Wilkes Booth.

On December 18, the Thirteenth Amendment, abolishing slavery, took effect.

*After the War:* The Civil War cost more American lives than any other war in history, including World War II. It ended slavery, which was good, but African-Americans, 180,000 of whom had fought bravely as soldiers during the war, were not yet free to participate fully in American life. Racist organizations such as the Ku Klux Klan were formed secretly in the South to terrorize blacks who wanted to vote, and legal segregation continued until the 1950s and 1960s. After the war, the U.S. government began to focus militarily on Americans they felt were hampering the settling of the West—the Indians.

**WORLD WAR I, also called the Great War
and the War to End All Wars**
**When:** 1914–1918
**Opponents:** Great Britain, France, Italy, Serbia, Russia, Japan, and the U.S. vs. Germany, Austria-Hungary, Bulgaria, and Turkey (the Central Powers).
**Who won:** Great Britain, France and their allies
**Why did they fight?:** The road to war began after France lost the Franco-Prussian war of 1870–1871. France had to give Germany $1 billion and the territories of Alsace and Lorraine. The French felt humiliated by this defeat and wanted revenge against Germany. France began to reorganize its armies and to rearm heavily. Meanwhile, Germany became a great political and military power in Europe. The European countries were also constantly at odds over who should control colonial territories in Africa, Asia, and the Middle East, and the Balkan countries such as present-day Yugoslavia and Greece. On June 28, 1914, Archduke Francis Ferdinand, heir to the Austrian throne, was fatally shot as he sat in his car in Sarajevo (in present-day Yugoslavia). The assassin was a Serbian student, Gavrilo Princip, who was one of a group of students who wanted independence for Serbia. Within days, Austria-Hungary declared war on tiny Serbia. Russia, Serbia's ally, mobilized its troops. Germany declared war on Russia and France and invaded Belgium. Great Britain declared war on Germany. Then Italy and Japan joined the war. The U.S. remained neutral for three years, but tensions between it and Germany increased after the 1915 sinking of the British passenger ship *Lusitania*. The ship was carrying many Americans, who perished in the sinking (many experts have said that the *Lusitania* was also carrying arms to Britain). German U-boats (submarines) repeatedly harassed American ships, and in 1917, the U.S. entered the war.
*About the war:* New and deadlier weapons were used in this war, such as poison gas and flamethrowers (developed by the Germans) and tanks (developed by the British), plus hand grenades and water-cooled machine guns. Battles were also fought by submarines and, for the first time, planes. Flying aces like American Eddie Rickenbacker and Germany's Baron von

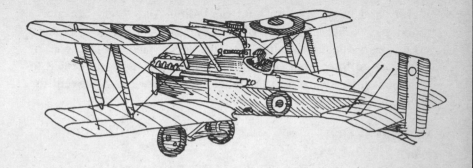

Richthofen (the "Red Baron") became legendary heroes of the war. The war was mostly fought on battlefields in Europe, especially in northern France and Belgium. Few of the battles were planned well by military leaders, and none of them ended with a real, decisive victory for either side. But by the end of 1917, the Allies were beginning to defeat the Central Powers. German war resources were becoming exhausted, severe food rationing in Germany caused hundreds of thousands of civilians to starve to death, and morale collapsed. There were mutinies in the German navy, army, and air force. By November 11, 1918, all the countries of the Central Powers had surrendered to the Allies. The German ruler, Kaiser Wilhem II, abdicated and fled to Holland. Ten million men had been killed in the war and 21 million had been wounded. The war had cost about $350 billion.

*And while all this was going on:* In 1917, the Russian Revolution took place, in which the Bolsheviks, led by Vladimir Ilich Ulyanov (known as Lenin) toppled the monarchy of the Tsars and replaced it with a communist government. In 1918, a worldwide flu epidemic took the lives of about 20 million people.

*After the war:* The Treaty of Versailles, which officially ended World War I, was signed at the Palace of Versailles in France. The main allied leaders at the treaty negotiations were French Premier Georges Clemenceau, Prime Minister David Lloyd George of Great Britain, and U.S. President Woodrow Wilson. The treaty stated that Germany had to dismantle much of its army and navy, give up land (including Alsace and Lorraine), and pay a huge amount of money in war damages. Eastern European countries gained independence, and the League of Nations, a forerunner of today's United Nations, was formed to prevent future wars. But the league was too weak to prevent the *next* World War.

## WORLD WAR II
**When:** 1939–1945

**Opponents:** Great Britain, the U.S., Russia, and France (the Allies) vs. Germany, Italy, and Japan (the Axis).

**Who won:** The Allies

**Why did they fight?:** The major powers of the Axis were Germany and Japan. Germany felt humiliated by its defeat in World War I and had become a poor and demoralized country in the 1920s. The National Socialist (Nazi) Party, led by Adolf Hitler, rose to power in the 1930s. The Nazis promised the German people that Germany would become economically and militarily powerful again. The Nazis created a secret police to crush political and intellectual opponents, and promoted the ridiculous and dangerous idea of a "Master Race" that would rule the world. Only gentiles (non-Jews) of "pure" Aryan (Nordic—Northern European) descent could be part of this "Master Race." The Nazis persecuted Jews, Slavs, communists, gypsies, homosexuals, Christians, the mentally and physically disabled, and other "enemies of the Reich (Empire)," took away their rights, and placed them in concentration camps. The Nazis banned free speech and a free press and secretly began to rearm heavily. They were preparing to spread their military power and their ideas worldwide.

Meanwhile, Japan had invaded China and had sunk the U.S. gunboat *Panay* and three oil tankers. By 1938, relations between the two countries were strained. Japan signed a military alliance with Germany and Italy, and in 1941, invaded Indochina. Japan wanted control of Asia and the Pacific and needed to destroy any U.S. influence in that region. Militarists were in control of the Japanese government and they chose a military, not a diplomatic, solution to this issue.

# Major Events and Battles
# of World War II

**1938**   German troops marched into Austria to "preserve order." Hitler reunited Germany and Austria as a result of this *"Anschluss."*

The British and French allowed Germany to take control of the Sudetenland, a German-speaking area of Czechoslovakia. British prime minister Neville Chamberlain thought Hitler would be satisfied and that there would be "peace in our time." He was wrong.

**1939**   Germany annexed the rest of Czechoslovakia and then invaded Poland. Great Britain and France declared war on Germany. Russia invaded Poland from the east, the result of an agreement between Germany and Russia. The U.S. wanted to stay out of the war, but signed the Neutrality Act, which allowed them to send arms and other aid to Britain and France.

**1940**   German submarines began torpedo attacks on Allied shipping, sinking nearly 4.5 million tons of ships in January and February. Italian dictator Benito Mussolini allied his country with Germany.

Between April 9 and June 22, Germany took control of Norway, Denmark, Luxembourg, Belgium, the Netherlands, and France. A pro-German government was set up in the French city of Vichy. A Free French government in exile, headed by General Charles de Gaulle, vowed to resist the invaders.

In July, German bombers began the Battle of Britain. They dropped a huge number of bombs on London and other strategic and nonstrategic areas of England. The Royal Air Force battled German planes and eventually took control of the skies. The battle resulted in heavy civilian and military losses. The German bombing of

Britain was called the "Blitz." After it failed to subdue the British, Hitler called off plans for an invasion of Britain.

U.S. president Franklin Delano Roosevelt announced an embargo on shipments of scrap metal to Asian countries. This was aimed at cutting off supplies to Japan.

**1941**    On June 22, Germany invaded the Soviet Union, breaking the nonaggression agreement between the two countries.

On December 7, the Japanese air force attacked the U.S. naval base at Pearl Harbor, Hawaii. The U.S., caught by surprise, suffered 2,403 casualties and the almost total destruction of its Pacific fleet. Japan also attacked Guam, Midway, Hong Kong, and Singapore, and declared war on the U.S. On December 8, Congress voted in favor of a declaration of war against Japan.

On December 11, Germany and Italy declared war on the U.S.

**1942**    On January 2, another U.S. possession, the Philippines, fell to the Japanese.

One of the most evil acts of genocide (murder of an entire people) in the history of humankind, the "final solution," was planned by Hitler and several German officers. The plan called for *all* European Jews to be rounded up and killed in concentration camps. About six million Jews, as well as many other prisoners, were murdered before the war was over.

In February, a U.S. plan to place Japanese-Americans in internment camps went into effect. The U.S. government was afraid that Japanese-Americans might help the enemy. Despite this humiliation, Japanese-American soldiers continued to fight for their country, the U.S.

On the Bataan Peninsula of the Philippines, 75,000 American and Philippine troops surrendered to the Japanese. They were forced to walk over 100 miles in the infamous "Bataan Death March." Thousands of soldiers were executed or died of hunger or thirst before they reached Japanese prison camps.

On June 3–6, the U.S. fought and won the Battle of Midway Island.

The U.S. Marines landed at Guadalcanal in the Solomon Islands in August. By February, 1943, U.S. Marines and the navy had taken control of the island.

On August 22, the Battle of Stalingrad took place. This Russian city withstood the German attack and siege for three months. Russian troops eventually pushed the Germans back.

**1943**    In February, U.S. forces in North Africa suffered defeat by the German Afrika Korps of Field Marshal Erwin Rommel. But U.S. troops regrouped under General George Patton and linked up with British forces, led by Field Marshal Bernard "Monty" Montgomery. Their combined armies finally defeated the Germans, who surrendered.

On July 10, the Allies, under the command of General Dwight D. Eisenhower, invaded Sicily, an island off the coast of Italy. From there they launched an attack on the Italian mainland and moved toward Rome. Mussolini was forced to resign, and Italy declared war on its onetime ally, Germany.

**1944**    The U.S. Army Air Corps began a massive bombing of Germany. The historic city of Dresden was almost totally destroyed in 1945, with great loss of life. Dresden was not an important military target, and its destruction raised serious questions about the bombing of civilian population centers.

On June 6, D-Day took place. This Allied invasion of Europe was code-named Operation Overlord and was planned in secret. The Germans knew there was going to be an invasion, but they weren't sure when or where it would occur. The largest invasion force in history—4,000 invasion ships, 600 warships, 10,000 planes, and more than 175,000 troops—attacked the French coastline at Normandy. The Allies suffered very heavy casualties, but forced the Germans back toward Germany. The Allies then began to advance toward Paris and Berlin.

On July 20, a group of German officers tried to assassinate Adolf Hitler with a bomb, but Hitler escaped injury, and the conspirators were arrested and executed.

French troops took control of Paris on August 25.

The U.S. retook Guam and won the Battle of Leyte Gulf, which eventually gave them control, once again, of the Philippines.

In December, the Battle of the Bulge was fought. It was the last attempt of the German Army to defeat the Allies. The armies battled for two weeks in brutal winter weather in the Ardennes Forest of Belgium. Germany lost the battle.

**1945**    At a February conference in Yalta in the Soviet Union, British Prime Minister Winston Churchill, Soviet leader Josef Stalin, and President Roosevelt met to discuss the postwar division of Europe and to agree on a peace organization that would eventually become the United Nations.

U.S. planes firebombed Tokyo, won the Battle of Iwo Jima, and successfully invaded the island of Okinawa. The Battle of Okinawa lasted almost three months and was the bloodiest battle of the Pacific war.

On April 11, U.S. troops met up with Russian forces at the Elbe River in eastern Germany. The next day, Roosevelt died and his vice-president, Harry S. Truman, became president. Soon after, Truman was told about the top-secret Manhattan Project—the development of the atomic bomb.

On April 30, as Russian troops shelled Berlin, Adolf Hitler and his bride, Eva Braun, committed suicide in Hitler's bombproof Berlin bunker.

On May 7, the Germans formally surrendered to General Eisenhower in France and to the Soviets in Berlin.

On August 6, a U.S. plane, the *Enola Gay*, dropped the first atomic bomb on the Japanese city of Hiroshima. The city was leveled, 80,000 people were killed immediately, and 100,000 were seriously wounded. On August 9, the U.S. dropped another atomic bomb on the city of Nagasaki. Many have questioned the necessity of using these bombs to force Japan to surrender.

On September 2, Japanese officials formally surrendered to the U.S. aboard the USS *Missouri* in Tokyo Bay. General Douglas MacArthur, Supreme Commander of Allied Powers in Japan, accepted the surrender. World War II was over.

*After the war:* In November, 1945, twenty-two high-ranking Nazis were put on trial at Nuremburg, Germany, for war crimes. Three were acquitted; the rest were convicted and either executed or imprisoned. A similar trial took place in Japan. Germany was divided into East and West, with the Soviet Union taking control of East Germany. Within a few years the Soviets also dominated the governments of Eastern European countries, such as Poland,

Hungary, and Czechoslovakia. A "Cold War" started between the U.S.S.R. and the U.S., marked by different ideologies (communism vs. capitalism), mutual distrust, and the buildup of weapons, especially nuclear weapons. The two superpowers managed to avoid going directly to war with each other and tried to ease tensions with summit talks and arms treaties. In the 1980s, Soviet-dominated countries in Eastern Europe and some Soviet republics began to rebel against control by the Kremlin (the center of Soviet government).

After the war, China underwent a revolution and became a communist country. In 1948, the Jewish state of Israel was created, and India, once part of the British Empire, became an independent country. The United Nations was formed to provide a forum where member nations could air their grievances and solve problems before resorting to warfare. Agencies of the U.N., such as UNICEF (United Nations Emergency Children's Fund) and WHO (World Health Organization) were created to help people in need worldwide. The U.S., West Germany, and Japan became economic superpowers.

## THE KOREAN WAR—also called the Korean Conflict
**When:** 1950–1953
**Opponents:** The United Nations supported by the U.S. vs. the communist Democratic People's Republic of Korea (North Korea)
**Who won:** Neither side
**Why did they fight?:** At the end of World War II, Korea was divided into two countries, communist North Korea and noncommunist South Korea. In 1950, North Korea invaded South Korea, hoping to unite the countries. The U.N. declared North Korea the aggressor and sent military aid to the South Korean army. General Douglas MacArthur commanded the U.N. troops, who were mostly American. MacArthur was later replaced as commander by General Matthew Ridgway. The U.S. won a major battle at Inchon, but troop reinforcements from the People's Republic of China allowed the North Koreans to regain lost territory. The war dragged on without decisive victory for either side and, in 1953, a truce was signed. The two Koreas remained divided.

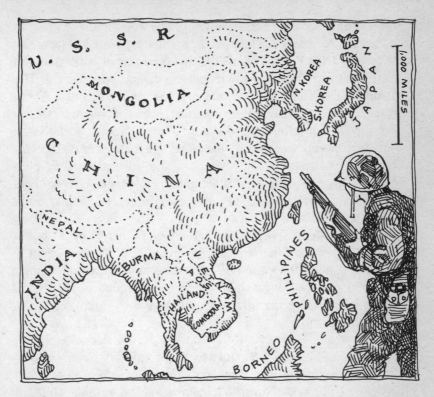

## THE VIETNAM WAR

**When:** 1954–1975

**Opponents:** North Vietnam supported by the Soviet Union and China vs. South Vietnam supported by the U.S.

**Who won:** North Vietnam

**Why did they fight?:** Since the late 1800s, Indochina (Vietnam, Laos, and Cambodia) had been a French colony. Before the end of World War II, the French announced plans for a Federation of Indochina, which would give the states greater self-government. Cambodia and Laos accepted the federation, but Vietnam demanded total independence. In 1947, Vietnamese and French troops began a war which lasted until the French defeat at Dienbienphu in 1954. The French withdrew from the region.

The Geneva Conference, a meeting of representatives from countries concerned in the conflict, including the U.S. and the Soviet Union, divided Vietnam into two countries, North and

South, until elections could be held. The communist north was headed by President Ho Chi Minh, and its capital was Hanoi. In 1955, Ngo Dinh Diem became the first president of noncommunist South Vietnam. The South Vietnamese capital was Saigon. The North wanted Vietnam to reunite as a communist country. About 10,000 North Vietnamese troops had been left in hideouts in South Vietnam after the division. These troops, called the Vietcong, were supported by the North Vietnamese government. The Vietcong first tried to overthrow the government of South Vietnam, then became guerilla fighters. (Guerillas are soldiers who make surprise attacks against enemy targets, then quickly leave the scene.)

U.S. president Dwight D. Eisenhower was fearful that a victory by North Vietnam would create a "domino effect," meaning that all the countries of Southeast Asia would topple, one by one, like dominos, and become communist. The U.S. began to provide economic and military aid to South Vietnam, Laos, and Cambodia.

*About the war:* Between 1961 and 1965, Presidents John F. Kennedy and Lyndon B. Johnson sent military advisors and U.S. Marines to South Vietnam. In 1964, after a skirmish between U.S. and North Vietnamese ships in the Gulf of Tonkin, Congress passed the Gulf of Tonkin Resolution, which allowed President Johnson to respond to any attacks against the U.S. and to prevent further attacks. The Vietcong attacked U.S. bases in South Vietnam, and in March, 1965, the first U.S. combat troops arrived there. Over the next eight years, the U.S. fought a ground war against the North Vietnamese army and Vietcong guerrillas, and U.S. planes bombed North Vietnam and Cambodia. Pilots used Agent Orange, a chemical defoliant, to destroy jungle cover and reveal enemy trails and bases. U.S. bombs and flamethrowers contained napalm, a material that burns intensely and sticks to its target. In the U.S., thousands of demonstrators protested the military draft and the war.

In 1968, the North Vietnamese began the Battle of Khe Sanh (a heavily fortified U.S. base) and then launched the Tet Offensive. Although the U.S. managed to repel the attackers both times and was able to capture the city of Hué, the troops began to realize that the North Vietnamese were determined to defeat them, whatever the cost. Peace talks began in Paris between the U.S. and North Vietnam. In 1969, Ho Chi Minh died. That same year, President Richard Nixon ordered the secret bombing of Cambodia and began to withdraw U.S. ground troops from South Vietnam. This was the first step in a plan called "Vietnamization," which would eventually turn the war over to the South Vietnamese army.

In 1970, the U.S. invaded Cambodia, sparking nationwide protests on college campuses. At Kent State University in Ohio, National Guardsmen opened fire on demonstrators, killing four. In 1971, the South Vietnamese, with American support, began attacking Vietcong supply lines in Laos. In 1972, the North Vietnamese launched a huge offensive into South Vietnam. By 1973, the U.S. had withdrawn all of its ground troops and ended the draft. POWs (prisoners of war) held in Hanoi were released, and Congress passed the War Powers Act, which restricted the president's power to send troops to foreign countries without Congressional approval. In 1974, President Nixon resigned over issues unrelated to the war (see Chapter 5, "World Leaders"). By 1975, North Vietnamese troops had overrun South Vietnam, the last Americans were evacuated from Saigon, and on April 30, communist forces took the city. The country was unified as the Socialist Republic of Vietnam, and Saigon was renamed Ho Chi Minh City.

*After the War:* The Vietnam War was a bloody and emotionally wrenching conflict fought on the ground in the difficult terrain of jungles and swamps. In the 1960s and early 1970s, the U.S. was sharply divided over whether or not the country should have been fighting the war. Many felt that communists were enemies who had to be fought whenever possible; others felt that the communists weren't a threat and that the U.S. should not be fighting the war. Most soldiers simply wanted to serve their country. It was the first war the U.S. had really lost, and for a time, the country just wanted to forget about it. Veterans felt abandoned by the country they had fought for, and many found it difficult readjusting to civilian life. Veteran support groups were formed, and the Vietnam Veterans Memorial was unveiled in Washington, D.C., in 1982. Veterans began to talk publicly about the war to college students and other groups. There are many people in the U.S. who claim that Vietnam is secretly holding American prisoners of war, but the U.S. government has continually denied the claim.

Another result of the war was the immigration of thousands of Vietnamese refugees into the U.S. and other countries, many of which were reluctant to receive them in such numbers.

## The Persian Gulf War—
## also known as Operation Desert Storm
**When:** 1991

**Opponents:** United Nations Middle East and European coalition forces, led by the United States, vs. Iraq

**Who won:** U.N. coalition forces

**Why did they fight?:** Since 1961, Iraq has claimed sovereignty (supreme power) over its neighbor, the small, oil-rich country of Kuwait. In July 1990, Iraq charged that Kuwait had stolen $2.4 billion worth of oil from an Iraqi oil field. Iraq's president, Saddam Hussein, claimed that Kuwait and other Arab states were in a conspiracy with the U.S. to keep oil prices low. In August, Iraq invaded and quickly conquered Kuwait. Iraqi forces began massing along the Saudi Arabian border, and fears that Iraq would invade Saudi Arabia grew. The U.N. condemned the Kuwaiti invasion, trade with Iraq and economic aid was cut off, and the U.S. began sending large numbers of troops to Saudi Arabia (known as "Operation Desert Shield"). The U.N. passed a resolution approving the use of force if Iraq did not withdraw from Kuwait by January 15, 1991. Iraq did not leave Kuwait by that date, and on January 16, coalition air forces attacked Iraq.

*About the war:* The war began with massive air strikes against military and communications targets throughout Iraq and its capital city, Baghdad. Civilian areas were also bombed. Airmen shot down by Iraq were forced to appear on Iraqi TV to condemn the coalition attacks. Iraq launched SCUD missiles against military and civilian targets in Saudi Arabia and Israel. Iraq hoped to draw Israel, an enemy of most Arab countries, into the war and thus break apart the coalition. But Israel, although outraged by the unprovoked attacks, did not enter the war. Patriot missiles were successful in destroying many SCUDs in the skies over Saudi Arabia and Israel. One SCUD hit an army barracks in Dahran, Saudi Arabia, killing 28 soldiers. Fears that the SCUDs (and conventional weapons) carried chemical or biological warheads proved to be unfounded. Iraq dumped millions of gallons of oil into the Persian Gulf and set Kuwaiti oil wells on fire, creating a huge environmental disaster. In February, a ground war began, and within a week, coalition forces had entered Kuwait City. By the end of February, Iraqi troops had been forced out of Kuwait.

*After the war:* The Gulf war was short and coalition casualties were relatively low. These factors, plus the allied victory, prompt release of POWs, and the almost universal condemnation of Saddam Hussein (widely recognized as a dangerous dictator), made this war generally popular. However, anti-war demonstrations did take place in the U.S. and elsewhere. TV news coverage of the war often replaced prime-time shows for millions of viewers, who sat spellbound, watching and listening to correspondents in Baghdad, Saudi Arabia, and Kuwait report on the war each day and sometimes around the clock. In war-torn Iraq, civil war threatened as anti-Saddam groups seized the opportunity to try to overthrow the existing government.

# Military Leaders Who Conquered the Most Territory

**ALEXANDER THE GREAT (356–323 B.C.)**
This young Greek king and military leader conquered about 2,180,000 square miles—an area approximately the size of Australia. His empire included the southern Balkan peninsula, Asia Minor, Egypt, and the entire Near East up to the Indus River. One of Alexander's greatest nonmilitary achievements was the founding of Alexandria, Egypt. The city became famous as a center of culture and learning.

## ATTILA THE HUN (c. 406–453)

This king of the Huns, the people who originated in North Central Asia, was called the Scourge of God by Europeans. Attila and his troops conquered about 1,450,000 square miles of territory in Europe from 433 to 453. Their empire included central and eastern Europe and part of western Russia. During World War I, the Germans were sometimes called "Huns" by Allied soldiers and civilians.

## GENGHIS KHAN (c. 1162–1227)

From 1206 to 1227, this Mongol chieftain conquered about 4,860,000 square miles of territory that stretched from the Pacific Ocean to the Caspian Sea. His empire included northern China, Mongolia, southern Siberia, and central Asia.

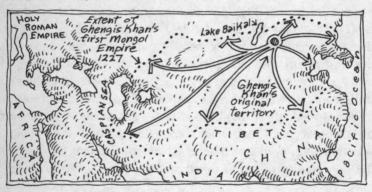

## TAMERLANE (c. 1336–1405)

Tamerlane, a Moslem Mongol chieftain, claimed to be a descendent of Genghis Khan. From 1370 to 1402, Tamerlane conquered about 2,145,000 square miles and created an empire which included most of the Near East from the Indus River to the Mediterranean Sea and from the Indian Ocean north to the Aral Sea.

## HERNANDO CORTÉS (1485–1547)

From 1519 to 1526, this Spanish explorer and military commander conquered the Aztecs of Mexico, seized the central and southern areas of their empire, and forced Guatemala and Honduras to accept Spanish rule. The grand total of his conquests was about 315,000 square miles.

## NAPOLEON BONAPARTE (1769–1821)

This French general and emperor conquered seven countries in Europe from 1796 to 1810, about 720,000 square miles. Napoleon's Grand Empire included France, Belgium, Holland, Italy, Germany (Prussia), Poland, Switzerland, and Spain.

# Types of Soldiers in History

## CAVALRY SOLDIERS

Cavalries were troops trained to fight from horseback. Cavalry was used by the ancient Egyptians, but it was more popular among such ancient Near Eastern peoples as the Hittites, Assyrians, Babylonians, and Persians. The ancient Greeks and Romans also used cavalry. Horse soldiers were especially useful in scouting and in pursuit of a fleeing enemy, but infantry (foot soldiers) were more effective as soldiers until the saddle was introduced in the fourth century A.D. The use of cavalry in Europe came at about the same time, with the invaders from Asia—the Huns, Magyars, Avars, and Mongols. In medieval Europe the knight on horseback became the typical warrior, and under Napoleon, the cavalry soldier became the elite of the fighting forces. Cavalry was also used a great deal during the U.S. Civil War and during the later wars against American Indian tribes.

## CENTURIONS

Centurions were officers of Ancient Rome who commanded a century—a subdivision of a Roman legion. A century consisted of 100 men. A legion was the main unit in the army and was made up of 3,000 to 6,000 foot soldiers and cavalry.

## INFANTRY SOLDIERS

These are soldiers who fight on foot and are equipped with hand-carried weapons. The ancient Greek *phalanx* was the first infantry to be organized into formations—rows of eight to sixteen men, their arms ready, made a solid block that could force its way through the less-organized ranks of the enemy. Infantry fighting grew less important with the emergence of cavalry, but units of pikemen and archers reappeared toward the end of the Middle Ages, because so many battles were being fought in Europe. Infantry fought in mass formations (groups of soldiers advancing at the same time toward the enemy) until the end of the nineteenth century. During World War I, mass-formation fighting gave way to trench warfare. More sophisticated and deadly small arms and artillery made it almost impossible for soldiers to attack in mass formation.

## KAMIKAZES

This Japanese word means "divine wind" and was the name given to the typhoon (hurricane) that destroyed Kublai Khan's fleet, foiling his invasion of Japan in 1281. In World War II, Kamikazes were Japanese suicide pilots, who crashed their bomb-laden planes into their targets, usually ships.

## KNIGHTS

In ancient Athens and Rome, knights (*equites*) were nobles of the second class, who, as soldiers, had to furnish their own horses and equipment. In Rome, knights ranked below senators and above ordinary citizens. A knight forfeited his status if his fortune fell below a certain level. In Medieval Europe, knights were armed and mounted warriors belonging to the nobility. Although all true nobles were knights, knighthood had to be earned. The son of a noble would first serve as page (attendant) to a knight, then as his squire (shield or armor bearer). A knight fighting under another's banner was called a knight bachelor; a knight fighting under his own banner was a knight banneret.

## SAMURAI

Samurai were Japanese knights, aristocratic warriors who arose during the twelfth century. Samurai were allowed to wear two swords, and at one time had the right to kill any commoner who offended them. They established a code of honor and behavior called *bushido,* the way of the warrior. The code stressed absolute loyalty to one's master, personal honor, and the virtues of austerity, self-sacrifice, and indifference to pain. The idea of military *bushido* lasted in Japan until very recent times.

# 8 Super Spies and One Famous Traitor

## BENEDICT ARNOLD—Traitor of the Revolution

Arnold's bravery during battles in the northern colonies and Canada earned him the rank of major general in George Washington's army. He was later court-martialed on four charges of misconduct, a court-martial he requested to disprove these charges. He was condemned on only one charge—misappropriation of army wagons. Arnold became commander of West Point, New York, but did not receive a promotion he had expected. With the help of British major John Andre, Arnold plotted to surrender West Point to the British. His price was £20,000 (English pounds—about $45,000). In 1780, Andre was captured and the plot was revealed. Arnold escaped and fought as an officer in the British Army. After the war, Arnold became a successful businessman in England.

## LYDIA DARRAH—One-Time Spy

In 1777, 15,000 British troops occupied Philadelphia. Darrah eavesdropped on a military meeting held between General William Howe and his officers in her home. She learned of plans for a surprise attack on George Washington and his army, camped nearby at Whitemarsh. She delivered information about the plan to Washington, who was ready for Howe when he attacked.

## NATHAN HALE—Schoolmaster Turned Spy

In 1776, Hale became a captain in Washington's Army and volunteered to spy on the British in New York. Dressed as a farmer, Hale entered enemy territory, drew maps, and recorded troop numbers. A relative of Hale's who worked for the British (American British sympathizers were called ''Tories'') recognized him and betrayed him to General Howe. Hale confessed and was hanged the next day. His famous last words were, ''I regret that I have but one life to lose for my country.''

## BELLE BOYD—''The Rebel Spy''

At the age of 17, Boyd killed a Union officer who tried to raise a U.S. flag over her home in Virginia. She often crossed Union lines with messages she delivered personally to Confederate General Thomas ''Stonewall'' Jackson. She was finally caught and imprisoned, but was sent back to Richmond under a prisoner-exchange arrangement. Boyd continued her espionage work and, before the war ended, married a Union officer whom she sweet-talked into becoming a Confederate agent. After the war, the 21-year-old Boyd toured the U.S. and England to give lectures on her wartime adventures. She was billed as ''The Rebel Spy.''

## EMMA EDMONDS—Mistress of Disguise

During the Civil War, Edmonds, a Union nurse, volunteered for espionage missions. But first she was asked to undergo a ''reading'' by a phrenologist—a person who analyzes someone's personality

by feeling the bumps on his or her head. The phrenologist decided
that Edmonds was capable of keeping a secret. Edmonds disguised
herself as a black laborer and crossed enemy lines into Yorktown,
Virginia, where she was given an axe, shovel, and wheelbarrow,
and put on a construction crew to help build the town's fortifica-
tions. She managed to sketch a map of the fort and noted the
number and size of the enemy's armaments. Then she hid her map
in the bottom of her shoe and walked back to the Union Army.
Edmonds completed ten other spy missions for the North, often
disguised as an Irish peddler woman or as a soldier.

## MATA HARI—Betrayed Spy
Mata Hari was born Margaretha Gertruida Zelle in Holland in
1876. At the age of eighteen, she married a Dutch colonel, Rudolf
MacLeod, and moved to Java with him. MacLeod treated her
badly, so she left him and moved to Paris. There, she joined the
chorus of a vaudeville show and later set herself up as a dancer
with her own act, calling herself Mata Hari. In 1907, she was
recruited by the German Secret Service, who paid for her lavish
lifestyle in exchange for her willingness to spy on the French
military. During World War I, Mata Hari spied for the Germans
and gave them many French military secrets. In time, the Germans,
tired of paying Hari's bills, betrayed her to the French. In 1917,
Mata Hari was executed by a French firing squad.

## KLAUS FUCHS—Russian Spy
During World War II, Fuchs, a German-born physicist, was
Russia's key informant on the development of the atomic bomb.
At the time, information on the bomb was shared only by the U.S.
and Great Britain. In 1941, Fuchs, a communist, was hired by the
British to do nuclear research. He immediately contacted Moscow
and offered his services as a spy. In 1943, he joined the U.S.-
British team that was secretly working on the bomb at Los
Alamos, New Mexico. Fuchs passed information about the bomb
to a Russian contact, who relayed it to Moscow. Fuchs and other
Russian spies involved in this mission were eventually caught.
Fuchs spent ten years in prison, then continued his nuclear re-
search in communist East Germany.

**BANDA MACLEOD—Mata Hari's Daughter**
MacLeod, a bright, outgoing teacher in Java, frequently entertained foreign diplomats, military officers, and journalists. When the Japanese invaded Java during World War II, Banda's uncle, in the service of the Japanese Army, threatened to expose her as Mata Hari's daughter unless she agreed to use her parties to gather information for Japan. MacLeod agreed, but became a double agent—appearing to spy for the Japanese, but actually spying for the Allies. With the help of another double agent and friend, Abdul, MacLeod passed information to the Allies. Through her, the Allies discovered plans for the Battle of Guadalcanal as well as other major Japanese attacks in the South Pacific. In 1950, MacLeod went to North Korea, where she accurately predicted the 38th-parallel invasion of South Korea. She was arrested by the North Koreans and was executed by a firing squad at 5:45 A.M., the same time as her mother had been executed many years before.

Most historians agree that there was a World War II spy named Banda, but some claim that she wasn't the daughter of Mata Hari.

# 10 Nobel Peace Prize Winners

These winners were honored for their efforts to bring peace and comfort during and after wartime or to prevent future wars:

| WINNER NATIONALITY | YEAR/REASON |
| --- | --- |
| **Jean H. Dunant,** Swiss | **1901:** Founded the International Red Cross |
| **International Red Cross** | **1917:** Put into place the Geneva Conventions, a set of international rules that govern the treatment of prisoners, the sick and wounded, and civilians during war; for its work in war relief during World War I. The IRC won the Prize again in 1944 and 1963. |

| WINNER<br>NATIONALITY | YEAR/REASON |
|---|---|
| **U.S. President Woodrow Wilson** | **1919:** For helping to set up the League of Nations, the forerunner of the United Nations. |
| **Fridtjof Nansen**<br>Norwegian | **1922:** Helped prisoners of war and refugees after World War I. Nansen, an Arctic explorer and relief worker, issued an identity card (the "Nansen Passport") which helped refugees find homes and work in new countries. |
| **Carl von Ossietzky**<br>Germany | **1935:** Founded antiwar organizations in Nazi Germany. Ossietzky, a newspaper editor, exposed Germany's secret rearmament. German dictator Adolf Hitler had him arrested and imprisoned in a concentration camp, where he died. |
| **Ralph Bunche**<br>American | **1950:** Negotiated an armistice in the 1949 Arab-Israeli dispute over Palestine, which had become the Jewish state of Israel in 1948. Arabs and Jews had, for the most part, been enemies for centuries, and the Arab countries went to war with Israel over Palestine, which they felt belonged to them. Bunche, an African-American and the grandson of a slave, had become the colonial affairs expert at the U.S. State Department. A skillful diplomat, Bunche successfully concluded an armistice between the seven Arab states and Israel. Bunche later served as undersecretary general of the United Nations. |
| **Lester Pearson**<br>Canadian | **1957:** In 1956, President Gamal Abdel Nasser of Egypt took control of the Suez |

| WINNER NATIONALITY | YEAR/REASON |
|---|---|
| | Canal and banned Israeli shipping there. Israeli, British, and French forces attacked Egypt. Diplomat Pearson created a U.N. peacekeeping emergency force to defuse the crisis. |
| **Dag Hammarskjold** Swedish | **1961:** For his work as secretary-general of the United Nations, 1953–1961. In 1956, he threatened to resign unless the warring forces in the Suez Crisis agreed to let Lester Pearson's peacekeeping force into the area. In 1961, Hammerskjold was killed in a plane crash in Africa. He was awarded his prize posthumously (after his death). |
| **Betty Williams and Mairead Corrigan** Irish | **1976:** Organized a movement called Peace People which sought to end the Protestant-Catholic fighting in British-ruled Northern Ireland. Civil war and terrorist activity has raged in this part of Ireland for many years. Two causes are Protestant-Catholic tensions and the demand of many citizens that the British gave up control of the area. Mrs. Williams, a Protestant, and Mrs. Corrigan, a Roman Catholic, organized peace marches throughout Ireland and England to protest violence. |
| **Menachem Begin** Prime Minister of Israel **Anwar Sadat** President of Egypt | **1979:** For signing an Egyptian-Israeli peace treaty which ended 30 years of war and established diplomatic relations between their countries. The treaty, sometimes called the Camp David Agreement, was spearheaded by U.S. president Jimmy Carter, who convinced the two leaders to come to Washington to discuss an agreement. |

# They Said It
## Quotes From Famous People About War and Peace

*"We must elect world peace or world destruction."*
### —U.S. statesman Bernard Baruch
**in a 1946 address to the United Nations Atomic Energy Commission.**

*"An army marches on its stomach."*
### —Napoleon Bonaparte
**on the need for soldiers to be well fed.**

*"Damn the torpedoes—full speed ahead!"*
### —Admiral David Farragut
**at the Civil War Battle of Mobile Bay, August 5, 1864.**

*"There never was a good war or a bad peace."*
### —Benjamin Franklin,
**in a 1773 letter to Josiah Quincy.**

*"We must all hang together, or assuredly we shall all hang separately."*
### —Benjamin Franklin,
**at the signing of the Declaration of Independence, July 4, 1776.**

*"Man must evolve for all human conflict a method which rejects revenge, aggression, and retaliation."*

**—Martin Luther King, Jr.,**
in his speech accepting the 1964 Nobel
Peace Prize.

*"To the memory of the Man, first in war, first in peace, and first in the hearts of his countrymen."*

**—Henry "Light-Horse Harry" Lee,**
cavalry commander and father of
General Robert E. Lee, on George
Washington, 1799.

*"Give peace a chance."*

**—Title of a song by Beatle John Lennon**

*"In war there is no substitute for victory."*

**—General Douglas MacArthur,**
commander of the U.S. forces in the Pacific
during World War II, in a 1951 address
to a joint meeting of Congress.

*"Sometime they'll give a war and nobody will come."*

**—U.S. poet Carl Sandburg**
in *The People, Yes.*

*"War is cruelty, and you cannot refine it."*

**—William Tecumseh Sherman**
in an 1864 letter to James M. Calhoun,
the mayor of Atlanta.

*"Peace Now!"*

**—Slogan of antiwar demonstrators during**
the Vietnam War.

# CHAPTER 4

# What a Disaster!

Here's a countdown of some of the deadliest disasters in history—
from ten terrible epidemics to one disaster mystery that has never
been solved.

# 10 Terrible Epidemics

**(Epidemics are outbreaks of diseases that strike large numbers of people.)**

**PLAGUE OF JUSTINIAN—Byzantine Empire, A.D. 500–650**
The bubonic plague, a deadly disease spread by rodents and transmitted to humans by fleas, raged throughout the Byzantine Empire during the reign of Justinian I. An estimated 100 million people died of the plague.

**BLACK DEATH—Europe, 1347–1351**
The bubonic plague struck in Europe during the 100 Years' War. Italian sailors carried the disease back to Genoa and other Mediterranean ports from the Crimea in Russia. The sick suffered swellings ("buboes") under the armpits, fever, pain, and bleeding, and they died quickly. The plague spread throughout Europe and killed an estimated 75 million people—about one-quarter of the population. The plague returned several times in the late 1300s, and smaller epidemics occurred until the 1700s. China and India suffered outbreaks of bubonic plague in the late 1800s and early 1900s. Today, the disease is rarely seen.

**ENGLISH SWEATS—England, 1485–1551**
This mysterious disease, which resembled the as yet unknown disease typhus, appeared in London two weeks after Henry Tudor had defeated Richard III at Bosworth Field and become king of

Richard III

England. Headache, chills, fever, chest pains, vomiting, and heavy sweating were symptoms of the disease. It only seemed to strike people of the upper classes and adults more often than children. The epidemic was so severe that Henry postponed his coronation for six weeks. The disease suddenly disappeared, only to reappear in 1507, 1517–1518, and 1528–1529, and 1551. By 1528, the disease had spread to the continent, and by the end of the epidemic, several million people had died of the English Sweats. It's thought that Henry Tudor and his soldiers were carriers of the disease and brought it with them from France, where Henry had lived before the battle.

**SMALLPOX—Mexico and Central America, 1500 and after**
This highly contagious disease was brought to the New World by the Spanish conquistadors. It caused the deaths of several million Indians in Mexico and Central America—possibly as much as half the population. Smallpox has been around since the beginning of human history. The last major epidemic occurred in India and Pakistan in 1967. The U.N.'s World Health Organization mounted a huge campaign in the 1960s to rid the world of smallpox, and by the late 1970s, the disease had been largely eradicated.

Europeans also introduced another disease to Mexican Indians in the 1500s—measles. In the epidemic of 1530–1545, some 1 million to 1.5 million Indians died from measles, to which they had no immunity.

**SAINT ANTHONY'S FIRE—Russia, 1722**
Also called Holy Fire, the scientific name of this disease is ergotism. It's an infection of the nervous system caused by a fungus, ergota, that grows on rye and other cereal grains. In 1722, 20,000 Russians died from eating bread made from diseased rye. Many of the victims were soldiers camped along the Volga River preparing for Tsar Peter the Great's invasion of the western lands. So many troops died that Peter had to call off the invasion.

**CHOLERA—United States, 1832 and 1848–1849**
Cholera is a severe intestinal disease that usually occurs in warm climates and slum areas where sanitation is poor. It comes from

food and water that has been contaminated by raw sewage. In 1832, the disease was brought to Canada from Europe. It then spread to the U.S. In October, a steamboat arrived in New Orleans carrying two men dying of cholera. Within ten days, the disease had spread through the city, killing about 6,000 people. Another epidemic of cholera began in 1848. It started in India in 1847, then spread to Berlin and London, and had crossed the Atlantic by 1848. The disease was brought to the U.S. by European immigrants. Thousands of people throughout the country died as a result of this epidemic.

## THE STRANGE CASE OF "TYPHOID MARY" MALLON— New York, 1906–1915

Mary Mallon, a cook, was the cause of a miniepidemic of typhoid fever in New York. She was immune to typhoid, but she carried the germ in her body and transmitted the highly contagious disease through the food she prepared. By the time she was arrested and quarantined in 1915, Mary Mallon had caused 51 cases of typhoid fever, which included three deaths from the disease. Mary Mallon became a lab technician at a hospital on North Brother Island in New York City and died of natural causes in 1938, aged 70.

## POLIO—United States, 1916 and 1946

Poliomyelitis, or Infantile Paralysis, was a viral disease that often caused paralysis of arms, legs, and the muscles that control swallowing, heartbeat, and breathing. There were outbreaks of the disease all through the first half of the twentieth century, but the worst epidemics took place in 1916 (27,363 cases) and 1946 (25,191 cases). Many people died from the disease, but most became disabled. Those who could not breathe were placed in iron lungs. An Australian nurse, Sister Elizabeth Kenny, came up with a successful physical therapy treatment for polio. Hot, moist applications were used, together with mild exercise, to stimulate paralyzed arms and legs. But the real breakthrough came in 1955, when the first polio vaccine was created by Dr. Jonas Salk. The Salk vaccine and the Sabin oral vaccine (created by Dr. Albert Sabin) of 1960 practically eradicated polio in the U.S.

**SPANISH INFLUENZA—Worldwide, 1918–1919**
No one is sure where this deadly form of the flu (short for "influenza") originally came from, but it was first identified as a virus at Fort Riley, Kansas. The epidemic began there in March, 1918, during World War I, and quickly spread to other army camps across the country. In April the flu hit American soldiers at Brest, France, and then spread throughout Europe and the rest of the world. The flu struck Spain so hard that the disease was named "Spanish Influenza." The only areas of the world that escaped the epidemic were the Atlantic islands of Tristan de Cunha and St. Helena and the Pacific island of New Guinea. By the time the Spanish Flu mysteriously vanished in 1919, over 20 million people had died.

**LEGIONNAIRE'S DISEASE—Philadelphia, Pennsylvania, 1976**
In July, 1976, 29 American Legion conventioneers died of a mysterious respiratory disease in Philadelphia. Fifty others became ill, but survived. In 1977, the "Legionnaire's disease" was shown to have been caused by a bacteria, but no one has ever been sure how the Legionnaires became infected. One theory was that the bacteria had been transmitted through the air vents in the hotel where the convention was being held. Other epidemics of the disease have occurred since 1976.

# 9 Horrible Hurricanes

**JAMESTOWN, VIRGINIA—August 27, 1667**
Jamestown had been founded in 1607 by Captain John Smith and was the first permanent English settlement in the New World. The Jamestown hurricane was the first in American history to be written up. A London pamphlet, *Strange News From Virginia*, described the storm as "The dreadful Hurry Cane."

**GREAT BRITAIN—November 26, 1703**
A fierce storm packing winds of more than 120 mph hit the coast of Wales. The hurricane swept across the island, felling thousands

of trees, stripping tiles off roofs, and toppling chimneys as far east as London. The Eddystone Light, a new and supposedly indestructible lighthouse off the coast at Plymouth, collapsed under the pounding of the waves and fell into the seas. The light's architect was inside the building when it fell. The Royal Navy lost fifteen warships, and one admiral and 1,500 seamen died.

### BENGAL, INDIA—October 7, 1737
In the second-deadliest storm in history, forty-foot sea waves roared up the Bay of Bengal and washed over land at the mouth of the Hooghly River near Calcutta. Thousands of shacks and huts along the coast were destroyed, 20,000 small boats capsized and sank, and 300,000 people were killed.

### LAST ISLAND, LOUISIANA—August 10, 1856
The rain was heavy and waves and winds were rising to hurricane force (74 mph) on Last Island, a sand spit near the mouth of the Mississippi River. But 400 partygoers danced on at a grand ball at the fashionable Trade Winds Hotel. Then, around midnight, the ballroom collapsed into the raging sea. The entire hotel washed away, along with 200 to 300 people.

### FLORIDA KEYS, FLORIDA—September 2, 1935
The full force of this ferocious Labor Day hurricane hit this group of tiny islands, which were linked to the Florida mainland by the Florida East Coast Railway. During the storm, a train set out for Key West, the city at the western tip of the Keys. As the train crossed Long Key above the open sea, a twenty-foot wave broke

over the causeway. The ten-car train overturned and the tracks and bridge were swept away. An estimated 150 people were killed in the incident. As the winds rose to 150–200 mph, destruction throughout the Keys was widespread, and hundreds of people were killed or injured. The rail link to the mainland had been destroyed, and residents had to wait three days until relief boats arrived with supplies and rescue workers.

**NEW YORK AND NEW ENGLAND—September 21, 1938**
People still talk about this fierce hurricane, which struck without warning. It moved across the Atlantic from Africa and headed for the Florida coast. Then it changed course and veered north. The Weather Bureau in Washington, D.C., didn't recognize the storm as a hurricane at first. But winds began to reach nearly 200 miles an hour, and barometers dropped to record lows. At 1:00 P.M. on September 21, the hurricane, with forty-foot waves, slammed into Long Island. After the eye passed over the island, the second half of the storm destroyed more property, including over 150 houses in Westhampton on the Island's East End. The hurricane, still strong, headed north to strike Connecticut, Rhode Island, and Massachusetts. Homes, businesses, and farms were damaged. On Cape Cod and the South Shore of Massachusetts, hundreds of miles of beachfront property were lost to the sea. About 16,000 shade trees in Springfield, Massachusetts, were toppled and four million bushels of apples were destroyed by the storm. The hurricane caused 700 deaths, injured 2,000 people, and made 63,000 homeless. The Weather Bureau, blamed for failing to give proper warning about the storm, was reorganized and new long-range prediction and tracking techniques were developed that would become today's national hurricane warning systems.

**HURRICANE CAMILLE—August 14–22, 1969**
Packing winds of over 170 mph and gusts up to 200 mph, Camille first hit Louisiana, Mississippi, and Alabama. Then it moved on to the mid-Atlantic states, dropping 27 inches of rain in 24 hours over parts of Virginia and West Virginia. Camille caused 255 deaths, mostly in the Mississippi Delta, where many residents ignored storm warnings. One hotel on the Gulf shore featured a "hurricane

party." As partygoers watched the raging storm, 20-foot waves began to batter the building, and the motel was soon smashed to bits.

## HURRICANE AGNES—June 14–23, 1972

First Agnes crossed the Gulf of Mexico from Cozumel Island, off the Yucatan Peninsula, and reached the west coast of Florida. Then it headed north toward New York City. Agnes didn't produce very high winds or waves, but it carried billions of tons of water and caused the worst flooding in U.S. history in five states. The famed Corning Glass Museum in Corning, New York, was totally submerged, and for several days Steuben County was cut off from the rest of the state. In Pennsylvania, the Susquehanna River rose thirty feet above normal, and the river at Wilkes-Barre crested to forty feet, three feet above the flood-control dikes. All told, Agnes flooded 4,500 miles of river and 9,000 miles of streams, and caused flood damage in twenty-five cities. More than 5,000 square miles were covered with water, about 330,000 people became homeless, and there were 122 deaths due to the hurricane.

## HURRICANE HUGO—September 16–22, 1989

Hugo swept through the Caribbean and hit the U.S. mainland in South Carolina. On the Caribbean island of Montserrat, 80 percent of property was destroyed and 99 percent of the island's 12,000 inhabitants became homeless. Looting of destroyed shops and homes became a problem on the Caribbean islands. Hugo's center hit the city of Charleston, South Carolina, with winds of 135 mph, and many historical buildings, along with other properties, were seriously damaged. Property damage was also severe along the South Carolina coast. Hugo caused fifty-one deaths, including twenty-four in the U.S.

# 8 Incredible Volcanic Eruptions

## MOUNT VESUVIUS, ITALY—August 24, A.D. 79

Vesuvius' first eruption blew pumice stone and ash high into the air. Citizens of the coastal city of Pompeii went about their normal business, some holding pillows or large pieces of bark on their heads to protect against falling stones. The eruptions which followed sent sand and lava streaming down from the crater and from other vents on the mountainside. Heavy rain, created by the hot clouds of volcanic dust in the upper atmosphere, created rivers of mud that mixed with lava. This sticky, 20-foot-deep mixture slid down the western slope and buried the city of Herculaneum. Then it was Pompeii's turn. A blizzard of black cinder fell on the city, crushing roofs and walls and suffocating many people in their homes. Pompeii was buried under 20 feet of ash. Some citizens managed to escape by sea, but most were trapped in the city because of damage to the docks and boat landings and the rough seas. An estimated 20,000 people died due to Vesuvius's eruptions.

## MOUNT ETNA, SICILY—March 25, 1669

First, a series of sharp earth tremors destroyed the city of Nicolosi on Sicily, an island off the coast of Italy. Then Mount Etna erupted, causing about 20,000 deaths as hot lava flowed over 14 other cities and towns. The huge wall of lava headed for Catania. About 140 million cubic yards of lava covered the city, in some places to depths of 40 feet. Approximately one million Sicilians have died because of Mount Etna's eruptions since the beginning of history. In 396 B.C., in the earliest recorded eruption, a 24-mile-long, 2-mile-wide stream of lava supposedly halted the invasion of the Carthaginian Army against the Romans.

## MOUNT SKAPTAR, ICELAND—June–August, 1783

After a series of earthquakes, lava flowed out of the 20-mile-long Laki fissure on the side of Mount Skaptar and poured into the Skaptar River Valley. The 50-mile-long valley was buried under 75 feet of lava. Then the lava fanned out over the coast, covering 200 square miles, damming lakes and rivers, destroying crops, and burying 20 villages. Dust, ash, and gases came with the lava flow, causing sulphur dioxide that suffocated livestock, killed plants, and made humans sick. Nearly 10,000 people—one-fifth of Iceland's population—died of starvation in the months following the eruption.

## TAMBORA VOLCANO, JAVA—April 5, 1815

The eruption of this volcano on the Javanese island of Sumbawa removed 4,000 feet from the volcano's summit and created a crater that was seven miles in diameter. It's said that the explosion was heard 1,000 miles away. About 36 cubic miles of volcanic material were blown out of Tambora, and the island was plunged into darkness for three days because of the huge amount of dust and ash in the air. Dust showers fell 900 miles away a week later. Meteorologists today think that the unusually cold and bad weather in the Northern Hemisphere the following year was caused by the eruption of Tambora. Almost one million people died on Sumbawa and the island of Lombox as a result of the eruption.

## KRAKATOA, INDONESIA—August 26–27, 1883

The first eruption of this volcano on the small island of Krakatoa took place at 1:00 P.M. on August 26. The volcano continued to erupt throughout the day and night, covering the land within a 100-mile radius with a thin coating of ash and cinders. Then, at 10:02 A.M. the next day, the volcano exploded with a force that blew about 5 cubic miles of rock ash out of its crater and sent red-hot boulders flying in an arc over the countryside. The sound of this explosion is said to be the loudest noise in recorded history. Many villages beneath the volcano vanished, and a number of ships in the Sunda Strait capsized and sank without a trace. Sea waves of 60 to 120 feet swept over Krakatoa and the islands on either side, Sumatra and Java. The tidal waves killed an estimated 36,000 people. Ash and cinders rained down on 30,000 square miles, and for a year after the eruptions, the amount of sunlight that reached the earth was only 87 percent of normal.

## MOUNT PELÉE, MARTINIQUE—May 8, 1902
Martinique is a resort island in the West Indies. In 1902, a popular vacation spot on Martinique was the sophisticated, bustling seaport of Saint-Pierre. Even though Mount Pelée loomed over Saint-Pierre, everyone in the city felt safe from the volcano, which had remained dormant (inactive) since 1851. But in April, 1902, Pelée began to give off low rumbling sounds. A scouting party headed up to the volcano and saw that lava was filling the crater floor. However, the scouts' report was largely ignored by the government. An election was coming up, and the party in power, the all-white Progress Party, was facing stiff opposition from the popular black Radical Party candidates. The Progress Party wanted to prevent white voters from fleeing the city. The local newspaper continued to stress the harmlessness of Mount Pelée, even though dust, ash, cinders, and gases blew out of the volcano, and a mud avalanche flowed down over a sugar plantation, killing 159 workers. Then, on May 8, Mount Pelée exploded, sending superhot steam, gas, and volcanic dust down onto Saint-Pierre. Only two people in the city of 30,000 survived the eruption.

## MOUNT KATMAI, ALASKA—June 1912
This eruption took place in the Alaska wilderness, but the ash and dust it produced destroyed vegetation 100 miles away at Kodiak and forced the evacuation of that city. Ash and cinder buried an area the size of Connecticut and created a vast wasteland of salt flats, geysers, mineral springs, and gas holes that is today the Katmai National Monument. The eruption was known in Alaska as the Valley of 10,000 Smokes.

## MOUNT ST. HELENS, WASHINGTON—May 18, 1980
The last time Mount St. Helens had erupted was in 1851, but geologists had been keeping an eye on this and other peaks in the Cascade Mountain Range. In March and April, earthquakes caused melted rocks, called magma, to shift inside Mount St. Helens, and a plume of steam and ash rose 6,600 feet above the cone. A bulge

began to grow in the mountain's side. Volcano experts watched carefully for signs that the mountain would split open. Then, on May 18, triggered by an earthquake, Mount St. Helens suddenly blew. Its entire north slope burst open along the upper edge of the bulge, releasing gases and magma and blasting rock and ash out and away from the mountain. Everything within five miles of the volcano was destroyed, and a 150-mile area around the mountain was flattened. Ash and dust dropped over central and eastern Washington, northern Oregon and Idaho, and parts of western Montana. Ranches and home were totally destroyed, 34 people were killed, 27 were missing, and thousands of animals died. Mount St. Helens continued to erupt until 1981 and remained a threat for years thereafter.

# 7 Earthshaking Earthquakes

**SHENSHI PROVINCE, CHINA—January 23, 1556**
This earthquake collapsed high loess (soft clay) cliffs in which million of peasants had carved artificial caves. Over 830,000 people were killed

**SAN FRANCISCO, CALIFORNIA—April 18, 1906**
The most famous earthquake in U.S. history registered 8.3 on the

Richter scale and happened at 5:12 A.M. on April 18. The earth shifted along the San Andreas Fault, causing the collapse of buildings and structures over a 400-square-mile area. Water, gas, and electrical lines broke, causing fires to break out all over the city. The fires destroyed more property and took more lives than did the actual earthquake. More than 75 percent of the city was destroyed, including about 38,000 buildings in a 4-square-mile radius. Up to 1,000 people died and 300,000 were left homeless. A new San Francisco was built on the ruins of the old one, and the city remained safe from a major quake for 83 years.

### ANCHORAGE, ALASKA—March 27, 1964

This earthquake registered 8.4 on the Richter Scale and occurred at 5:36 A.M. A 200,000-square-mile area, about the size of Illinois and Indiana, was shifted by the quake, and in some places, the land was raised 30 feet or more. The energy released by the quake was nearly 10 million times greater than that of the atom bomb that was dropped on Hiroshima in 1945. The city of Anchorage suffered the most damage. There were rock slides, snow avalanches, and landslides around the city, and about 30 blocks of buildings were totally destroyed. Tidal waves wiped out several small settlements and Eskimo villages along the Gulf of Alaska and caused destruction on the west coasts of Canada and the U.S. The death toll was 131.

### NORTHERN PERU—May 31, 1970

At 3:23 P.M. this Sunday, an earthquake registering 7.5 on the Richter Scale rocked northern Peru and destroyed most of the coastal city of Chimbote. The earthquake also touched off an avalanche of ice, rock, and mud from the slopes of Mount Huascarán in the Andes Mountains. The city of Yungay and its 20,000 inhabitants were buried beneath 100 million cubic yards of mud. All told, between 50,000 and 70,000 people died as a result of this earthquake.

### GUATEMALA CITY, GUATEMALA—February 4, 1976

More than 24,000 people were killed and 50,000 were injured in this earthquake, which registered 7.5 on the Richter Scale. The first shock occurred at 3:04 A.M., collapsed thousand of poorly constructed buildings, and cut communication lines and highways linking the government with outlying areas. A series of violent aftershocks did more damage and further hindered relief efforts. It was estimated that one-sixth of Guatemala's six million people were made homeless by the quake.

## TANGSHAN, CHINA—July 28, 1976
The Chinese had been successful in predicting earthquakes before, but this one struck without much warning. Just before the first tremor, at 3:42 A.M., the sky over Tangshan lit up in a display of flashing multicolored lights that was seen up to 200 miles away. When the quake occurred, fences and roads moved several yards out of line, and many people were thrown six feet into the air. Rows of buildings collapsed at the same time, like houses of cards. Railroad lines became twisted tangles of iron, trees were uprooted, and deep, craterlike sinkholes were formed. The quake, measuring 7.8 on the Richter Scale, killed 655,000 people and injured 780,000. An area about the size of Manhattan Island, New York City, was demolished.

## SAN FRANCISCO, CALIFORNIA—October 17, 1989
Minutes before the start of the third game of the World Series between the Oakland A's and the San Francisco Giants, an earthquake registering 6.9 on the Richter Scale hit the San Francisco Bay area. It lasted 15 seconds, killed 59 people, and injured 3,000. Seven counties in Northern California were declared disaster areas. The worst damage came when a more than mile-long section of the upper level of the two-level Nimitz Freeway collapsed onto the lower level. Over 30 people were killed, and others were trapped in their cars. The narrow space between the two levels made it difficult for rescue and medical teams to aid the trapped victims. A 30-foot section of the San Francisco-Oakland Bay Bridge also collapsed, killing one person. The estimated 50 million Americans watching the series on TV saw the image on their screens shake as the earthquake started. Candlestick Park did not suffer major structural damage, but the stadium was evacuated, and the game postponed until late October.

# 6 Severe Tornadoes

**WASHINGTON, D.C.—August 25, 1814**
The U.S. was at war with Britain (the War of 1812), and British troops had set fire to the White House and the Capitol building. While the buildings burned, a tornado struck the heart of the city, killing about 30 soldiers and some residents who had not fled.

**SOUTH-CENTRAL U.S.—February 9–19, 1884**
A series of twisters swirled up the U.S. from the Gulf of Mexico to Illinois within a ten-day period, leaving about 600 people dead.

**ST. LOUIS, MISSOURI—May 27, 1896**
At 5:00 P.M. that Wednesday, lightning crackled in the overcast sky above St. Louis, heavy rains began to fall, and winds rose to 80 miles per hour. Then the sky turned an eerie green and the twister struck. It zig-zagged through the city, destroying a large number of buildings and causing over 300 deaths.

**MIDWESTERN U.S.—March 18, 1925**
At least eight deadly tornadoes sped at 60 miles per hour in a loop through Missouri, southwest Indiana, Illinois, Kentucky, and Tennessee. Within three hours, 689 people had been killed, 13,000 injured, and $16 million to $18 million worth of property had been destroyed. It was the worst tornado disaster on record.

## MISSISSIPPI AND GEORGIA—April 5–6, 1936

The town of Tupelo, Mississippi, was totally destroyed by a twister on April 5. The next day, two more tornadoes hit the shopping district of Gainesville, Georgia, destroying a large number of stores and businesses and killing 203 people.

## WICHITA FALLS, TEXAS—April 10, 1979

This twister cut a quarter-mile-long, five-mile-path through the city, destroying both shopping malls and more than 2,000 homes. The tornado sucked up people and property, tossed cars around in the air, and leveled tall buildings. It was said that the winds were so fierce, dentures had been pulled from the mouths of some people.

# 5 Famous Fires

## GREAT FIRE OF LONDON—September 1–5, 1666

Since 1665, London had been suffering from a severe epidemic of the bubonic plague. Then, just before midnight on Saturday, September 1, 1666, a fire broke out in a wooden frame house on Pudding Lane. The house was owned by Thomas Fraynor, a baker for King Charles II, and the fire may have started in an oven on the bottom floor. The fire quickly spread through a nearby section of wharves and warehouses on the Thames River. By early the next morning, the fire was out of control and threatened to destroy most of the city north of the river. On Monday, as the fire continued,

Charles II

King Charles and his brother went out into the streets to hand out gold coins to the firefighters. On Tuesday, the king and his brother joined the bucket brigade. Firefighting efforts had become hampered by a lack of water, after the wooden water wheels on the Thames that provided the city's supplies burned. Buckets had to be dipped into the river, then passed along a line of firefighters.

On Tuesday, riots broke out against foreigners and Catholics whom many citizens incorrectly blamed for starting the fire on purpose. Thousands of homeless people fled to the fields outside the city. On Wednesday, the Great London Fire finally ended. The London of the Middle Ages had disappeared. Eighty percent of the Medieval city had been totally destroyed, including 90 percent of the housing. At least 200,000 people were homeless. But the fire also destroyed the bubonic plague and paved the way for a new London, rebuilt with a healthier sewer system.

## PESHTIGO FOREST FIRE—October 8, 1871

In 1871, Peshtigo, Wisconsin, was a thriving town of 2,000 people. On the Peshtigo River was a prosperous sawmill that handled 150,000 feet of lumber a day. But that summer there had been a serious drought, and a number of small fires had burned through the early autumn. The hand-drawn fire wagon and bucket brigades had not been able to put out the fires—there were too many of them. Then, on October 8, a huge fire started in the forest west of Peshtigo; within ten minutes the town was engulfed in flames. A blast of superhot air shook every building, and houses, barns, trees, and grass burst into flames. The town disappeared, and 1,300 residents died. The fire spread across northern Wisconsin and upper Michigan, destroying 1,280,000 acres of timberland north of Green Bay and killing an estimated 1,500 people.

## GREAT CHICAGO FIRE—October 8–10, 1871

The drought of 1871 caused small fires to break out in Chicago, a fire-hazard of a city with narrow streets, flimsily constructed wooden buildings, and a population of 334,000. On October 7, a sixteen-hour fire had raged over Chicago's West Division, damaging three pieces of firefighting equipment. The exhausted firefighters thought they'd never have to battle such a blaze again. They were wrong. On the night of October 8, a fire started in a cow barn belonging to Patrick O'Leary. (Legend has it that one of Mrs. O'Leary's cows kicked over a kerosene lamp, which started the fire.) Engine Company No. 6 and its powerful "Little Giant" pumper arrived, but firefighters could not contain the flames. The fire spread south, toward the gasworks. Firefighters drained the gas into reservoirs and sewers to prevent an explosion, but the gas fumes running through the sewers probably helped spread the fire. By October 9, an army of firefighters, police, militia, and private citizens led by Civil War hero General Philip Sheridan, were battling the blaze.

Then the fire headed north, leveling everything in its path, including the huge McCormick Reaper works. Thousands of people fled to the waters of Lake Michigan, and looters broke store windows and helped themselves to whatever they wanted. Firefighters arrived from Milwaukee, Wisconsin, and from Ohio, but even their help couldn't stop the flames. Finally, on October 10, the fire burned itself out. Over 2,124 acres of property had been burned, 17,450 buildings had been destroyed (but not the O'Learys' house), between 200 and 250 people had been killed, 200 were missing, and 100,000 were homeless. The newly built Chicago Historical Society was one of the buildings destroyed; inside it had been the original draft of Abraham Lincoln's Emancipation Proclamation.

The city recovered quickly. General Sheridan declared martial law (the military took charge of law and order in the city) and set up a tent city for the homeless. Food, money, and other supplies poured in from people around the country. Within a year, half the city had been rebuilt, and by 1880, all traces of the fire had vanished and Chicago's population had grown to over half a million.

## TRIANGLE SHIRTWAIST FACTORY FIRE—March 25, 1911

In the early years of the twentieth century, many young women, mostly immigrants, worked as garment sewers in factories called "sweatshops." The Triangle Shirtwaist Factory was a sweatshop located in the Asch Building in Greenwich Village, New York City. The building had no sprinkler system, and had wooden floors and window sashes and only two staircases instead of the three the city fire code required. The fire escape exited only to the roof. On the eighth, ninth, and tenth floors, 850 young women bent over tightly packed rows of sewing machines. The tables were covered with piles of cloth and tissue paper, and scraps of oil-soaked rags littered the floors. The women worked six thirteen-hour days and could earn ten dollars a week for making ladies' shirtwaists (blouses).

On March 25, the women were working overtime to fill a special order. Just before the closing bell that afternoon, a fire started in a pile of scrap material. It was thought to have been started either by a carelessly discarded cigarette, or by a spark from one of the sewing machines. The fire quickly spread to shirtwaists hanging overhead. The women tried to escape, but the narrow exit quickly became blocked. One of the fire escapes collapsed under the weight of twenty women and fell to the ground. Others simply jumped from the windows into the fire nets, which ripped from the hands of the rescuers. Some women died of shock and smoke inhalation. Firefighters had arrived quickly, but their hoses and ladders could not reach the upper floors. Finally, firefighters with hand extinguishers and axes raced up the stairs and doused the fire in 18 minutes. But 145 people had died.

The tragedy strengthened the labor movement in New York, and legislation to eliminate sweatshops and improve fire laws was eventually enacted. The owners of the Triangle Shirtwaist Factory, Isaac Harris and Max Blanck, were brought to trial, but were found not guilty of manslaughter.

## COCOANUT GROVE FIRE—November 28, 1942

The Cocoanut Grove nightclub in Boston was styled to look like a South Sea island, with paper palm trees and bamboo groves, imitation leather wallpaper, and blue satin skies. On November 28, guests at the Cocoanut Grove included Boston College football fans—who had decided to celebrate even though their team had lost in an upset to Holy Cross, 55–12—and soldiers who would soon ship out for Europe to fight in World War II.

About 10:00 P.M., busboy Stanley Tomaszewski tried to replace a lightbulb in the Melody Lounge, a bar on the bottom-floor nightclub. He couldn't find the socket in the dimly lit room, so he struck a match. The match flame accidentally ignited one of the paper palm trees, and flames quickly jumped up and across the cloth ceiling. The 100 people in the bar hurried to the door that led upstairs to the revolving exit door, which became jammed. At that moment, flames shot up through the floor of the upstairs dining room and ignited the flimsy wall coverings and fabric ceiling. Smoke swirled across the room. Most patrons became trapped in the blazing, smoke-filled building, and firefighters were hampered in their rescue and firefighting efforts by the crush of people that jammed the foyer of the nightclub. About 60 people escaped, 451 were killed, and 150 were injured in the blaze.

# 4 Weird Weather Disasters

**THE GREAT BLIZZARD OF 1888—March 12–13, 1888**
The newspaper weather report for New York City on March 12 read: "Light snow, then clearing." By the next morning, 24 inches of snow had fallen, the temperature was 15° F, and winds with 40-mile-per-hour gales had created 20-foot drifts in the city's streets. Many New Yorkers enjoyed the opportunity to skate, ski, and sled in the center of the city, and to slide across the ice bridge that had formed across the East River from Manhattan to Brooklyn. But many others suffered from food, water, and fuel shortages as delivery wagons failed to get down snow-packed streets. More than 200 New Yorkers died from the extreme cold and storm conditions; 600 more died due to the blizzard in other areas along the East Coast.

**THE MIDWESTERN DROUGHT—1932–1937**
Since the late 1800s, the rich prairie lands of the U.S. Midwest had been plowed under to raise wheat and corn, or overgrazed by cattle. The fertile topsoil began to blow away, causing a Dust Bowl in that area by the 1930s. In 1932, the U.S. was in the middle of a deep economic depression. The price of crops fell, and the spring was marked by a late freeze, violent storms, and a plague of insects. Then a drought affected about 50 million acres in Kansas, Oklahoma, Texas, New Mexico, Colorado, and parts of Nebraska

and the Dakotas. Huge dust storms, or "black blizzards," began in 1933, blotting out the sun for three or four days at a time. Great black dust drifts formed around homesteads and blocked highways and railroad lines. Reduced visibility forced the closing of airports throughout the Midwest. Hundreds of people and heads of livestock died as a result of the dust storms, and crops grew brown and stunted. Thousands packed up and left, abandoning their barren farms.

The drought ended in 1937, and as the weather got better, farming began to return to normal. Prices for crops rose as the country emerged from the Great Depression, and once again, farmers were able to make a living in the Midwest.

## THE LONDON KILLER FOG—December 1952

London, England, had always been famous for its "pea-souper" fogs. The novelists of the 1800s, including Arthur Conan Doyle, the creator of superdetective Sherlock Holmes, frequently featured thick, mysterious fogs in their stories. But the fog that plagued

Londoners in December 1952, wasn't the kind you read about in stories.

On December 4, a high-pressure weather system spread southeast over Britain, bringing light winds, dry air, and cold temperatures. That night, the winds stopped completely, and cold air became trapped near the ground under a layer of warm air. Heavy fog began to form. During the next four days, about 2,000 tons of sulphur dioxide and other pollutants from coal-burning industrial furnaces and home heating systems entered the trapped air mass. The sky turned yellow, then amber, brown, and finally, almost black. The poisoned air became difficult to breathe, and visibility outdoors dropped to a few feet. All told, thousands of Londoners died as a result of the killer fog. The fog finally lifted when the weather changed and strong winds blew the air away.

## THE DROUGHT OF THE SAHEL, CENTRAL AFRICA—1965 and Beyond

The Sahel is the vast semiarid zone between the Sahara Desert and Equatorial Africa. An extended drought there has caused the deaths of hundreds of thousands and possibly millions of Africans since 1965. The deaths have been due to famine, starvation, forcible relocation, and war. In Ethiopia in the 1970s, the 200,000 deaths caused by the drought, plus the loss of huge numbers of cattle, caused a rebellion of army officers against Emperor Haile Selassie, whose government had done little to relieve conditions. In the 1980s, relief efforts from around the world were hampered by warring factions in Ethiopia. In 1985, a 17-hour rock concert, "Live Aid," was held to raise money for the hungry people of Africa.

# 3 Notable Nuclear Accidents

## WINDSCALE—October 7, 1957

A fire in the Windscale plutonium production reactor north of Liverpool, England, spread radioactive material throughout the countryside. In 1983, the British government said that 39 people probably died of cancer as a result of the accident.

## THREE MILE ISLAND—March 28, 1979

The worst commercial nuclear accident in the U.S. occurred at the Three Mile Island nuclear reactor in Middletown, Pennsylvania, when equipment failure and human mistakes led to a loss of coolant and a partial core meltdown. Radioactive gases escaped through the plant's venting system. No one knows yet what the effect of the accident on the population around the reactor will be.

## CHERNOBYL—April 25, 1986

A serious accident at the Chernobyl nuclear plant about 60 miles from the city of Kiev in the Soviet Union sent clouds of radiation spreading over several European countries. Twenty-three people were killed by the accident and 40,000 were evacuated from the area.

# 2 Awful Avalanches

## PLURS, SWITZERLAND—September 4, 1618

This avalanche of snow destroyed the town and 1,500 inhabitants. The only survivors were four people who happened to be away from Plurs that day.

## ITALIAN-AUSTRIAN ALPS—December 13, 1916

More than 10,000 soldiers of both Italian and Austrian forces fighting World War I were killed in 24 hours by avalanches. The avalanches were the result of heavy snows which had fallen the day before.

# 1 Really Mysterious Disaster

## THE TUNGUSKA FIREBALL—June 30, 1908

At dawn on June 30, a falling star flashed into sight over western China. It landed with a huge explosion in a region of peat bogs and pine forests near the Tunguska River in central Siberia, Soviet Union. Witnesses reported seeing a blinding light and hearing a series of deafening thunderclaps. That night, the sky lit up over parts of Europe, and ships could be seen for miles out to sea. European scientists decided that these "northern lights" were due to solar flares. The explosion wasn't investigated by the Soviets until 1927; it had been delayed by World War I and the Russian Revolution. Russian scientists thought the explosion had been caused by the fall of a huge meteorite, but when the expedition reached the blast site, there was no sign of a crater a meteorite would have made. Instead, the scientists saw that to a 12-mile radius from the center of the explosion, the pine forest was leveled and blackened. Uprooted trees lay parallel to one another, their tops pointed away from the blast. At a 5-mile radius, the wrecked forest appeared to have been burned instantly from above. At the center was an island of blackened trees, stripped of bark and branches.

No one is sure what the "Tunguska Fireball" really was, but the most popular theory is that it was a comet, which evaporated in an explosion near the ground. But some scientists have said that a comet large enough to have caused the explosion would have been seen by astronomers long before it struck the earth. One Russian engineer turned writer, Aleksander Kazantsev, suggested that the Siberian explosion was caused by a nuclear-powered alien space-ship attempting to land. Another, more scientific, explanation is that the explosion was caused by a fast-moving tiny "black hole" that struck the earth. (A black hole is thought to be a collapsed star which is so dense with gravity that neither light nor matter can escape from it.) The black hole caused a nuclearlike explosion, then passed through the earth like a bullet. None of these theories have really satisfied scientists, and the Tunguska Fireball has remained the most mysterious natural disaster in history.

# CHAPTER 5

# Historical VIPs

In this chapter, you'll get the facts on the forty U.S. presidents—what they did for a living *before* they became president, their nicknames, achievements, presidential firsts, and more. There are also facts on first ladies, famous world leaders, and young rulers.

# Presidents of the U.S.

## GEORGE WASHINGTON, 1789–1797

**Born:** February 22, 1732, Westmoreland County, Virginia.
**Died:** December 14, 1799, Mount Vernon, Virginia
**Occupations:** Surveyor, planter, general of the Continental Army during the American Revolution.
**Highlights of administrations:** Created Department of Foreign Affairs, national bank, patent laws, Post Office, Treasury; Bank of U.S. chartered.
**Nickname:** Father of His Country.

## JOHN ADAMS, 1797–1801

**Born:** October 30, 1735, Braintree (now Quincy), Massachusetts
**Died:** July 4, 1826, Braintree
**Occupations:** Schoolteacher, lawyer, vice-president of the U.S.
**Highlights of administration:** Established the Library of Congress, Marine Corps, Navy, and public health services.
**Nickname:** Colossus of Debate.

## THOMAS JEFFERSON, 1801–1809

**Born:** April 13, 1743, Albermarle County, Virginia
**Died:** July 4, 1826, at Monticello, his home in Virginia.
**Occupations:** Writer, inventor, lawyer
**Highlights of administrations:** Purchased the Louisiana Territory; authorized the Lewis and Clark expedition; ended African slave import (although Jefferson himself kept slaves).
**Nickname:** Father of the Declaration of Independence.

## JAMES MADISON, 1809–1817

**Born:** March 16, 1751, Port Conway, Virginia
**Died:** June 28, 1836, at Montpelier, his home in Virginia.
**Occupations:** Lawyer, statesman
**Highlights of administration:** Issued the first war bonds; U.S. defeated England in the War of 1812.
**Nickname:** Father of the Constitution.

## JAMES MONROE, 1817–1825
**Born:** April 28, 1758, Westmoreland County, Virginia
**Died:** July 4, 1831, New York City
**Occupations:** Lawyer, writer
**Highlights of administrations:** Purchased Florida; issued Monroe Doctrine (a warning to Europe to stop colonizing America); Missouri Compromise.
**Nickname:** Last of the Cocked Hats.


## JOHN QUINCY ADAMS, 1825–1829
**Born:** July 11, 1767, Braintree, Massachusetts. He was the son of president John Adams and Abigail Adams.
**Died:** February 23, 1848, Washington, D.C.
**Occupations:** Lawyer, statesman
**Highlights of administration:** Opened western America for settlement with the building of canals, highways, and railroads; helped establish the Smithsonian Institution.
**Nickname:** King John the Second.


## ANDREW JACKSON, 1829–1837
**Born:** March 15, 1767, Waxhaw, South Carolina
**Died:** June 8, 1845, at the Hermitage, his home in Tennessee.
**Occupations:** Soldier
**Highlights of administrations:** Introduced the "spoils system," by which friends were awarded government jobs; reopened U.S. trade with the West Indies.
**Nickname:** Old Hickory.


## MARTIN VAN BUREN, 1837–1841
**Born:** December 5, 1782, Kinderhook, New York
**Died:** July 24, 1862, Kinderhook
**Occupations:** Lawyer, statesman
**Highlights of administration:** Created independent treasury system to deal with the economic panic of 1837.
**Nickname:** Little Magician.

## WILLIAM HENRY HARRISON, 1841 (35 days in office)

**Born:** February 9, 1773, Charles City County, Virginia

**Died:** April 4, 1841, in the White House

**Occupation:** Soldier

**Highlights of administration:** Harrison caught pneumonia during his inauguration and died 35 days later.

**Nickname:** Old Tippecanoe.

## JOHN TYLER, 1841–1845

**Born:** March 29, 1790, Charles City County, Virginia

**Died:** January 18, 1862, Richmond, Virginia

**Occupation:** Lawyer

**Highlights of administration:** Annexed Texas; established uniform election day; signed treaty with China.

**Nickname:** Honest John.

## JAMES KNOX POLK, 1845–1849

**Born:** November 2, 1795, Mecklenburg, North Carolina

**Died:** June 15, 1849, Nashville, Tennessee

**Occupation:** Lawyer

**Highlights of administration:** Established the Department of the Interior; purchased California, New Mexico, Arizona, Nevada, Utah, and parts of Colorado; settled Oregon boundary dispute with Great Britain; was president during the Mexican-American War of 1846, in which the U.S. fought Mexico for disputed Texas lands settled by Mexicans.

**Nickname:** Handy Jim of Tennessee.

## ZACHARY TAYLOR, 1849–1850
**Born:** November 24, 1784, Orange County, Virginia
**Died:** July 9, 1850, Washington, D.C.
**Occupation:** Soldier. He had served in the War of 1812, two Indian wars, and the Mexican-American War.
**Highlights of administration:** Signed a treaty with the Hawaiian Islands; Compromise of 1850; died after 16 months in office.
**Nickname:** Old Rough and Ready.

## MILLARD FILLMORE, 1850–1853
**Born:** January 7, 1800, Cayuga County, New York
**Died:** March 8, 1874, Buffalo, New York
**Occupation:** Lawyer
**Highlights of administration:** Sent Commodore Matthew Perry to Japan to open up U.S. trade with that country; Fugitive Slave law enacted.
**Nickname:** His Accidency.

## FRANKLIN PIERCE, 1853–1857
**Born:** November 23, 1804, Hillsboro, New Hampshire
**Died:** October 8, 1869, Concord, New Hampshire
**Occupations:** Lawyer, politician
**Highlights of administration:** Signed treaty with Japan; Gadsden Purchase of Mexico border land; Kansas-Nebraska Act (states were allowed to choose whether or not to be slave states; the border was Kansas).
**Nickname:** Handsome Frank.

## JAMES BUCHANAN, 1857–1861
**Born:** April 23, 1791, Cove Gap, Pennsylvania
**Died:** June 1, 1868, at Wheatland, his home in Pennsylvania
**Occupations:** Lawyer, statesman
**Highlights of administration:** Dred Scott decision enacted, which deprived Congress of the right to end slavery; Pony Express begun, in which riders carried mail from St. Joseph, Missouri, to Sacramento, California.
**Nickname:** Bachelor President.

## ABRAHAM LINCOLN, 1861–1865

**Born:** February 12, 1809, Hogdenville, Kentucky

**Died:** April 15, 1865, Washington, D.C. Lincoln was fatally shot by actor and Confederate John Wilkes Booth as he watched a performance of the play *Our American Cousin* at Ford's Theatre.

**Occupation:** Lawyer

**Highlights of administration:** Civil War was fought; issued the Emancipation Proclamation; established the Department of Agriculture; proclaimed Thanksgiving Day a national holiday; Homestead Act approved, granting free family farms to settlers.

**Nickname:** Honest Abe.

## ANDREW JOHNSON, 1865–1869

**Born:** December 29, 1808, Raleigh, North Carolina

**Died:** July 31, 1875, Carter's Station, Tennessee

**Occupations:** Tailor, politician

**Highlights of administration:** Purchased Alaska from Russia; 13th amendment (abolishing slavery) and 14th amendment (guaranteeing rights of citizens) passed.

**Nickname:** Great Commoner.

## ULYSSES SIMPSON GRANT, 1869–1873

**Born:** April 27, 1822, Point Pleasant, Ohio

**Died:** July 23, 1885, Mt. McGregor, New York

**Occupations:** Farmer, soldier. Grant was a Union general during the Civil War.

**Highlights of administration:** Created the Department of Justice; transcontinental railroad finished; financial panic of 1873; political scandals.

**Nickname:** United States Grant.

## RUTHERFORD BIRCHARD HAYES, 1877–1881

**Born:** October 4, 1822, Delaware, Ohio

**Died:** January 17, 1893, Fremont, Ohio

**Occupation:** Lawyer

**Highlights of administration:** Women were allowed to practice law before the Supreme Court; the last Federal troops were removed from the South.
**Nickname:** Fraud President.

## JAMES ABRAM GARFIELD, 1881
**Born:** November 19, 1831, Orange, Ohio
**Died:** September 19, 1881, Elberon, New Jersey. On July 2, 1881, Garfield was shot by a mentally disturbed office seeker, Charles Guiteau, while entering a railroad station in Washington, D.C. He was taken to Elberon, where he died on September 19.
**Occupations:** Teacher, minister
**Highlights of administration:** Established the American Red Cross
**Nickname:** Boatman Jim.

## CHESTER ALAN ARTHUR, 1881–1885
**Born:** October 5, 1830, Fairfield, Vermont
**Died:** November 18, 1886, New York City
**Occupation:** Lawyer
**Highlights of administration:** Signed treaty with Korea; civil service reform act passed; standard time adopted; first Labor Day celebration; Chinese Exclusion Act, which prohibited the further immigration of Chinese workers to the U.S.
**Nickname:** Dude President.

## GROVER CLEVELAND, 1885–1889 and 1893–1897
**Born:** March 18, 1837, Caldwell, New Jersey
**Died:** June 24, 1908, Princeton, New Jersey
**Occupations:** Lawyer, politician
**Highlights of administration:** Interstate Commerce Commission established; gold standard maintained; financial panic of 1893; western U.S. homesteaded.
**Nickname:** Uncle Jumbo.

## BENJAMIN HARRISON, 1889–1893
**Born:** August 20, 1833, North Bend, Ohio
**Died:** March 13, 1901, Indianapolis, Indiana

**Occupation:** Lawyer

**Highlights of administration:** Pan-American Conference between North and Latin American countries held; Sherman Antitrust Act, which broke up business monopolies, passed; Washington, Idaho, Montana, Wyoming, North Dakota, and South Dakota entered the Union.

**Nickname:** Grandfather's Hat.

## WILLIAM McKINLEY, 1897–1901

**Born:** January 29, 1843, Niles, Ohio

**Died:** September 14, 1901, Buffalo, New York. McKinley was shot on September 5 by anarchist Leon C. Czolgosz while welcoming citizens at the Pan-American Exposition in Buffalo.

**Occupation:** Lawyer

**Highlights of administration:** Spanish-American War won, whereby the U.S. acquired the Philippines, Puerto Rico, and Guam from Spain; Hawaii annexed by the U.S.

**Nickname:** Wobbly Willie.

## THEODORE ROOSEVELT, 1901–1909

**Born:** October 27, 1858, New York City, New York

**Died:** January 6, 1919, at Sagamore Hill, his home in Oyster Bay, New York.

**Occupations:** Rancher, politician

**Highlights of administration:** Created the Department of Commerce and Labor; Pure Food and Drug Act and Meat Inspection Act passed to protect consumers; Panama Canal Zone leased to the U.S. for use of the canal.

**Nickname:** Teddy.

## WILLIAM HOWARD TAFT, 1909–1913

**Born:** September 15, 1857, Cincinnati, Ohio

**Died:** March 8, 1930, Washington, D.C.

**Occupation:** Lawyer

**Highlights of administration:** Established postal banks and parcel post; Congress given the power to tax citizens' incomes.

**Nickname:** Big Bill.

## WOODROW WILSON, 1913–1921

**Born:** December 28, 1856, Staunton, Virginia
**Died:** February 3, 1924, Washington, D.C.
**Occupation:** Teacher
**Highlights of administration:** Purchased Danish West Indies (now the U.S. Virgin Islands); Federal Trade Commission and Federal Reserve System created; the 19th amendment (women's voting rights) passed; World War I fought.
**Nickname:** Professor.

## WARREN GAMALIEL HARDING, 1921–1923

**Born:** November 2, 1865, Corsica, Ohio
**Died:** August 2, 1923, San Francisco, California
**Occupation:** Newspaper editor
**Highlights of administration:** Created the Bureau of the Budget; first immigration quota passed; administration rocked by political scandals.
**Nickname:** Great Handshaker.

## CALVIN COOLIDGE, 1923–1929

**Born:** July 4, 1872, Plymouth, Vermont
**Died:** November 5, 1933, Northhampton, Massachusetts
**Occupation:** Lawyer
**Highlights of administration:** Created the U.S. Foreign Service and U.S. Radio Commission; U.S. citizenship granted to Native Americans; the "Roaring Twenties" in the U.S., a decade of economic prosperity, easy credit, stock-market speculation, short skirts and greater liberation for women, and such products as autos, radios, and telephones available to more Americans.
**Nickname:** Silent Cal.

## HERBERT CLARK HOOVER, 1929–1933

**Born:** August 10, 1874, West Branch, Iowa
**Died:** October 20, 1964, New York City
**Occupation:** Engineer
**Highlights of administration:** Created the Veterans Administration; adopted the "Star-Spangled Banner" as the national anthem; stock market crash of 1929, which led to a serious economic collapse and depression and resulted in millions of unemployed Americans.
**Nickname:** Grand Old Man.

## FRANKLIN DELANO ROOSEVELT, 1933–1945

**Born:** January 30, 1882, Hyde Park, New York
**Died:** April 12, 1945, Warm Springs, Georgia
**Occupation:** Lawyer
**Highlights of administration:** Brought U.S. out of the Great Depression; spearheaded government relief and work programs; government reform and expansion through programs such as the Social Security Act and Minimum Wage Laws; U.S. entered World War II.
**Nickname:** F.D.R.

## HARRY S. TRUMAN, 1945–1953

**Born:** May 8, 1884, Lamar, Missouri
**Died:** December 26, 1972, Kansas City, Missouri
**Occupations:** Haberdasher (he ran a men's furnishings store), politician
**Highlights of administration:** U.S. dropped atom bombs on Japan; World War II ended; Korean War began; U.N. charter

ratified; North Atlantic Treaty Organization (NATO) established; Truman Doctrine (halted Soviet expansion into Europe and Asia).

**Nickname:** Give 'Em Hell Harry.

## DWIGHT DAVID EISENHOWER, 1953–1961

**Born:** October 14, 1890, Denison, Texas

**Died:** March 28, 1969, Washington, D.C.

**Occupations:** Army officer. Eisenhower graduated from West Point and, as general, became supreme Allied commander in Europe in 1943, during World War II.

**Highlights of administration:** Korean War ended; racial integration of schools enforced; created National Aeronautics and Space Administration (NASA) which launched first U.S. satellites.

**Nickname:** Ike.

## JOHN FITZGERALD KENNEDY, 1961–1963

**Born:** May 29, 1917, Brookline, Massachusetts

**Died:** November 22, 1963, Dallas, Texas. Kennedy was fatally shot by former U.S. marine and onetime Soviet citizen Lee Harvey Oswald while riding through the city in an open-car motorcade.

**Occupation:** Politician

**Highlights of administration:** Created Peace Corps to help people in developing countries; established "hot line," a direct telephone line between U.S. and Soviet leaders; mounted an unsuccessful invasion of Cuba by anti-Castro Cubans at the Bay of Pigs; forced the Soviet Union to remove missiles from Cuba; saw first American launched into space.

**Nickname:** J.F.K.

## LYNDON BAINES JOHNSON, 1963–1969

**Born:** August 27, 1908, Stonewall, Texas

**Died:** January 22, 1973, at the LBJ Ranch, Johnson's Texas home.

**Occupations:** Teacher, politician

**Highlights of administration:** Escalated U.S. involvement in Vietnam; passed legislation on civil rights and tax reduction; established antipoverty and conservation programs.

**Nickname:** L.B.J.

## RICHARD MILHOUS NIXON, 1969–1974

**Born:** January 9, 1913, Yorba Linda, California

**Occupation:** Lawyer

**Highlights of administration:** First person on the moon; established relations with the Peoples' Republic of China; withdrew U.S. troops from Vietnam; Watergate scandal, which started when Nixon campaign committee employees broke into Democratic party headquarters in the Watergate office complex in Washington, D.C. to obtain information; first resignation from office of a U.S. president.

**Nickname:** Tricky Dick.

## GERALD RUDOLPH FORD, JR., 1974–1977

**Born:** July 14, 1913, Omaha, Nebraska

**Occupations:** Lawyer, politician

**Highlights of administration:** Pardoned former President Nixon; passed Federal Campaign Reform Act; proposed statehood for Puerto Rico; U.S. celebrated Bicentennial

**Nickname:** Mr. Nice Guy.

## JAMES EARL CARTER, 1977–1981

**Born:** October 1, 1924, Plains, Georgia

**Occupations:** Peanut farmer, statesman

**Highlights of administration:** Pardoned Vietnam draft resisters; led negotiations for peace in the Middle East; signed treaty which gave the Panama Canal back to Panama in the year 2000; hostages taken at the U.S. embassy in Iran; imposed grain embargo and boycotted the 1980 Summer Olympics in Moscow after the Soviets invaded Afghanistan; challenged nations' abuses of human rights.

**Nicknames:** Jimmy.

## RONALD WILSON REAGAN, 1981–1989

**Born:** February 6, 1911, Tampico, Illinois

**Occupations:** Actor, politician

**Highlights of administration:** Ordered U.S. invasion of Grenada; sent U.S. marines to Beirut, Lebanon; Iran-Contra scandal; U.S. bombed Libya for alleged terrorist activities; economic boom caused by stock market speculation and lower interest rates,

energy costs, and inflation; stock market crash of 1987; U.S. hostages held in Lebanon; huge government budget deficit and trade deficit.
**Nickname:** Great Communicator.

**GEORGE HERBERT WALKER BUSH, 1989–**
**Born:** June 12, 1924, Milton, Massachusetts
**Occupations:** Oil man, politician
**Highlights of administration:** Savings and Loan crisis; in 1990, sent U.S. troops to Saudi Arabia after the Iraqi invasion of Kuwait.
**Nickname:** Poppy.

# Presidential Trivia

**PRESIDENTS WHO PLAYED FOOTBALL FOR THEIR COLLEGE TEAMS**
Dwight D. Eisenhower—West Point
Richard M. Nixon—Whittier College
Gerald Ford—University of Michigan
Ronald Reagan—Eureka College

**PRESIDENTS WHO NEVER WENT TO COLLEGE**
George Washington
Andrew Jackson
Martin Van Buren
Zachary Taylor
Millard Fillmore
Andrew Johnson
Grover Cleveland
Harry S Truman

## PRESIDENTS WHO WERE BALD

John Quincy Adams
Martin Van Buren
Dwight D. Eisenhower

## PRESIDENTS WHO OWNED SLAVES

George Washington
Thomas Jefferson
James Madison
Andrew Jackson
John Tyler
James K. Polk
Zachary Taylor
Andrew Johnson
Ulysses S. Grant

## PRESIDENTS WHO WERE ONCE GOVERNORS OF A STATE

**California:** Ronald Reagan
**Georgia:** Jimmy Carter
**Massachusetts:** Calvin Coolidge
**New Jersey:** Woodrow Wilson
**New York:** Martin Van Buren, Grover Cleveland, Theodore Roosevelt, Franklin D. Roosevelt
**Ohio:** Rutherford B. Hayes, William McKinley
**Tennessee:** James K. Polk, Andrew Johnson
**Virginia:** Thomas Jefferson, James Monroe, John Tyler

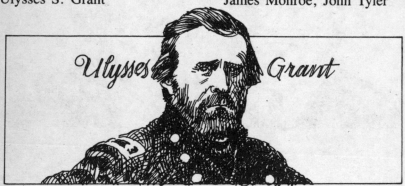

*Ulysses Grant*

# Presidential Firsts

**First to put up a Christmas tree in the White House:** Franklin Pierce, in 1856

**First to watch a professional baseball game:** Benjamin Harrison, on June 6, 1892, when Cincinnati beat Washington, 7–4, in 11 innings

**First to throw out the first pitch:** William Howard Taft, on April 14, 1910, when the Washington Senators beat the Philadelphia Athletics, 3–0

**First to live in the White House:** John Adams

**First and only son of a president to become a president:** John Quincy Adams

**First to be born in a log cabin:** Andrew Jackson

**First to be born a U.S. citizen:** Martin Van Buren. The first 7 presidents had been born British subjects.

**First elected from a state west of the Mississippi River:** Zachary Taylor. He lived in Louisiana.

**First and only president to be granted a patent for an invention:** Abraham Lincoln, patent 6469, in 1849. Lincoln invented a floatable device to allow steamboats to pass over shallow waters.

**First to change his name:** Ulysses S. Grant. He dropped his original first name, Hiram, because he disliked it.

**First to use a telephone while in office:** Rutherford B. Hayes

**First to be left-handed:** James Garfield

**First to win the Nobel Peace Prize:** Theodore Roosevelt, 1906, for mediating the peace between Russia and Japan. The two countries had fought the Russo-Japanese War in 1905.

**First disabled president:** Franklin D. Roosevelt. A case of polio in 1921 had paralyzed his legs, but he learned to walk again with the aid of leg braces and a cane.

**First to appear on TV:** Franklin D. Roosevelt

**First to be born in the 20th century:** John F. Kennedy

**First to resign from office:** Richard Nixon

**First movie actor to become president:** Ronald Reagan

# 9 Notable First Ladies

### ABIGAIL SMITH ADAMS (1744–1818)
Abigail Adams, the wife of the second president, John Adams, is remembered for her strong views on women's rights. Long before they were accepted ideas, Abigail spoke out for women's right to vote and women's right to equal education. Some called her "Mrs. President" because of her influence over her husband.

## DOROTHEA PAYNE MADISON (1768–1849)

One of the most popular first ladies, fashionable "Dolley" Madison was a very lively and gracious White House hostess. She was responsible for starting the traditional Easter egg roll for kids. During the War of 1812, Dolley Madison bravely stayed in the White House to make sure that important papers and other treasures were removed before the advancing British troops burned the house in 1814.

## JULIA GARDINER TYLER (1820–1889)

Julia, the second wife of John Tyler, was the first president's wife to have her portrait hung in the White House. On a return visit to the White House during Andrew Johnson's presidency, she convinced him to hang her portrait with those of the presidents, thus starting the tradition of first-lady portraits. A young and fun-loving first lady, Julia Tyler was also the first to introduce dancing at White House receptions. Julia's nicknames were "Rose of Long Island" and "Fairy Girl" (given to her by her husband).

## LUCY WARE WEBB HAYES (1831–1889)

Lucy, the wife of 19th president Rutherford Hayes, was the first president's wife to be called the first lady. A newspaper columnist used the term when describing her at her husband's inauguration. She was also the first president's wife to graduate from college. Well known for her charity work, she spent a great deal of time as first lady visiting schools, prisons, and mental institutions. An exceptional woman, Lucy was praised in poems by American poets Henry Wadsworth Longfellow and Oliver Wendell Holmes. Lucy's nickname, "Lemonade Lucy," was given to her because she served no liquor in the White House. She also did not allow smoking, dancing, or card playing.

## HELEN HERRON TAFT (1861–1943)

Helen Taft is best remembered for having three thousand cherry trees planted in Washington, D.C. The now famous trees of the nation's capital were a gift to her from the mayor of Tokyo, Japan.

### ANNA ELEANOR ROOSEVELT (1884–1962)

Eleanor Roosevelt was one of the most active and influential first ladies. She wrote a daily newspaper column, held press conferences, and served as the U.S. delegate to the United Nations. At the U.N., she was head of the Commission on Human Rights. Known and loved the world over, Eleanor Roosevelt was called "The First Lady of the World."

### JACQUELINE BOUVIER KENNEDY (b. 1929)

"Jackie" Kennedy brought cultural programs and an historic renovation to the White House and conducted the first televised tour of the newly restored house.

### CLAUDIA TAYLOR JOHNSON (b. 1912)

"Lady Bird" Johnson toured the U.S. campaigning for a more beautiful America and lecturing on ways to improve the environment. It was her suggestion to beautify the roadsides by removing billboards and planting trees and wildflowers.

### ROSALYNN SMITH CARTER (b. 1927)

Rosalynn Carter was the first first lady to represent the administration on visits to foreign countries on her own. She also worked hard for mental health programs and for passage of the Equal Rights Amendment. She was nicknamed "Steel Magnolia," because she's from the South and is perceived as strong and capable.

# Kids in the White House

- Abraham and Mary Todd Lincoln's youngest son, Thomas, was nicknamed "Tad," because his father thought he looked like a tadpole. The White House staff called Tad "Little Tyrant," because he was spoiled and always wanted to have his own way. During the Civil War, Tad was given his own Union lieutenant colonel's uniform, and he would march White House guards and staff around for hours.

- Chester and Ellen Arthur's daughter, Nellie, hosted the first White House Christmas party for needy children in 1883.

- Grover and Frances Cleveland's daughter, Ruth, often played on the front lawn of the White House. This was stopped after too many tourists picked her up and passed her around. From then on, Ruth played out of sight of tourists, causing newspaper columnists to write that she must be "deformed," since no one ever saw her anymore.

- Theodore and Alice Roosevelt's daughter, Alice, was known as "Princess Alice." She was an outspoken, mischievous girl, who startled dignitaries by such pranks as sliding down the White House banisters or pulling a garter snake out of her purse. All of the president's six children were lively and full of mischief. They were known as the "White House Gang." Kermit and Quentin Roosevelt once sneaked family pet Algonquin, an Icelandic calico pony, up the White House elevator. They thought Algonquin would cheer up their brother, Archie, who had the measles.

- When the famous rock group the Beatles made its American debut on TV's "The Ed Sullivan Show," President Nixon's daughters, Tricia and Julie, were in the audience.

- Gerald and Betty Ford's son, Steven, played the role of Andy Richards in the CBS TV soap opera "The Young and the Restless."

- During a dinner for the president of Mexico, Jimmy and Rosalynn Carter's nine-year-old daughter, Amy, read a Nancy Drew mystery at the table in between courses.

# Lineup of Notable World Leaders
# in History

| LEADER | YEARS AND HIGHLIGHTS OF RULE/ ACHIEVEMENT |
|---|---|
| **David**<br>King of the ancient Hebrews | **died 972 B.C.:** Reign marked the change of the Jews from a confederation of tribes to a settled nation; moved his capital from Hebron to Jerusalem. |
| **Pericles**<br>Athenian statesman, leader, ancient Greece | **c. 495–429 B.C.:** Created a democracy in Athens; patron of the arts; the Parthenon, a temple which served as a model for much Greek and Roman architecture, built; Peloponnesian War fought between Athens and Sparta. |
| **Alexander**<br>King of Macedonia, military commander | **356–323 B.C.:** Conquered much of Asia, the Middle East, and Egypt; spread Greek culture throughout his huge empire; founded the city of Alexandria in Egypt, which became a center of culture and learning; one of the greatest generals and most powerful leaders of all time. |
| **Julius Caesar**<br>Roman general, dictator | **c. 102–44 B.C.:** Became popular with the Roman people after conquering Gaul (France) and Britain. The Roman senate, fearing his power, ordered him to disband his army, but Caesar refused and crossed the Rubicon River into Italy. He won battles against forces opposing him and made himself dictator. He was assassinated by his friend Brutus and others on the Ides of March, 44 B.C. |
| **Cleopatra**<br>Queen of Egypt | **69–30 B.C.:** Led a revolt against her brother for the throne of Egypt, which she won with the help of Julius Caesar, who fell in |

| LEADER | YEARS AND HIGHLIGHTS OF RULE/ ACHIEVEMENT |
|---|---|
| | love with her; later married Roman soldier and politician Marc Antony. The two tried to defeat an invasion of Roman forces led by Octavian, but were defeated. Antony committed suicide; soon after, Cleopatra killed herself by allowing an asp, a poisonous snake, to bite her. |
| **Augustus Caesar** Roman emperor | **63 B.C.–A.D. 14:** Adopted son of Julius Caesar; first emperor of Rome; oversaw the Pax Romana (Roman Peace), during which no wars were fought; the arts flourished and it was a golden age for literature in Rome; Jesus was born. |
| **Constantine the Great** Roman emperor | **c. A.D. 288–337:** Founded the city of Constantinople (present-day Istanbul, Turkey), which became the capital of the Byzantine Empire; made Christianity a lawful religion (Christians had been persecuted earlier); first Christian emperor. |
| **Charlemagne** King of France, Emperor of the Holy Roman Empire | **c. 742–814:** Ruled over large part of central and western Europe; encouraged trade and education; established schools for children of all classes; preserved classical Greek and Roman literature; was considered a model for Christian rulers of the Middle Ages. |
| **Haroun al-Rashid** Caliph, Arab Empire | **c. 764–809:** Descended from the uncle of Muhammad, the Arab founder of Islam; empire included all of southwest Asia and the northern part of Africa; had diplomatic relations with China and Charlemagne; patron of art and literature; made Baghdad a great cultural center. |

| LEADER | YEARS AND HIGHLIGHTS OF RULE/ ACHIEVEMENT |
| --- | --- |
| **William I, the Conqueror** Duke of Normandy; later king of England | **c. 1027–1087:** Norman Conquest of England, during which William defeated King Harold and his forces at the Battle of Hastings in 1066 and became king of England; started the system of feudalism in England, whereby the king gave land (called fiefs) to nobles in exchange for their loyalty. |
| **Lorenzo de Medici** Ruler of Florence | **1449–1492:** Patron of the great artists and sculptors of the Italian Renaissance, such as Michelangelo, Botticelli, and Leonardo da Vinci; known as "Lorenzo the Magnificent." |
| **Ferdinand and Isabella** King and queen of Spain | **1452–1516, 1451–1504:** Defeated the Moors, who had invaded and occupied the southern part of Spain, and united the country; sponsored the exploration of the New World by Christopher Columbus. |
| **Henry VIII** King of England | **1491–1547:** England changed from a Catholic country to a Protestant country. Henry, with the support of Parliament, made himself the head of the Christian church in England instead of the Pope. The Pope wouldn't let Henry divorce his wife, Catherine of Aragon, and marry Anne Boleyn. Henry had four more wives after Anne. Of Henry's six wives, two were divorced by him, one died after giving birth to his son, two were beheaded (including Anne), and the sixth outlived him. |
| **Elizabeth I** Queen of England | **1533–1603:** Henry VIII and Anne Boleyn's daughter; reigned during a cultural golden age (the Elizabethan Period in literature), which featured such brilliant writers as |

| LEADER | YEARS AND HIGHLIGHTS OF RULE/ ACHIEVEMENT |
|---|---|
| | William Shakespeare and Edmund Spenser; war with Spain and England's defeat of the Spanish Armada (fleet) in 1588; enactment of the poor laws, which attempted to remedy widespread poverty; encouraged commerce, exploration, manufacturing; a popular, shrewd ruler, known as "Good Queen Bess." |
| **Oliver Cromwell** English Puritan general, later Lord Protector of England | **1599–1658:** Led the army of Parliament to victory over King Charles I in the English Civil War; wars with Holland and Spain; persecution of most non-Puritain Protestants; harsh suppression of rebellion in Ireland. The monarchy was restored in 1660, when King Charles II returned to England from exile in Holland (called the Restoration period). |
| **Cardinal Richelieu** French cardinal, statesman, and chief minister to Louis XIII | **1585–1642:** Controlled the government of France; established absolute monarchy—rule by one person who is above the law; Thirty Years' War fought in Europe; French Protestants (Huguenots) persecuted. Richelieu is featured as a character in the famous adventure story *The Three Musketeers*, by 19th-century French author Alexandre Dumas. |
| **Louis XIV** King of France | **1638–1715:** Invited French nobles to live at court, thereby removing them as threats to his power; encouraged foreign trade and industry; built up the French army and navy; patron of the arts; the lavish royal palace of Versailles was built; Louis was known as the "Sun King," because of the brilliance of his court. |

| LEADER | YEARS AND HIGHLIGHTS OF RULE/ ACHIEVEMENT |
|---|---|
| **Peter the Great** Tsar of Russia | **1672–1725:** Tried to modernize Russia by introducing customs, culture, and ideas from western European countries; Peter personally cut off the long beards of the nobles and made them replace their traditional robes with European dress; built up the army and navy; moved the capital from Moscow to a new city he had built, St. Petersburg (now Leningrad). |
| **Louis XVI and Marie Antoinette** King and queen of France | **1754–1793, 1755–1793:** Last king and queen of France; dethroned by the French Revolution, convicted of treason and guillotined (beheaded by the guillotine). |

| **Maximilien Robespierre** Leader of the French Revolution | **1758–1794:** Headed the Committee of Public Safety after the downfall of the monarchy; the committee served as the government of France and conducted a Reign of Terror, during which thousands of aristocrats (nobles), their families, and other "enemies of France" were guillotined without trial. After public reaction against his policies, Robespierre was executed without a trial. |
|---|---|
| **Napoleon Bonaparte** French general, first consul, emperor | **1769–1821:** Overthrew the government in the coup d'etat of 1799; crowned himself emperor in 1804; conquered and placed his |

| LEADER | YEARS AND HIGHLIGHTS OF RULE/ ACHIEVEMENT |
|---|---|
| | brothers and sisters on the thrones of Holland, Spain, and Italy; lost two-thirds of his army in a disastrous invasion of Russia; defeated by allied forces at Leipzig and exiled to the island of Elba; returned to France with a small army and was defeated by the British at Waterloo; exiled to the island of St. Helena; while emperor, created the Napoleonic Code of laws. |
| **Simon Bolivar** Venezuelan revolutionary | **1783–1830:** Fought Spanish troops for the independence of countries in northern South America (present-day Venezuela, Colombia, Ecuador, Peru, and Bolivia); called "The Liberator." |
| **Otto von Bismarck** Chancellor of Germany | **1815–1898:** United the German states into a single empire ruled by a kaiser (emperor); expansion of German commerce and industry; acquisition of overseas colonies; known as the "Iron Chancellor." |
| **Victoria** Queen of England | **1819–1901:** Because of Victoria, her husband, Prince Albert, and her outstanding prime ministers, Britain became a world power; industrial, military, and colonial expansion took place. The British Empire included a large number of colonies, such as Australia, Canada, India, New Zealand, and large portions of Africa. The Victorian Period was also marked by scientific advances, artistic and literary greatness, and stern morality. |
| **Nicholas II** Tsar of Russia | **1868–1918:** Last Tsar; the Russian Revolution of 1917 toppled the monarchy and substituted a communist government. Nicholas, his wife, and their children were |

| LEADER | YEARS AND HIGHLIGHTS OF RULE/ ACHIEVEMENT |
|---|---|
| | executed. It was rumored that one child, Anastasia, survived, but no one has ever been able to prove this. |
| **Lenin (Vladimir Ilyich Ulyanov)** Russian revolutionary leader, chief of the Soviet Government | **1870–1924:** Leader of the Russian Revolution; founder of the modern Soviet state. |
| **Mohandas K. "Mahatma" Gandhi** Indian political and spiritual leader | **1869–1948:** Led India's campaign for independence from Great Britain; used methods of passive resistance and nonviolent disobedience such as boycotts and hunger strikes to influence the British rulers (called the "Raj," a shortened form of "rajah," meaning an Indian Prince) and to stop fighting between Hindus and Moslems; assassinated by a Hindu fanatic who was angered at Gandhi's tolerance of Moslems. The title *mahatma* means "great soul." |
| **Josef Stalin** Leader of the U.S.S.R. | **1879–1953:** Became leader after Lenin's death in 1924; totally abolished private ownership of industries and farms, which became collectives, run by the workers but owned by the government; conducted brutal "purges," in which millions of "enemies of the state" were executed or sent to *gulags* (labor camps); World War II fought; expanded Soviet influence in Eastern Europe, which contributed to the Cold War between East and West. |
| **Adolf Hitler** German dictator | **1889–1945:** Founder of the Nazi Party and Führer (leader) of Germany; came up with the terrible idea of a "master race" of "pure" Aryans who would rule the world |

**LEADER**

**YEARS AND HIGHLIGHTS OF RULE/ ACHIEVEMENT**

for a thousand years as the Third Reich (empire); persecuted, imprisoned, and murdered millions of political opponents and other "enemies of the Reich"; started World War II, lost the war, and committed suicide. He was one of the most evil and mentally unbalanced rulers in history.

Adolf Hitler

**Winston Churchill**
Prime Minister of
Great Britain

**1874–1965:** Led the country through World War II; symbolized the fierce determination of the British to resist conquest by the Germans and to win the war.

**David Ben-Gurion**
Prime Minister of
Israel

**1886–1973:** Helped Israel become a state (1948) and was made its first prime minister.

**Haile Selassie**
Emperor of Ethiopia

**1891–1975:** Led troops in 1935 against the invasion forces of Italy; worked for greater cooperation and unity among African countries, especially through the Organization for African Unity (OAU); overthrown by the Ethiopian military in 1974.

**Mao Tse-tung**
Chinese revolutionary
leader

**1893–1976:** Founded the People's Republic of China, a communist republic; became chairman of the communist party;

| LEADER | YEARS AND HIGHLIGHTS OF RULE/ ACHIEVEMENT |
|--------|-------------------------------------------|
| | established the Cultural Revolution, during which many government officials and teachers were sent out to work in the fields alongside the peasants. Mao's "Little Red Book," *Quotations from Chairman Mao*, contained his thoughts on communist ideology and was required reading for children in school. |
| **Ayatollah Ruhollah Khomeini** Iranian religious and political leader | **1900–1989:** Exiled by the Shah of Iran; returned to Iran in 1979 after the shah was deposed; proclaimed Iran an Islamic republic and began to exercise complete authority in the nation; war with Iraq (1980–1988); holding of U.S. hostages (1979–1981). |
| **Nelson Mandela** South African political leader | **b. 1918:** Lawyer and black nationalist who fought against apartheid (white-racist policy that denies civil, social, and economic equality to blacks and other nonwhites); sentenced to life imprisonment in 1964 for political activities; released, 1990. Mandela's civil-rights cause has been celebrated worldwide. |
| **Lech Walesa** Polish labor leader | **b. 1943:** Dismissed as an electrician at the Gdansk shipyard in 1976 for antigovernment protests; in 1980, striking workers won his reinstatement; became the leader of an independent (not state-run) union, Solidarity, which gained many concessions from the government. Walesa was arrested and imprisoned during the military crackdown of 1981, but was released in 1982; won the Nobel Peace Prize, 1983; elected president of Poland in 1990. |

# Nicknames of Kings and Queens

**Louis the Fat**

Louis VI was King of France from 1108 to 1137. In his forties, he gained so much weight that he could not mount his horse. However, he was also known as "Louis the Wide-Awake" because of the peace and prosperity of his reign.

Other Louises in French history:
Louis II—"the Stammerer"
Louis V—"the Sluggard"
Louis VII—"the Young"
Louis X—"the Quarrelsome"
Louis XI—"the Cruel"

**Ivan the Terrible**

Ivan IV, Russian ruler from 1547 to 1584, was called "the Terrible" because of his reign of terror and fits of fury. He killed his son, Ivan, in a rage and disposed of seven wives.

Mary I Queen of England

**Bloody Mary**

Mary I, Queen of England (1553–1558), earned her nickname because of her religious persecution of Protestants.

**Peter the Mad**

Peter III, ruler of Russia (1761–1762), earned his nickname because of his many temper tantrums. He was also said to be mentally unbalanced.

**Silly Billy**    William IV, King of Great Britain from 1830 to 1837, was dubbed "Silly Billy" because of his eccentric behavior.

# Young Rulers

**TUTANKHAMEN—Ruler of Ancient Egypt, circa 1358 B.C.**
Tutankhamen became Pharaoh (king) of Egypt when he was about eight or nine and ruled until his death nine years later. "King Tut" is remembered more for his tomb than for his reign. In 1922, the unopened tomb was discovered, containing four rooms full of treasures and a coffin of solid gold. The treasures of "Tut" have been shown in museums throughout the world.

**EDWARD V—King of England, 1483**
At the age of eighteen, Edward V became king. Within a short time, his uncle, Richard, Duke of Gloucester, imprisoned Edward, along with his younger brother, in the Tower of London and took over the throne.
    The young king and his brother disappeared, and to this day, no one knows exactly what happened to them. It is widely believed that the boys were smothered to death in their sleep by order of Richard. However, some sources suggest that Henry VII, the king who ruled after Richard, had the boys killed.

**EDWARD VI—King of England, 1547–1553**
Edward VI was the son of King Henry VIII and his third wife, Jane Seymour. Edward VI became king at the age of ten when his father died. He reigned for six years under the control of his uncle, Edward Seymour. He is remembered for founding English grammar schools. Edward died at the age of sixteen from tuberculosis.

**LADY JANE GREY—Queen of England, 1553**
Lady Jane became queen at the age of fifteen and reigned for nine days. Her succession to the throne was arranged by English nobles who didn't want Edward VI's sister, Mary, to become queen. However, the English people rallied to the cause of Mary, and Jane was imprisoned and beheaded.

## FRANCIS II—King of France, 1559–1560

Fifteen-year-old Francis became king when his father, Henry II, died of a head wound sustained in a lancing bout in a tournament. The death of his father had been predicted by the famous psychic Nostradamus four years earlier. Francis II died of a high fever at age sixteen, having reigned less than eight months.

## PETER I—Ruler of Russia, 1682–1725

At age ten, Peter ruled Russia with his half brother, Ivan. When he was seventeen, he assumed full power. Known as Peter the Great, he is most remembered for westernizing Russia.

## PU YI—The Last Emperor of China, 1908–1912

Pu Yi became emperor when he was two years old. He spent most of his youth pampered and protected inside the Forbidden City of Peking. After he abdicated, he became the emperor of the Japanese-ruled state of Manchuria until the end of World War II. In the 1950s, Pu Yi was imprisoned by the Chinese communist government and later became a gardener in Peking. Pu Yi died in 1967.

# They Said It
# Quotes From World Leaders

*"The die is cast."*

**—Julius Caesar**
**As he crossed the Rubicon River into Italy**

*"I am the state."*

**—Louis XIV**
**King of France**

*"The care of human life and happiness . . . is the first and only legitimate object of good government."*

*"When angry, count ten before you speak; if very angry, an hundred."*

**—Thomas Jefferson**
**Third U.S. president**

*"One man with courage makes a majority."*
### —Andrew Jackson
**Seventh U.S. president**

*"As I would not be a* slave, *so I would not be a* master. *This expresses my idea of democracy."*
### —Abraham Lincoln
**Sixteenth U.S. president**

*"We are not amused."*
### —Victoria
**Queen of England, after seeing a groom-in-waiting do an imitation of her.**

*"Speak softly and carry a big stick."*
### —Theodore Roosevelt
**Twenty-sixth U.S. president.**

*"The chief business of the American people is business."*
### —Calvin Coolidge
**Thirtieth U.S. president**

*"The only thing we have to fear is fear itself."*
### —Franklin D. Roosevelt
**Thirty-second U.S. president, first inaugural address.**

*"No one can make you feel inferior without your consent."*
### —First Lady Eleanor Roosevelt

*"I have nothing to offer but blood, toil, tears, and sweat."*

*"We shall never surrender."*
### —Winston Churchill
**Prime minister of Great Britain, in speeches during World War II.**

*"Ask not what your country can do for you; ask what you can do for your country."*
### —John F. Kennedy
**Thirty-fifth U.S. president, during his inaugural address.**

# 29 Influential Americans of the Past

Each of the notable Americans below holds an important place in U.S. history. They deserve special mention for their great contributions to society, and for their ideas, courage, and determination.

**Jane Addams**
**1860–1935**

Addams was a social worker who founded Hull House, a community center for the poor in Chicago. Hull House influenced community centers (called settlement houses) throughout the country. Addams worked for social reforms for the poor, for world peace, and for women's rights. She received the Nobel Peace Prize for her reforms in 1931.

**Susan B. Anthony**
**1820–1906**

Anthony was an abolitionist and women's rights (then called women's suffrage) activist. She and fellow suffragette Elizabeth Cady Stanton succeeded in bringing about New York State laws guaranteeing women rights over their children and control of property and wages (until then, legally controlled by men). In 1872, Anthony led a group of women to the polls in Rochester, N.Y., to vote. She was arrested, tried, and fined. Other women followed Anthony's example, forcing the issue of women's right to vote to the U.S. Supreme Court. The case was decided against them, and voting rights for women did not become law until 1920.

**Clara Barton
1821–1912**

Founder of the American Red Cross. Barton nursed in army camps and on battlefields during the Civil War and was known as the "Angel of the Battlefield." During the Franco-Prussian War of 1870, she worked behind German lines for the International Red Cross. She organized the American Red Cross in 1881 and headed it until 1904.

**Daniel Boone
1734–1820**

Frontiersman who blazed the famous Wilderness Road, explored Kentucky, and founded a settlement there—Boonesboro. In 1778, Boone was captured and enslaved by the Shawnee Indians, who nicknamed him "Big Turtle." He escaped and traveled 160 miles to safety. Boone's pioneer adventures have become legendary, and he is considered one of the greatest frontierpersons in U.S. history.

**Louis Brandeis
1856–1941**

Lawyer and Associate Justice of the Supreme Court from 1916 to 1939, Brandeis secured social, political, and economic reforms that benefited American workers. He was a leader of the Zionist movement in the U.S. (the movement to establish a Jewish national home in Palestine), supported President Franklin D. Roosevelt's New Deal to help end the Great Depression, and crusaded for labor unions against big business.

**George Washington Carver**
**c. 1860–1943**

Carver was a chemist, botanist, and educator born the son of slaves in Missouri. While a researcher at Alabama's Tuskegee Institute, he developed hundreds of industrial uses for such crops as peanuts and sweet potatoes. Carver's research ended the South's overdependence on cotton as a cash crop and helped the region become more stable economically.

**Dorothea Dix**
**1802–1887**

Dix was a social reformer who crusaded for the scientific and humane treatment of the mentally ill. In 1841, Dix was shocked to see mental patients in prisons with criminals, and she launched a successful campaign to establish mental hospitals.

**Frederick Douglass**
**1817–1895**

Douglass, an escaped slave, became a leading abolitionist and orator, lecturing for an antislavery society in Massachusetts. Fearing capture as a fugitive slave, Douglass traveled to England and Ireland, where he spoke out against slavery. In 1847, he returned to the U.S. and purchased his freedom. During the Civil War, Douglass helped to organize two black Massachusetts regiments and urged other blacks to join the Union ranks. After the war, he pressed for civil rights for blacks and held government posts, including that of minister to Haiti.

**W.E.B. (William Edward Burghardt) Du Bois 1868–1963**

Civil rights leader, college professor, author, and a cofounder of the National Association for the Advancement of Colored People (NAACP). Du Bois spoke out in favor of political and social equality for blacks, as well as economic opportunity. He lived in Ghana the last two years of his life. There he edited the *African Encyclopedia for Africans*.

**Ralph Waldo Emerson 1803–1882**

Poet and essayist who stressed the importance of individuality and self-reliance. His writings and lectures encouraged people to rely on their own judgment.

**Benjamin Franklin 1706–1790**

Franklin was a statesman, diplomat, writer, printer, publisher, and inventor. He was a founder of the United States, a signer of the Declaration of Independence, and helped draft the Constitution. Among his inventions were the Franklin stove, bifocal glasses, and a glass harmonica. His famous magazine, *Poor Richard's Almanack*, was published from 1732 to 1767. The sayings of "Poor Richard" stressed prudence, common sense, and honesty, and became standard American proverbs. Well-known examples are "Early to bed and early to rise, makes a man healthy, wealthy, and wise" and "A word to the wise is enough."

**Marcus Garvey**
**1887–1940**

Black leader and orator who stressed the importance and greatness of the African heritage. He believed that African Americans could establish in Africa a state with its own culture and civilization that would be free from the domination of the white majority in the U.S.

**Samuel Gompers**
**1850–1924**

Labor leader who was the first president of the American Federation of Labor. Gompers successfully campaigned for wage increases, shorter hours, and greater freedom for workers (most of whom had been underpaid and overworked).

**Alexander Hamilton**
**1755–1804**

Hamilton was a founder of the United States, a leader in the drafting of the Constitution, and served as the first U.S. secretary of the treasury. Hamilton favored a strong national government that would guide the industrial development of the nation and regulate the excesses of business owners. His closest political rival was Thomas Jefferson, who believed that the United States economy should be based on agriculture, and that state and local governments should have the power to regulate citizens.

**William Randolph**
**Hearst**
**1863–1951**

Journalist and publisher who established a huge publishing empire that included 18 newspapers in 12 cities and 9 magazines. Hearst was a pioneer in the kind of sensational newspaper reporting often called "yellow journalism." His reporters would make an event sound more dramatic than it actually was in order to get readers to buy Hearst's newspapers. Articles also featured pictures that highlighted the drama. Hearst's newspapers stirred up public hatred of the Spanish after reporting on the alleged mistreatment of Cuban citizens by Spanish soldiers. The reports led to U.S. military involvement in the Spanish-American War. Hearst was also known for his huge estate in California, San Simeon. It cost $50 million to build and featured a castle with elevators, pools, movie rooms, and enormous dining halls.

**Oliver Wendell Holmes, Jr. 1841–1935**

Holmes was a judge and Supreme Court Justice known for his wit and legal wisdom. He thought that the law should be used to respond to the needs of society. He supported minimum-wage laws and the right of Americans to freedom of speech, and was an opponent of censorship.

**Helen Keller 1880–1968**

Keller was an author and lecturer who had become blind and deaf at the age of 20 months after contracting a high fever. When she was seven, her parents hired a special teacher, Anne Sullivan, to work with her. After some time, Anne was able to communicate with Helen by using the sense of touch. Anne spelled out words with her fingers pressed into the palms of Helen's hands. Helen also learned to speak, and she went on to graduate with honors from Radcliffe College. She then became a spokesperson for the disabled and raised money for schools and research. She also wrote books, including *The Story of My Life* and *Midstream—My Later Life*.

**Martin Luther King, Jr. 1929–1968**

Clergyman and probably the greatest leader of the civil-rights movement in the twentieth century. King supported nonviolent methods of protest against segregation, such as boycotts of segregated city buses and sit-ins at lunch counters. (At a sit-in, demonstrators would occupy seats visible to the public and then refuse to vacate them. Blacks were expected to stand if they wished to be served.) These protests were a way of forcing people to confront the injustice of segregation. King also helped organize the 1963 civil rights march on Washington. Hundreds of thousands of people listened as King gave his now-famous speech ("I Have a Dream") describing a future of racial harmony. Martin Luther King was assassinated in April 1968 in Memphis, Tennessee. A national holiday is observed in his honor each January, the month of his birth.

**Charles Lindbergh 1902–1974**

Aviator who, in 1927, made the first solo nonstop flight across the Atlantic Ocean in his plane *The Spirit of St. Louis*. Nicknamed the "Lone Eagle" and "Lucky Lindy," Lindbergh influenced the future of aviation.

**Thomas Paine 1737–1809**

Paine was a leading patriot of the American Revolution and an author. His popular and very influential pamphlet *Common Sense* (1776) urged the American colonists to declare their independence from English rule.

**Rosa Parks 1913–**

On December 1, 1955, Parks, a black seamstress, sat down in the whites-only section of a Montgomery, Alabama, city bus and refused to give up her seat to a white man who boarded later. The act and her arrest sparked a year-long bus boycott by blacks, which ended in a Supreme

Court decision declaring bus segregation
unconstitutional.

**William Penn
1644–1718**

In 1681, Penn, a Quaker, was given a
large province of land in America by King
Charles II in payment of a debt owed to
Penn's father. Penn called his province
Pennsylvania and established a colony there
notable for its religious tolerance and political freedom. Thousands of European
Quakers, who had been persecuted for
their beliefs in their own countries, emi-
grated to Pennsylvania.

**Frances Perkins
1882–1965**

Perkins was the first woman to become a
U.S. cabinet member. From 1933 to 1945
she served as secretary of labor under
President Franklin D. Roosevelt. She was
instrumental in the adoption of the Social
Security Act, and she promoted many labor reforms to aid workers.

**Sitting Bull
c. 1831–1890**

Native American leader of the Sioux tribe
and a leader in the armed resistance against
the forced resettlement of the Sioux onto
reservations. Sitting Bull and an army of

Tatanka
Yotanka
(Sitting Bull)

Sioux warriors won a decisive victory over U.S. Army general George Armstrong Custer and Custer's cavalry at the Battle of Little Bighorn in Montana on June 25, 1876. Custer and all his men were killed, and Sitting Bull escaped to Canada with some of his warriors. He returned to the U.S. in 1881 on the promise of a pardon and encouraged the Sioux not to sell their lands.

**Henry David Thoreau 1817–1862**

Writer, philosopher, and naturalist who stressed the importance of individuality and of living in harmony with nature. In his famous essay "Civil Disobedience," Thoreau wrote that people have the right to break the law in order to protest the actions of government they believe are unjust, but he also cautioned that protestors should be prepared to go to jail if they do disobey the law. Thoreau himself was jailed for refusing to pay his poll tax in 1845. He didn't want his taxes to be spent on the Mexican War, because he felt that slavery would be extended to the West if the U.S. won the war.

Henry David Thoreau

**Sojourner Truth**
**c. 1797–1883**

A slave until her escape in 1827, Sojourner Truth traveled throughout the North speaking out in favor of black emancipation and women's rights. After the Civil War, she worked to resettle freed slaves in Washington, D.C. A powerful personality and a gripping speaker, Sojourner Truth remained unable to read and write all her life.

**Harriet Tubman**
**c. 1820–1913**

Tubman was an escaped slave. After 1850, she helped over 300 slaves to freedom in the northern states and Canada via the Underground Railroad, a network of houses and other hiding places. Escaped slaves traveled from one "station" of the railroad to the next under cover of night. Harriet Tubman was called "Moses," after the Biblical character who led the Hebrew slaves out of Egypt to the Promised Land. During the Civil War, Tubman worked as a nurse, a laundress, and a spy for the Union forces.

**Booker T.**
**Washington**
**1856–1915**

Educator, born into a slave family, who founded the Tuskegee Institute, a college for black students, in Alabama. The institute opened in 1881 and was one of the first to educate freed slaves.

**Emma Hart Willard**
**1787–1870**

In 1814, Willard, a teacher, opened a women's school in her home, where she taught subjects not then available to women, such as science and mathematics. In 1821, she founded the Troy Female Seminary, which offered collegiate education to women and opened up new opportunities for women teachers. The school was later renamed in her honor.

# They Said It
## Quotes by Influential Americans

*"Join the union, girls, and together say* Equal Pay for Equal Work.*"*
**—Susan B. Anthony**

*"Our government is the . . . teacher. For good or ill, it teaches the whole people by its example."*
**—Louis Brandeis**

*"No man can put a chain about the ankle of his fellow man without at last finding the other end fastened about his own neck."*
**—Frederick Douglass**

*"Believe in life! Always human beings will live and progress to greater, broader, and fuller life."*
**—W.E.B. Du Bois**

*"The only way to have a friend is to be one."*
**—Ralph Waldo Emerson**

*"No barrier of the senses shuts me out from . . . my book friends. They talk to me without embarrassment."*
**—Helen Keller**

*"I have a dream that my four little children will one day live in a nation where they will not be judged by the color of their skin, but by the content of their character."*
**—Martin Luther King, Jr.**

*"These are the times that try men's souls."*

**—Thomas Paine,**
**Common Sense**

*"What treaty that the white man ever made with us have they kept? Not one. . . . Where are the warriors today? Who slew them? Where are our lands? Who owns them? . . . What law have I broken?"*

**—Sitting Bull**
**(Tatanka Yotanka)**

*"When I found I had crossed that line, I looked at my hands to see if I was the same person. There was such a glory over everything."*

**—Harriet Tubman**
**On her first escape from slavery**

# 6 Really Rich People in History

## CROESUS—King of Lydia
Croesus, the last king of Lydia (560 to 546 B.C.), was responsible for the creation of a state treasury made up of pure gold coins. Earlier Lydian coins had been made of electrum, a natural combination of gold and silver, and their trade value was always questionable. The Lydians mined and refined huge amounts of gold which made their country—and especially Croesus, who controlled the treasury—incredibly wealthy. Today, wealthy people are sometimes said to be "as rich as Croesus."

## CRASSUS—Businessman of Rome
Marcus Licinius Crassus was born in 115 B.C. into a wealthy Roman family. Crassus was smart and had an attractive personality, but he was also greedy and ambitious. He created Rome's first fire department by putting a 500-man bucket brigade together to rush to burning buildings. However, the firefighters had to wait while Crassus bargained with the building's owner over the price of his service. If the owner couldn't come up with a satisfactory price, Crassus and his men would simply let the building burn down. Crassus usually got the price he asked for. Another business

venture of Crassus's was a school for slaves. He bought unskilled bondsmen (slaves), had them trained, and then sold them for handsome profits. Crassus also owned huge tracts of land, which Roman generals had captured during the Civil War of 88 to 82 B.C. Crassus was allowed to buy the land at bargain prices. It's estimated that Crassus was worth about 170 million sesterces (a unit of Roman currency), a sum almost equal to the entire annual income of the Roman treasury.

## CORNELIUS VANDERBILT—"The Commodore"

Vanderbilt was born in 1794 in Staten Island, New York. He quit school at eleven and at sixteen bought a small boat with money borrowed from his parents. He began to ferry passengers from Staten Island to New York City. He enlarged his fleet to three sailing ships, but then sold the ships in 1817 to learn the steamboat business. In 1829, Vanderbilt started his own steamboat fleet, and by 1846, he was a millionaire. Vanderbilt did it by charging lower fares and offering better service than his competitors. He established a network of steamboat lines along the New York and New England seaboard and created a monopoly in American transportation. During the California Gold Rush, Vanderbilt founded the Accessory Transit Company to take prospectors by ship to Panama, then overland to the Pacific and California. "The Commodore" (a commodore is a ship's commander) had made $11 million by 1853. In 1860, Vanderbilt quit the shipping business to go into railroads. He merged the mismanaged New York and Harlem and New York and Hudson River Lines into one profitable line. Then he acquired the New York Central railroad line and established the first New York-to-Chicago rail system. When Vanderbilt died in 1877, he was the richest man in the U.S., worth more than $100 million.

## HETTY GREEN—World's Biggest Miser

Born Henrietta Howland Robinson in 1835, Hetty inherited about $10 million from her parents. Her mother's family, the Howlands, had made millions in the shipping business, and Hetty's father had increased the fortune. Hetty devoted her life to increasing it further and she became the richest woman in the U.S. When she married millionaire Edward Green in 1867, she made him sign a contract stating that her fortune would remain solely in her possession. The couple separated after a few years, and he eventually went bankrupt. Instead of living in luxury, Hetty and her son occupied a rundown apartment in Hoboken, New Jersey. Hetty dressed in ragged clothing and rode the ferry to her office in New York City each day. She ate cold oatmeal because she was too stingy to pay for fuel to heat it up. When her son's knee became infected, Hetty refused to pay for a doctor. She dressed him in rags and took him to Bellvue Hospital in New York as a charity patient. When doctors recognized her and demanded payment, Hetty took her son home. The boy never received medical treatment, and several years later, his leg had to be amputated. When Hetty died in 1916, she left a fortune of more than $100 million. Hetty Green was known as the "Witch of Wall Street."

## JOHN D. ROCKEFELLER—The Billionaire Who Gave Away Dimes to Kids

Rockefeller was born in 1839 on a farm outside Richford, New York. In 1853 his family moved to Cleveland, where John attended B.S. Folsom's Commercial College. He worked as a clerk and then started his own business in 1859 selling grain, hay, and meats on the Cleveland docks. But Rockefeller realized that there was a lot of money to be made refining the oil that had just been discovered in western Pennsylvania. He and a partner built a refinery that quickly became the largest in Cleveland. In 1870, Rockefeller's business became a corporation called the Standard Oil Company of Ohio. During the next two decades, Standard Oil became a monopoly. Competitors were given a choice: merge with Standard Oil or be driven out of business. In 1896, Rockefeller was worth about $200 million. When Standard Oil began to produce kerosene for lighting and gasoline for automobiles, profits zoomed, and before long Rockefeller was a billionaire. A great philanthropist (a person who donates money to promote human welfare), Rockefeller gave away about $500 million during his lifetime. He founded the University of Chicago in 1892, the Rockefeller Institute of Medical Research in New York City in 1901, and the Rockefeller Foundation in 1913. Toward the end of his life, Rockefeller was known for giving away dimes to children he happened to see on the street.

## HENRY FORD—His Cars Made History

The man who once said that "History is bunk" (nonsense) was born on a farm near Dearborn, Michigan, in 1863. He served as an apprentice in a Detroit machine shop and later worked as an engineer for Thomas Edison at the Edison Illuminating Company. Ford began to tinker with internal-combustion engines in his home workshop and eventually created a fast Ford 999 racing automobile. In 1903 he formed the Ford Motor Company to produce cheap, efficient automobiles for every American. The first Model T Ford, the "Tin Lizzie," made its debut in 1908 and was an instant success. This sturdy little car cost $850—about half the price of most of its competitors. In 1913 Ford introduced the conveyor-belt assembly line. By 1915 half a million mass-produced cars were rolling off the assembly line, each one selling for less than $500. Most Americans wanted and could afford Ford cars, and Henry Ford became the largest automobile producer in the world. Over 15 million Model Ts were sold between 1908 and 1928, when the model was discontinued. The Model A was created to meet growing competition from other automakers. Ford also manufactured war materiel for the U.S. during both World Wars. Ford employees were better paid than workers at other factories, and they could join a profit-sharing plan, but Ford did this mainly to discourage his workers from forming a union. Ford, with his son, Edsel, established the Ford Foundation, a philanthropic organization. When Henry Ford died in 1947, he left a fortune of more than $1 billion.

# CHAPTER 6

# It's the Law

Did you know that it's still against the law in Kentucky to carry an ice cream cone in your pocket? Or that you can't hitch your bike to an airplane in Utah? These are just two of the wild, wacky laws of the past you'll come across in this chapter. On a more serious note, there are facts on famous law codes, important Supreme Court decisions, and a history of the police, plus famous prisons, stupid criminals, and a Crooks Hall of Shame that features a lineup of some of the most notorious lawbreakers in history.

# Lawmakers

## Famous Codes of Law

Throughout history, leaders of countries or empires have come up with rules to regulate the behavior of citizens. Without rules, people might do whatever they wanted; they might not respect the rights of others. But it wasn't enough just to say "Don't steal," or "Don't dump your trash in your neighbor's yard." These rules had to be written down as the laws of the land or community. Codes of law were written statements of rules that every citizen had to obey—even the leaders themselves. Below are some famous law codes in history.

**CODE OF HAMMURABI—18th century B.C., Babylonia**
Hammurabi was the king of Babylon, a city in the ancient kingdom of Babylonia in Mesopotamia (present-day Iraq). Hammurabi's law code was carved on an eight-foot-tall rock column in 3,600 lines of cuneiform, an ancient kind of writing made up of wedge-shaped characters rather than letters. There were 282 laws written into the code, and they dealt with such legal matters as commerce, marriage, theft, slavery, and debts. Punish-

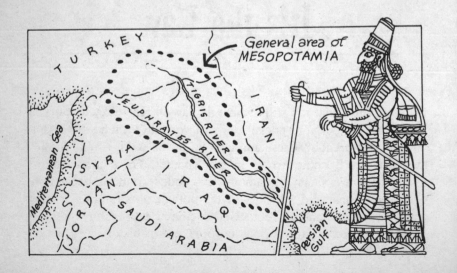

ment for disobeying these laws was harsh and followed the Biblical law of "an eye for and eye and a tooth for a tooth." If someone caused the blindness of another, he or she would be blinded; if a person was hit by another, the assaulter would have his or her fingers broken; a thief's own property would be confiscated.

## TWELVE TABLES—450 B.C., Rome

This early Roman law code was written after the plebeians (the common people) complained that the patrician (rich, aristocratic) judges were discriminating against them. Because the laws hadn't been written down, the judges had to try to remember them, or might even make up new ones that would favor the wealthy and powerful. The tables were written in Latin on twelve wooden tablets, and they gave the plebeians more legal power in Roman society and government.

## MAGNA CARTA—1215, England

In 1215, forty English nobles, angry at King John for abusing their rights and privileges, prepared to dethrone their ruler. John quickly decided to compromise and met with the nobles in a meadow at Runnymede, outside London. There, John was forced to sign a list of rights and privileges written up by the nobles. According to the Magna Carta (Latin for "Great Charter"), the king could not levy taxes without the consent of his parliament (the English legislature, similar to the U.S. Congress), and no free man in England could be deprived of liberty or property except through a trial or other legal process. Even though the Magna Carta originally benefited the nobles, it limited royal power and eventually served as a model for English common law.

## THE U.S. CONSTITUTION—1787–1791

During the American Revolution, delegates from the Thirteen Colonies—the Continental Congress—governed under a set of laws called the Articles of Confederation. After the war, the Constitutional Convention was held to draft a Constitution that would establish a strong central government in the new United States of America. The convention designed a government with separate Legislative, Executive, and Judicial branches. States also adopted this form of government.

The convention established Congress as a lawmaking body with two houses: the Senate and the House of Representatives. The Judicial branch was given the power to interpret those laws, to try criminal cases in court, and to hear appeals from citizens. The highest court of appeals was the Supreme Court. The Executive branch included the president, who had the power to approve or veto federal bills, carry out laws, appoint judges and other high officials, make foreign treaties, grant pardons and reprieves to federal offenders (spies or impeached presidents, for example), and act as commander-in-chief of the armed forces.

But the framers of the Constitution didn't want any one branch of government to become too powerful. They came up with a system of "checks and balances" that gave one branch the power to block a decision made by another branch. That way, everyone in government could have a say in how the country should be governed. Each branch could become involved in such issues as what laws should be enacted, when and if the U.S. should declare war on another country, or whether or not a president should be impeached.

The original seven articles of the Constitution set down the laws on how the U.S. government was to be formed. But several states refused to ratify the new Constitution unless a bill of rights for all citizens was attached to it. The first Congress agreed, and the first ten amendments, called the Bill of Rights, were added to the Constitution. They guaranteed all U.S. citizens freedom of the press, speech, religion and assembly; the right to a speedy trial and trial by jury; states' rights; that soldiers could not be quartered in private homes; the regulation of search and seizure of private property; and the right to keep and bear arms. By 1791, all thirteen states had ratified the Constitution.

By 1971, there were twenty-six amendments to the Constitution. Some important amendments since the Bill of Rights are: the abolition of slavery (1865); voting rights of every adult male citizen (1870); income taxes authorized (1913); women's right to vote (1920); repeal of Prohibition (1933); and lowering the voting age to eighteen (1971).

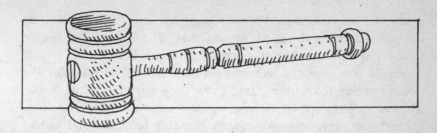

# 4 Famous Supreme Court Decisions

The Supreme Court, the highest (most important) court in the U.S., was established by the Constitution to have the final say on the interpretation of laws and of the Constitution itself. The Court has had a great impact on American society because of the decisions it has handed down. Below are some of the most famous Supreme Court decisions.

### 1857: *Dred Scott v. Sanford*
In 1834, a U.S. army surgeon, Dr. John Emerson, left Missouri, a slave state, and moved to Illinois, a free state, where slavery was against the law. Then he moved to Fort Snelling in Wisconsin Territory, also a free area. With him on his journeys was his slave, Dred Scott. Emerson and Scott moved back to Missouri in 1838, and in 1846, Emerson died. Dred Scott sued Mrs. Emerson for freedom for himself and his family. Because he had been a resident of a free state and a free territory, he felt his bondage should be ended. The case finally went to the Supreme Court. The Court was split over the decision, and it was Chief Justice Roger Taney, a former slaveowner, who tipped the balance against Dred Scott. Taney ruled that slaves were property—like a mule or a horse— and could not be citizens of any state or of the United States. Dred Scott and his family were doomed to remain slaves. The "Sanford" in the case was J.F.A. Sanford, Mrs. Emerson's brother, who was the legal administrator of his sister's property.

### 1896: *Plessy v. Ferguson*
In 1890, a Louisiana law separated railroad-coach passengers by race. When Homer Plessy tried to sit in an all-white railroad

coach, he was arrested. Plessy fought his arrest all the way up through the courts to the Supreme Court. The Court ruled against Plessy and in favor of segregation of the races: States could legally segregate public places like railroad cars and public schools. The Court's ruling led to the "Jim Crow" laws in the South, which widened segregation to include separate areas in restaurants, buses, and waiting rooms and separate drinking fountains and factory entrances. The law said that blacks were "separate but equal." But that phrase didn't make sense, if you think about it, because blacks couldn't *possibly* be equal to whites if they didn't have the same rights. They couldn't sit in the front of a bus, for example. *Note:* "Jim Crow" was a demeaning name for African-Americans and was featured in a racist song written by Thomas Dartmouth Rice that was sung by white entertainers made up to look like black men.

## 1954: *Brown v. Board of Education*

Linda Brown, a young black schoolgirl living in Topeka, Kansas, had to travel over two miles to attend a black elementary school, even though there was a white school four blocks from her home. Linda's parents sued the school district for its policy of school segregation, and the case finally reached the Supreme Court. The Court ruled that schools had to open their classrooms to *all* children. The Court called for the desegregation of schools "with all deliberate speed."

## 1966: *Miranda v. Arizona*

Ernesto Miranda, a high-school dropout with a long criminal record, was arrested in Arizona in 1963 for kidnapping. He was identified in a police lineup, and he signed a confession in which he said he had been told his rights by the police. But at the trial, Miranda's court-appointed lawyer argued that his client *hadn't* been told he had the right to a lawyer. The American Civil Liberties Union, an organization of lawyers that takes on cases perceived as threatening to the civil liberties of U.S. citizens or groups, took the case to the Supreme Court. In 1966, the Court ruled that before suspects can be questioned, the police must tell them they have the right to remain silent, that any statement they make can be used against them, and that they have the right to a lawyer, which the state will provide if they can't afford to pay for one. The reading of a suspect's rights became known as the Miranda warnings.

### 1973: *Roe v. Wade*
In the 1960s, "Jane Roe" (so called to protect her privacy) sued her home state of Texas to try to overturn the antiabortion laws, in the hope that abortion would become legal. The case reached the Supreme Court, which ruled in her favor and said that states could not ban abortions up to the third month of pregnancy. This Supreme Court decision is probably the most controversial in U.S. history. Many Americans feel that abortions are murder; many others feel it is a woman's choice whether or not to have an abortion, and that the government should not interfere in this choice; still others believe that abortions should be legal only in certain cases, as when the mother's life is in danger.

# 12 Really Weird Laws

These wacky laws were created many years ago, but for some strange reason, lawmakers never decided to repeal them. However, it's pretty unlikely that you'd be arrested today for breaking them—or that you'd even *want* to break most of them!

- In California, it's against the law to enter a restaurant on horseback.
- Donkeys can't sleep in bathtubs in Brooklyn, New York.
- Pickles must bounce in Connecticut.
- It's against the law in Kentucky to carry an ice cream cone in your pocket.
- In New Jersey, horse racing on the New Jersey Turnpike is prohibited by law.
- You're not allowed to plow a cotton field with an elephant in North Carolina.
- And in Dover, North Carolina, it's illegal to keep pigs outside your kitchen window.

- Don't auction off your turtle in Kansas City, Missouri. It's against the law.
- It's against the law in Green, New York, to walk backward on a sidewalk while munching peanuts at an outdoor concert.
- In Oklahoma, it's against the law to take a bite of another person's hamburger.
- Kids can't hitch their bikes to airplanes in Utah.
- And last but not least: If your pet goldfish makes a disturbance, it will not be allowed to ride buses in Seattle!

# Law Enforcers

## Police in History

### ATHENS AND ROME

In these ancient cities, unpaid magistrates were appointed by assemblies of citizens to keep law and order. Magistrates judged cases, but private citizens arrested wrongdoers and carried out punishments. In A.D. 6, the Roman *vigiles* were created. This was a large force of police who patrolled Rome's streets night and day.

### EUROPE IN THE MIDDLE AGES

Before the twelfth and thirteenth centuries, soldiers were put on "watches" at certain times of the day to keep an eye out for wrongdoings. Manors—the houses of nobles, sometimes castles, that functioned as self-sufficient villages—used their own soldiers to defend themselves. In Paris in the 1300s, King Louis IX appointed a provost who directed the night watch and commanded a mounted guard. In 1356, mounted patrols were formed to make the highways safe from bandits. They were the state troopers of the

Middle Ages. In the Scandinavian countries, a group called the *gjaldkere* was responsible for keeping law and order, and in rural towns, a *lensman* enforced the law and collected taxes.

## RUSSIA

In 1564, Russian ruler Ivan the Terrible created a group called the *oprichniki* to keep the boyars (nobles) from becoming too powerful. Tsar Peter the Great appointed a police chief in the capital city of St. Petersburg in 1718. In towns, military officers of the tsar supervised a paid police force, and in rural areas, officials used volunteers from the peasant class to keep law and order.

## ENGLAND

In the 1200s, kings appointed sheriffs to fine people who broke the law. Able-bodied men over fifteen formed the *posse comitatus,* which could be called out to capture fleeing criminals. Constables assisted sheriffs and magistrates and kept law and order. This system lasted for centuries.

## SCOTLAND YARD—And Why British Police Officers Are Called "Bobbies"

In 1829, Sir Robert Peel, a member of Parliament, reformed England's criminal laws and established the London police force. In his honor, police officers came to be known as "Peelers" or "Bobbies." The force's headquarters, Scotland Yard, was set up at the site of a palace used in the 1100s as a residence for visiting Scottish kings. The street on which the palace had been built was called Scotland Yard. The Yard (police headquarters) moved to a new building along the Thames River in 1890 and was renamed New Scotland Yard. In 1967, it moved to another building in the same area. Scotland Yard has become famous throughout history for solving baffling cases and catching notorious criminals.

# Law and Order in North America

## ROYAL CANADIAN MOUNTED POLICE

The RCMP was formed as a constabulary in 1873 and was first called the Northwest Mounted Police. Its job was to bring law and order to the Canadian west and especially to keep Native Americans from fighting settlers who had moved to their land. In 1920, the corps' name was changed to the Royal Canadian Mounted Police. The RCMP originally numbered 300 men and gained a legendary reputation for its daring exploits and determination in tracking down criminals. They came to be known as "Red Coats," "Riders of the Plains," and the "Mounties." The RCMP later included the police forces in all the provinces except Ontario and Quebec. Today, the RCMP performs police functions throughout Canada.

## THE U.S. "WILD" WEST

Cities had police forces or a militia to enforce the law, but keeping law and order in the newly settled West wasn't so easy. Settlers faced attacks by Indian tribes, who were very understandably angry that their land was being taken away from them. Homesteads, banks, and businesses were frequently robbed, and gun duels were common occurrences. Such towns as Dodge City, Kansas, and Tombstone, Arizona, became famous for their lawlessness. Government wasn't very well organized in the West of the 1800s, and for the most part, settlers took the law into their own hands. Vigilante committees were formed in frontier communities to enforce the law and punish wrongdoers, and the U.S. Army waged war against Native Americans for most of the century. In the 1870s, marshals and sheriffs like Wyatt Earp and Bat Masterson kept law and order in Western towns. Sheriff William Barclay Masterson, a gambler known for his dapper appearance, often used his gold-tipped cane to stop Kansas lawbreakers instead of his Colt .45 gun, earning him the nickname "Bat." But he and other law enforcers were just as ready to use their guns to "keep the peace."

Judges traveled from town to town to hear cases and pronounce sentences. A former cattle rustler (thief) and gambler, Roy Bean, set himself up as "Justice of the Peace" in Vinegaroon, Texas. His courtroom was in a saloon (bar) and he tried cases with the aid of one law book. He was known for his wit and common sense in dealing with crooks.

## THE TEXAS RANGERS

This famous mounted fighting force was organized in 1835 during the Texas Rebellion against Mexico. The Rangers fought in the Mexican War of 1846 and 1848 and in the Civil War. In the late 1850s, the Rangers battled the Comanche Indians. After the Civil War, their job was to control outlaws and feuding ranchers, and to keep law and order along the Rio Grande River. In 1874, the Rangers were split into two battalions: one battalion had the responsibility of settling range wars between ranchers; the other controlled cattle rustling on the Texas-Mexico border. By the 1900s, the Texas Rangers weren't really needed as a police force, and in 1935, they were merged with the state highway patrol.

# Lawbreakers
## Crooks Hall of Shame

There have been more crooks in history than you can throw the book at. (To "throw the book" at someone means to give him or her the most severe sentence the law allows.) Below are eight notorious criminals who definitely belong in the Hall of Shame.

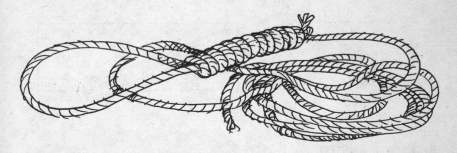

## WILLIAM H. BONNEY—better known as "Billy the Kid"

Born in 1859, Bonney was dubbed "the kid" because of his youth and small size. He was a notorious robber and gunslinger of the Old West and at one time headed a gang of cattle rustlers. He was captured twice and escaped twice, and finally caught for the last time by Sheriff Pat Garrett in 1881.

## AL "SCARFACE" CAPONE

Born in Naples, Italy, in 1899, Capone grew up in New York City, where he became involved in organized crime. In 1920, he moved to Chicago and became a notorious "bootlegger," a smuggler of liquor. At that time, it was against the law in the U.S. to sell or drink alcohol. Capone smuggled liquor from Canada to the U.S. and sold it to "speakeasies," bars that sold alcohol illegally and in secret. Patrons often needed to use a password in order to get into a speakeasy. Amazingly, business people, politicians, and some members of the police force secretly supported Capone and ignored the murders and other crimes committed by the gangster and his men. Government agent Elliot Ness was sent to Chicago to stop Capone, but Ness and his officers, known as the "Untouchables," had a tough time pinning any crimes on Al. Then the Untouchables discovered that Capone had never paid any income tax. Al was indicted for income-tax evasion and sentenced to eleven years in prison, where he died in 1947. Capone was nicknamed "Scarface" because of a knife wound he had received during a fight in Brooklyn, New York.

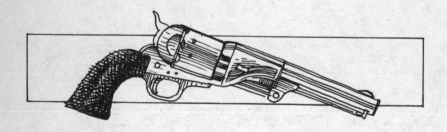

## BUTCH CASSIDY

This famous train and bank robber of the Wild West was born George LeRoy Parker in Utah in 1866. He took the last name "Cassidy" in honor of Mike Cassidy, who taught him cattle rustling and horse theft. He worked for awhile as a butcher (the only legal job he ever had) and was nicknamed "Butch." Cassidy, his friend Harry Longabaugh (the "Sundance Kid"), and their gang, the Wild Bunch, roamed the West robbing trains until the law finally caught up with them. Butch and Sundance fled to Bolivia, where it's said they died in a shoot-out with the Bolivian cavalry in 1909. But Butch's sister claimed that her brother came home to Utah in 1925, went straight, and died in 1937.

**FERDINAND WALDO DEMARA, JR.—The "Great Imposter"**
Demara, born in 1920, was a high-school dropout, but that didn't stop him from having several careers. However, he didn't have the proper and legal credentials for any of the careers he chose. During the 1940s, Demara posed as a Trappist monk in a Kentucky monastery, a psychology professor at a Pennsylvania college, a biologist at a cancer research institute near Seattle, and the recreational officer at a maximum security prison in Texas. But his greatest feat occurred during the Korean War, when he posed as a lieutenant-surgeon with the Canadian Navy. With the aid of medical books, Demara successfully performed operations on soldiers. He was eventually discovered, discharged, and deported to the U.S. In 1956, Demara was arrested in Maine for posing as a teacher in a local school. He later became a legitimately ordained minister.

**JOHN DILLINGER**
Dubbed "Public Enemy Number One" by the FBI, this vicious criminal of the 1930s and his gang robbed more banks in one year than Wild West outlaw Jesse James did in sixteen years. Dillinger's life of crime was cut short in 1934 outside a Chicago movie theatre, where he was apprehended by FBI agents.

**ELMYR DE HORY**
Born in 1906, De Hory was a Hungarian artist who wasn't having much luck selling his own paintings, so he decided to forge (illegally imitate) paintings in the style of famous artists. Hundreds of his fakes hang in famous museums and art galleries around the world; thousands are in private collections. All are "signed" by such famous artists as Henri Matisse, Pablo Picasso, and Paul Gauguin. De Hory was exposed as an art forger in 1967, but was never arrested for his crime. He died in 1976 on the Spanish island of Ibiza, where he had lived and painted since 1962.

## JESSE JAMES

Born in Missouri in 1847, Jesse fought in the Civil War with a Confederate guerrilla band. In 1866, with his brother, Frank, Jesse headed a notorious band of outlaws who robbed banks and trains. Most of the gang were captured or killed in 1876, but the James brothers escaped. The Governor of Missouri offered a reward for their capture, dead or alive. A former gang member, Robert Ford, tracked Jesse down and killed him to collect the reward money. Frank James surrendered, was tried for his crimes and acquitted, and settled peacefully on a farm in Missouri.

## ROBERT STROUD—"The Birdman of Alcatraz"

Sentenced to life imprisonment in 1916 for killing a prison guard, and kept in solitary confinement, Stroud found two baby sparrows one day in the exercise yard at Leavenworth Penitentiary, Kansas. He raised the sparrows with the aid of books on birds. Stroud became an expert on birds, corresponded with bird lovers all over the world, and gained a reputation for curing birds of diseases. He even published a book—*Stroud's Digest on the Diseases of Birds*—that is still in public libraries. Prison officials allowed him to keep more birds, a typewriter, a microscope, and books and magazines on the subject. But during the 1940s, Stroud was transferred to Alcatraz prison in California and ordered to leave his birds behind. At Alcatraz, Stroud continued his research through books and studied French and law. He died at Alcatraz in 1963.

## 5 Famous Prisons

### ALCATRAZ
This rocky island in San Francisco Bay was discovered by the Spanish in 1769 and named for its large pelican colony. The Spanish built a fort there, which the U.S. military later used as a prison. Alcatraz became a Federal prison for criminals in 1933. It was said to be impossible to break out of, and no one who attempted to escape ever succeeded. Alcatraz's nickname was "The Rock." The prison was closed in 1963.

### BASTILLE
This fortress in Paris was used mainly as a prison for nobles and political prisoners, who could be sent there at the king's whim. The dreaded *lettre de cachet* ("secret letter") would arrive from the king and order imprisonment for the receiver. In 1789, at the start of the French Revolution, a Paris mob of 20,000 stormed the Bastille to capture arms and ammunition to fight the king's regiments, which had been called out to keep law and order in the city. In the process, they freed seven prisoners. The Bastille, a hated symbol of royal power and tyranny, was soon demolished.

### DEVIL'S ISLAND
This infamous French Prison was an island in the Caribbean Sea off the coast of French Guiana. Founded in 1852 as a penal colony for political prisoners, Devil's Island was known for its unsanitary conditions and harsh treatment of prisoners who were condemned to hard labor there. Devil's Island was phased out as a prison between 1938 and 1951.

### THE GULAGS OF THE SOVIET UNION
These prison camps inside the U.S.S.R. were used mainly for political prisoners, who were sentenced to hard labor. In the 1930s, when Josef Stalin led the Soviet Union, millions of prisoners died from starvation and ill treatment in these camps. The Gulag prison camps are still in existence today. *Gulag* is a Russian

acronym, which in English means Chief Administration of Corrective Labor Camps.

## TOWER OF LONDON

Built around 1078, the Tower was a fort used as a royal residence in the Middle Ages, and then as a prison for the nobility and other notable people. Among those imprisoned there were Princess Elizabeth (later Queen Elizabeth I), jailed briefly by her sister, Mary; two wives of Henry VIII; Lady Jane Grey; and Sir Walter Raleigh. The Tower was sometimes called the "Bloody Tower," because of the executions which took place there, and ghosts were said to walk the battlements. Today the Tower of London is a museum that houses a collection of British crowns and jewels. In 1675, a swashbuckling highwayman (a thief who robbed coaches in the 1600s and 1700s) named Colonel Thomas Flood tried to steal the British Crown Jewels, but was caught while fleeing the Tower.

# 3 Famous Trials

## GALILEO—1633

This famous 69-year-old scientist was put on trial in Rome for heresy. He had written a book in which he agreed with the Polish scientist Copernicus that the sun was the center of the universe, not the earth. This theory was true, but it conflicted with the teachings of the Roman Catholic Church at that time. Galileo was threatened with torture and forced to confess that the theory was false.

## THE SALEM WITCH TRIALS—1692–1693

People were superstitious back then, and such phenomena as magic and witchcraft were widely feared. In Salem, Massachusetts, about ten girls accused certain men and women of making them act strangely by bewitching them. The girls' accusations were rarely questioned. About 150 "witches" were arrested, but only 31 were tried in 1692. All 31 were sentenced to death. By May, 1693, the trials had stopped, and the untried "witches" were released.

## THE "MONKEY" TRIAL—1925

In 1925, high-school teacher John Scopes was put on trial in Tennessee for teaching Charles Darwin's theory of evolution. In part, the theory states that humans evolved from a common ancestry with apes, and the teaching of it was against the law in Tennessee. People believed that the Bible story of human creation should be interpreted literally (many still believe that). Scopes was defended by the brilliant attorney Clarence Darrow; fiery orator and politician William Jennings Bryan spoke for the prosecution. The trial drew huge crowds who came to listen to the two famous lawyers match wits. In the end, the jury found Scopes guilty, and he was fined $100.

# 3 Really Stupid Crooks

The crooks below should have realized that breaking the law was a bad idea in the first place!

- In 1978, three shoplifters entered a home furnishings store in Barnsley, England, and stuffed some curtains into their plastic bags. They tried to leave by separate exits, but were immediately caught by store detectives. They hadn't noticed that the shop was hosting a convention of store detectives that day.

- In 1982, Carlos Aralijo decided to burglarize a McDonald's in downtown Los Angeles. In the early morning hours, he climbed to the roof and slid down the chimney. However, about halfway down, he got stuck in the narrow, grease-coated pipe. He yelled for help for hours before someone heard him. It took firefighters and paramedics half an hour to free this would-be hamburglar.

- After Clive Bunyan stole about $350 from a store's cash register in Cayton, England, he made his getaway on his motorcycle. To hide his identity, Bunyan wore his full-face crash helmet as a mask. However, he forgot that the words "Clive Bunyan—Driver" were printed clearly across the front of his helmet. Bunyan was arrested and ordered to pay for his crime by doing 200 hours of community service.

# CHAPTER 7

# Lifestyles

. . . . . . . . . . . . . . . . . . . . . . . . . . . . . . . . . . . . . . . . .

Take a trip back into the past and find out what your life would have been like if you had lived in Ancient Egypt, during the Middle Ages, in an Iroquois Indian village, or as a pioneer during the settling of the American West. Then, check out the origins of celebrations such as birthdays, holidays like Halloween, and favorite foods like hot dogs and potato chips. You'll also find a history of clothes, including a list of hot styles of the past that will probably never be popular again!

# What if You and Your Family Lived In...:
## Ancient Egypt

**WHERE DID YOU LIVE?**
Wealthy Egyptians who lived in the countryside built large villas (estates) with high walls around them. The house of a villa featured a reception room where business was conducted and guests were received, a central hall where the family entertained their friends, and the family's private living quarters, including bedrooms and the bathroom. Outside, in separate areas, were the kitchens, well, stables, servants' quarters, storerooms, a chariot house, and cattle pens. There was a family chapel on the grounds, and a shady garden with a pool. Less wealthy families lived in similar houses, but they were smaller and did not have gardens. The family spent a lot of time on the roof to catch the breeze and escape the dust and heat below.

Houses were made of mud bricks. Rich, sticky mud from the Nile River was mixed with sand or chopped straw, then shaped in rectangular molds and dried in the hot sun. Poor families lived in small, one-room houses probably made from reeds, wood, and mud.

**WHAT DID YOU WEAR?**
Egyptian clothes were made of linen. Women and girls wore straight dresses with two broad shoulder straps. Men and boys wore loincloths and short kiltlike skirts. The skirts of wealthy Egyptian men of the old kingdom (around 3500 B.C.) were pleated, and women's dresses were often covered with beads. By 2100 B.C., during the New Kingdom, clothing had become fancier. Both men and women wore draped and pleated robes. Men and women sometimes wore sandals, but most Egyptians went barefoot.

Egyptian men and women wore wigs made of human hair, palm-leaf fibers, or wool. Many men and some women shaved their heads. Jewelry was popular, and Egyptians of all ages wore circlets on their heads, and earrings, necklaces, rings, bracelets, and anklets. Jewelry was made from gold, silver, semiprecious stones, glazed beads, shells, and colored polished pebbles. Both men and women wore makeup and perfume. Oils were used to keep the skin from drying in the hot sun, and kohl was worn as eyeliner and eyeshadow. Kohl also acted as a kind of sunscreen to protect the eyes.

## WHAT KIND OF JOB DID YOU HAVE?

Most Egyptians were farmers; most women ran the household and took care of the children. Some Egyptian men were craftspeople such as painters and sculptors. The most skilled craftspeople worked for the pharaoh (king), at a religious temple, or for nobles who had workshops on their estates. The sons of craftsmen and carpenters were expected to follow their fathers' professions and to be trained by them. Training started early, and sons had to learn how to use the tools of the trade, which were made of copper, bronze, or stone with wooden handles.

## WHAT DID YOU DO FOR FUN?

Wooden animals, dolls, and leather balls were favorite children's toys. Pictures in tombs show kids dancing, playing team games, and leap-frogging. Games resembling chess and checkers were enjoyed by Egyptians of all ages. Other popular pastimes included wrestling, hunting, fishing, swimming, and chasing hippos or crocodiles. Since most people lived near the Nile River, water sports were favored forms of recreation. One river sport was similar to fencing, except that the players used sticks. Teams were formed in boats and competitors tried to push each other into the river with their poles.

## HOW DID YOU GET AROUND?

Chariots—light, open, horse-drawn, wheeled vehicles—were used by some Egyptians for transportation, but mainly for war. The most popular way to travel and trade was by boat up and down the Nile. Ships varied in size from small reed boats, propelled by sails, poles, and oars, to large merchant ships and warships. Many ships used oarsmen to move them along, as well as a sail. The

pharaoh and nobles traveled in elegant barges that were brightly painted and gilded.

## WHERE DID YOU GO TO SCHOOL?

Egyptian girls weren't allowed to go to school. Some boys went to school to learn how to become scribes. A scribe was a very important person in ancient Egypt. He knew how to write hieroglyphics, which was the Egyptian system of writing, and he kept household and government records. He also recorded the activities of the pharaohs. One Egyptian's advice to his son around 2000 B.C. was: "Understand that I am putting you in school for your own good. A scribe never knows poverty, and from his childhood is treated with respect." However, boys who were studying to become scribes were also advised to "love writing, hate dancing, and not to set their hearts on playing."

# Ancient Rome

## WHERE DID YOU LIVE?

The houses of well-to-do families who lived in Rome were airy and cool, with little furniture. Floors, walls, and ceilings were fancily decorated, often with mosaic tile. The Romans liked statues and busts (head-and-shoulder statues), and wealthy families displayed them in their houses. Gardens contained more statues, fountains, pools, birds, trees, and plants. During the winter, Romans heated their houses with *hypocausts,* an early type of central heating. Hot air from a furnace under the floors traveled up through hollow walls to heat the rooms.

Many Romans also lived on farms in the countryside. There were three types of farms: large estates owned by nobles; medium-sized farms; and small holdings worked by a single peasant family. A noble would leave his farm to serve in the Roman Senate or the army, but would return home as soon as his duties were over.

The households of all but the poorest families included slaves to do the chores. Children had their own slaves who dressed them, played with them, and took them to school. Slaves were usually men, women, and children captured in countries throughout the Roman Empire. They were bought and sold in the marketplace and worked as servants for no wages.

## WHAT DID YOU EAT?

The Romans ate three meals a day. The main meal, called the *cena,* was eaten at midafternoon and sometimes lasted for several hours and included as many as seven courses. Wealthy families enjoyed such "delicacies" as peacocks, stuffed sow's udders, flamingoes boiled with dates, and dormice stuffed with pine nuts. Poor families ate bread and hot cereal for almost every meal. Families who lived on farms ate more sensibly, because they supplemented their diets with the fruits and vegetables they grew. Everyone, including children, drank wine with meals. Wine for children was usually watered down or mixed with honey to make it sweeter.

## WHAT DID YOU WEAR?

Romans wore tunics—robes that were fastened at the shoulders and tied at the waist. A child and man's tunic was usually knee-length; a woman's tunic, called a *stola*, fell to the floor. A large cloak, called a *pallium* (men) or *palla* (women), was worn outdoors and could be used as a blanket if necessary. Romans also

wore *togas,* cloaks that hung over the left shoulder and wrapped around under the right arm. Only Roman citizens were allowed to wear the toga; slaves and exiled citizens were forbidden to wear it. Freed slaves had to get special permission to wear a toga. Women and children wore shoes or sandals; men wore sandals or boots.

Roman shoemakers were the first to fashion footwear for the right and left feet. Children wore a locket called a *bulla* as a good luck charm. Boys wore the *bulla* until manhood; girls wore it until they got married.

## WHAT DID YOU DO FOR FUN?

Popular children's games were leap-frog, blindman's bluff, dice, and jacks. Nuts were rolled like marbles and dolls were popular. Some Roman dolls had movable joints. Families went to the public baths to gossip, meet their friends, and eat and drink, as well as to get clean. There were three kinds of baths: the *frigidarium*, which was very cold; the warm *tepidarium*; and the hot *caldarium*. Romans also attended entertainments at large stadiums called *amphitheatres*. The biggest amphitheatre in Rome was the Colosseum, which could hold 55,000 people. Such bloodthirsty "entertainments" as battles between gladiators and animal fights were held in amphitheatres. Prisoners were sometimes thrown to starving animals as audiences watched. But there were also chariot races, exhibitions of ostriches, hippos, and rhinos, and performing animals. Plays and mime shows were also popular entertainments.

## WHERE DID YOU GO TO SCHOOL?

At the age of seven, the boys and some girls of well-to-do Roman families went to elementary school. They then went on to grammar school and sometimes rhetoric school (college). Roman children and teens learned reading, writing, arithmetic, Latin, Greek, hunting, riding, shouting, fighting, public speaking, philosophy, and logic. Most girls stayed home and were taught by their mothers how to be good wives and homemakers. They also learned such skills as singing, dancing, cooking, and sewing. Students in school read from scrolls and wrote on wax-coated wooden tablets with a pointed writing instrument called a stylus.

Teachers were often Greek slaves who had been given their freedom. They were badly paid and rarely treated with respect. Teachers were strict in Roman times and beating was a common form of punishment in schools.

## Europe During the Middle Ages
## (The 400s to the 1400s)

**WHERE DID YOU LIVE?**

Life in the Middle Ages was based on the idea of feudalism. Here's how feudalism worked. Until the eleventh century, Europe was constantly invaded by Vikings from the Scandanavian countries. No community felt safe unless it was protected by soldiers. To help keep order, kings granted large pieces of land, called fiefs, to important nobles and lords in exchange for their loyalty and willingness to fight for the king. A lord would grant parts of his fief to less important nobles, called vassals. Vassals had to swear loyalty and to fight in the lord's army when called. But most people during the Middle Ages weren't lords and vassals; they were serfs—peasants who lived and worked on the land belonging to the nobles.

Most nobles and serfs lived on a manor, a village made up of the lord's fief, which included the lord's manor house or castle, serfs' cottages, and a church. Cottages had dirt floors and were made of strips of wood woven together and covered with mud plaster. Windows were small holes that were usually shuttered against the weather. Roofs were thatched with bundles of straw that were pegged down on a framework of wooden rafters. The thatched roofs kept the one- or two-room cottages warm in winter and cool in summer. Each cottage had a *toft* or vegetable garden. Some of the family's animals such as pigs, cows, or hens, were either kept in the cottages at night or in a shed built onto the cottage.

Manor houses were larger and made of wood. Castles were part stone, part wood. By the middle of the thirteenth century, there were at least 300 castles in England. Castles were built as fortresses where a lord could defend himself, his family, and the manor from enemies. A castle was surrounded by a moat, a deep, wide trench filled with water, and had high walls and towers. Inside was an outer courtyard, called the outer bailey, and a walled inner courtyard with a huge stone tower called a donjon or keep. The donjon had many levels. The lord and his family lived in it,

and people from the manor hid there during an attack. Inside the castle walls were the garden, kitchen, well, stable, blacksmith's forge, and a barracks for the lord's knights. To get to the inner courtyard, a visitor had to cross the moat on a large wooden ramp that was lowered and enter through a raised spiked iron gate called a portcullis.

## WHAT DID YOU WEAR?

During the early Middle Ages, men and women wore simple tunics and cloaks. The woman's tunic developed into a long dress that was laced to fit the upper part of her body closely. Men wore loose breeches under their tunics and various kinds of tight leg coverings. During the 1100s and 1200s, women wore metal hairnets, veils, and draped throat covers called wimples. Men wore hoods that had long tails called liripipes. Both men and women wore an outer tunic called a surcoat that had been adopted from the Crusaders' garments. Some surcoats were sleeveless and cut with low armholes. Knights wore these surcoats over chain-metal armor. Women's surcoats were long and worn over long-sleeved gowns; men wore sleeveless surcoats of varying lengths.

During the 1300s, the clothing of the wealthy became fancier. Trimmings such as buttons were popular on men's outerwear. Men began to wear a close-fitting, low-waisted jacket called a cote-hardie, with an expensive jeweled belt. Women wore long, high-waisted dresses with long flaring sleeves called a houppelande. Toward the end of the Middle Ages, men and women trimmed their clothes with fur. Children of the Middle Ages wore simple versions of adult clothing.

## WHAT KIND OF JOB DID YOU HAVE?

People of the Middle Ages were merchants, teachers, weavers, blacksmiths, masons, carpenters, millers, bakers, shepherds, swine-herds, dairymaids, knights, and farmers. A steward managed the lord's household; a wardrober was in charge of the castle's household possessions. The reeve and the bailiff made sure the village ran smoothly. The serfs worked their own land, but they also had to spend time doing chores for the lord. For example, a man might have to spend three days a week tilling the lord's fields, repairing his buildings, or running his mill. Women often worked in the noble's house, spinning or weaving. Serfs could not leave the land without the lord's permission. A serf couldn't even get married without the lord's approval.

## WHAT DID YOU DO FOR FUN?

Popular toys of the Middle Ages included toy soldiers and horses made of wood or clay, dolls, hobbyhorses, tops, whistles made in the shape of birds, paper windmills, marbles, and hoops. Festivals with food, dancing, singing, and plays were held in villages. Probably the most popular entertainment in Medieval times was the town fair, which was attended by nobles and serfs alike. All kind of goods for sale were displayed at the fair, and jugglers and tame dancing bears entertained fairgoers. One of the greatest attractions at a fair might be a man wearing a doctor's robe and hood who sold little lead bottles, supposedly containing water from the River Jordan in the Holy Land, which he claimed could cure any illness. The "doctor" was probably a quack, and the water was just plain water, but the people of the Middle Ages knew little about medicine and were willing to believe his claims.

## HOW DID DOCTORS TREAT YOU WHEN YOU WERE SICK?

The standard treatment used by doctors for many diseases was bleeding. A vein was opened, and the doctor applied cups to catch the blood flow. Sometimes bloodsucking worms called leeches were attached to the patient's body. Bloodletting was thought to cleanse the body of the harmful substances that were causing the illness. The treatment usually failed. Doctors also used charms as cures. The charms might be magical symbols written on a piece of parchment, which the patient swallowed.

Herbs, plants, and drugs were widely used by doctors. Some of them were known to be useful in treating illness; others were only soothing temporarily or totally useless. For example, one Medieval recipe for curing toothache called for burning the seeds of sea holly in a candle made of mutton fat. The heat of the seeds supposedly made the worms that were causing the pain to drop out of the tooth. It's not surprising that with "cures" like this one, doctors often collected their fees *before* treating their patients. However, one Medieval treatment for fevers frequently worked— extract made from the bark of the willow tree. Doctors didn't know it then, but willow bark contains acetylsalicylic acid—the main ingredient in aspirin.

## HOW DID YOU GET AROUND?

The Romans had built roads throughout their European empire. Some were still paved and straight, but most roads were dirt tracks that became impossible to travel in the snowy winter, or because of mud. People also dug up dirt and clay from the roads to use for building repairs, which left huge potholes. Journeys often took weeks to complete because of bad roads.

The most common methods of travel were by foot, horse, or mule. Well-to-do women sometimes traveled in luxurious carriages with silken drapes, carpets, and even beds with cushions. The carriages resembled the covered wagons used by the American pioneers of the 1800s and were drawn by as many as five horses. But since springs hadn't been invented yet, these carriages weren't very comfortable.

## WHERE DID YOU GO TO SCHOOL?

Girls didn't attend school in Medieval times. They were brought up by their nurses and mothers to be well-mannered and obedient, to run the household, and to learn such hobbies as needlework. The daughter of a noble was married at about the age of fifteen— to a nobleman her parents picked out for her.

Boys of noble families went to school or trained to become knights. A knight in training left home at the age of seven to become a page in another lord's household. The lord might be the overlord of the boy's father, or the father's friend or relative. Pages ran errands, waited on the ladies of the household, learned how to play an instrument and sing for the ladies, were taught table manners, and carried messages. When a page became older, he began to practice using weapons, riding and caring for horses, and studying hawking and hunting. He might also be taught to spell a few words and to write the alphabet and learn a little geography, a few Latin prayers, and some arithmetic.

At the age of fourteen, a page became a squire. Each squire served one knight, taking care of his horse and polishing his armor. Squires continued their riding lessons and became more skillful at using swords and lances. They were on call at all hours and followed knights into battle. If a squire served his knight well, he was made a knight himself at the age of twenty. Kneeling before his lord, the new knight promised his loyalty and agreed to fight when needed.

Most of the boys who attended schools in the Middle Ages planned to become monks. Many schools also accepted children from local villages or towns whose parents paid a small fee. Sometime the sons of knights went to school as well. Schools were usually church-run and classes were taught by priests. Students learned their ABCs from a hornbook, which was a piece of parchment on which were written the letters of the alphabet and the Lord's Prayer. The parchment was covered over with a transparent piece of horn (made from the horn or hoof of an animal). The boys also studied reading, writing in their own language, Latin, and some arithmetic. Discipline was severe and beatings were common. Some students went on to the universities in Paris or Oxford, or to seminaries at abbeys or cathedrals to study for the priesthood.

## An Iroquois Tribe in pre-Colonial America

### WHERE DID YOU LIVE?

The Iroquois, along with the other Indians of the Americas, were descendants of the people who migrated to the Americas from Asia between about 18,000 and 14,000 B.C. The Iroquois were one of a group of Woodland Indians. They lived in the forests of the eastern U.S., around the lower Great Lakes in Northern Ohio, Pennsylvania, and New York, and farther north into Canada. There were five tribes in the Iroquois Nation: the Seneca, Cayuga, Onondaga, Oneida, and Mohawk. The tribes frequently fought each other, until the League of the Iroquois was formed, probably sometime between 1350 and 1600.

The Iroquois lived in longhouses made from the bark of the elm tree. Longhouses were constructed on a framework of poles that were lashed together. Over the frame were overlapping sheets of elm bark to hold it in place. Longhouses had rounded roofs and doors at either end. The average size of a longhouse was 25 feet by about 80 feet, but some were smaller or larger. Longhouses were arranged in a circle to make up the Iroquois village.

Each longhouse was divided into apartments, with a central corridor running the length of the building. Each apartment contained two families, one on either side of the corridor. In the center of each apartment was a cooking fire. A typical longhouse had three to five fires and housed six to ten families.

Foot-high platforms were built in each longhouse to keep people off the damp floor. Platforms were covered with woven reed mats or fur and were used for sitting and sleeping. Above the platforms were storage shelves, and between the apartments were storage areas for food.

## WHAT DID YOU WEAR?

The Iroquois made all their clothes from the skins of animals. The skin of the deer, called buckskin, was used most frequently. In summer, women wore buckskin skirts and leggings; in winter they wore buckskin dresses, leggings, and moccasins. Men wore kilts or breechcloths (two flaps of cloth that hung down from the waist in front and back) in summer and buckskin leggings, breechcloths or kilts, shirts, and moccasins in winter. Men also wore derbylike caps with feathers in them. Both men and women wore furs in the winter to keep warm. Children wore the same clothing as adults.

## WHAT KIND OF JOB DID YOU HAVE?

Iroquois men were hunters, farmers, and warriors. Women tended the fields, cooked meals, looked after the children, smoked the meat, and made pottery, baskets, and clothing. The favored weapons for hunting and fighting were bows and arrows. Spears and hard wooden clubs called war clubs were also used as weapons.

When Europeans began to arrive in America and trade with the Indians, the Iroquois started to use guns.

The Iroquois also participated in tribal and village government. At the top of the social structure was the League Council, which was made up of a set number of members from each of the five tribes. The council members were called sachems. Sachems inherited their positions through their families. The head mother, with the help of the other women in her family, chose the sachem. The women could also remove the sachem from the council if they decided he wasn't doing a good job.

There were also special council members called Pine Trees— men and women of the tribes who had distinguished themselves in some way. Often they were famous warriors. Pine Trees were allowed to speak at council meetings, but only sachems were allowed to vote on issues. The council's main duty was to keep the peace among the tribes of the League. The League saw itself as uniting the five tribes into one longhouse family. The Iroquois referred to themselves as the People of the Longhouse.

Benjamin Franklin was said to be so impressed by the Iroquois League's structure of government that he adopted aspects of it to form the government of the new United States of America.

## WHAT DID YOU DO FOR FUN?

Children often played with dolls made of corn husks. They played games like lacrosse and developed a type of lacrosse stick that is still in use today. "Snowsnake" was a winter game. To play it, the Iroquois made a long, narrow track in the snow, then sprinkled the track with water to freeze it. The player stood at the end of the track and slid a slim wooden snowsnake up the icy track. The player who made the snake slide farthest was the winner. Players often made their snakes with weighted tips so that they would slide farther.

## HOW DID YOU GET AROUND?

The territory of the Iroquois stretched for hundreds of miles. The Iroquois traveled mainly on foot; long trails crisscrossed the Iroquois homelands, and the Central Trail connected the Five

Nations. It began near present-day Albany, New York, passed through villages, and ended at what is now Buffalo, New York.

Iroquois hunters and warriors were swift travelers who could cover great distances quickly, even in winter. The Iroquois wore snowshoes to travel through the snow and felt that they could move faster on these shoes than they could on bare ground on foot. Hunters would regularly travel as far as fifty miles a day on their snowshoes.

The Iroquois usually built their villages on high ground near a source of water—a stream, river, or lake. They used canoes made of elm or hickory bark to travel on water. Canoes ranged in size from one-person 12-footers to thirty-person 40-footers. Canoes were used in the fur trade and also to transport warriors. The Iroquois traveled long distances along the rivers in search of fur-bearing animals. The pelts were often traded to Dutch, French, and English settlers.

## WHERE DID YOU GO TO SCHOOL?

The Iroquois didn't have schools as the Romans or people of the Middle Ages did, or as we know them today. But the education of children was very important to the Iroquois. Children were taught about their religion, and they learned about work and correct behavior through watching adults. Girls were encouraged to work alongside their mothers and, as soon as they could, began to help with the household chores. Fathers and uncles were usually responsible for teaching boys the skills they would need to become good hunters and warriors.

During the winter, children were taught by the elders of the longhouse. The elders told them stories that were intended to teach them the correct way to behave, or stories about the religion or history of the Iroquois. Stories weren't told in the summer, because the animals of the forest might stop to listen to them and not get their work done. Bees would not make honey, beavers would stop making dams, and of course, children might be too engrossed in the stories to do their chores. One summertime chore for children was to stay in a tree hut in the fields and keep away crows and other birds that might eat the crops.

# The U.S. During the Settling of the West in the 1800s

**HOW DID YOU TRAVEL WEST?**

As the western frontier opened, men with strings of pack horses hauled freight for settlers. Two men could take ten horses, and each horse might carry 200 pounds of nails, iron, or salt.

When roads were cut through the forest, wagons could be driven over the rough terrain. The most popular wagon for families was the horse or oxen-drawn covered wagon, which was specially built for traveling over the mountains. The wagon bed was higher in the front and back to keep the load inside from sliding when the wagons went up- or downhill. There was plenty of room under the tall canvas cover for boxes and barrels. Men and sometimes women drove the wagons; children and women often walked beside them. It was more comfortable to walk than to ride inside the bumpy wagons. Wagon trains were led by a wagon master, and a scout kept settlers informed of streams, type of terrain, and

Indian war parties ahead. Travelers camped out at night, or stayed in people's homes or homes that had been converted into taverns.

Another way of traveling West was by flatboat along rivers. Families arriving at the Ohio River in Pittsburgh could place their belongings on the flatboat and float West until they found a good spot to settle. Families sometimes shared the cost of having a large flatboat built for them.

## WHAT KIND OF HOUSE DID YOU LIVE IN?

The two most popular types of houses built by the settlers were log cabins and the ''soddy.''

For some families who had traveled all summer, there wasn't time before the winter to build a house. These families built lean-tos, with the open side facing the fire and away from the wind. The back of a lean-to consisted of a large fallen log. The builder placed two forked poles in the ground to hold the front of the roof and laid a long pole across the forks. More poles were placed on the crosspole, reaching down to the large log. The top and sides were covered with brush and mud to keep out rain, snow, and wind. Piled inside the shelter were buffalo robes and other skins, plus the family's belongings.

Log cabins usually had one room and a hard-packed dirt floor. The walls were built from round logs notched at each end to lock them together. Sticks were used to fill in the spaces between the logs, and mud and moss filled in the cracks. The cabin's roof was made of thin pieces of wood split from a tree stump.

The ''soddy'' was a popular type of house built on the prairie, where there were few trees. Settlers cut chunks of sod (the upper layer of soil, fastened by grass and plant roots into a thick mat) from the grasslands and stacked them to make the walls and roof of the houses.

Windows of settlers' houses were either fitted with glass, or covered with the thin skin of an animal or oiled paper. The fireplace, probably the most important feature of a settler's house, was usually made of mud or clay, but field stones might be used if they were found on the land.

The settlers used wood to build furniture and to whittle spoons, bowls, and plates. Pegs were driven into the walls of log cabins to support one side of a bed. Boards or rope held the mattresses, which might be stuffed with leaves, shredded cornhusks, straw, or feathers.

## WHAT KIND OF FOODS DID YOU EAT?

The settlers produced almost all their own food. They hunted wild animals such as deer, bear, and turkey, and raised farm animals for food. They planted corn, squash, pumpkins, turnips, carrots, peas, beans, cabbage, melons, wheat, and apple trees. Apples were used for cider, applesauce, apple butter, pies, and baked apples. The pioneers dried apples to bake into pies in the winter. Maple syrup was tapped from trees in the winter during "maple sugaring time."

The settlers would sometimes travel as far as twenty miles on foot or horseback to the nearest store or settlement to purchase items they couldn't produce themselves, such as sugar, coffee, tea, chocolate, and tobacco. Often they would trade butter, cheese, and ham for these items. In the late 1800s, when railroads began to cut through the wilderness, trains brought food and other goods to the settlers' towns from the East.

Salt was an important seasoning and necessary for the curing of meat. The settlers found salt licks, or springs, and boiled the water from them until only the salt was left.

Corn, the primary crop of the pioneers, was prepared in a variety of ways. Settlers ate hasty pudding—cornmeal mush flavored with milk, butter, syrup, or gravy. Other popular corn dishes were corn bread, corn cakes (also called corn "dodgers," "corn pone," or "Johnnycake," depending on the area of the frontier) and corn hominy.

Vegetables and fruits were stored in the family's root cellar, a pit dug in the ground or in the side of a hill near the house. A small stone springhouse was often built over a cold spring that supplied the family's water. Milk and butter were stored in the springhouse to keep them from spoiling.

## WHAT DID YOU WEAR?

The pioneers wore simple, practical dresses, trousers, and shirts made from milkweed fibers, buffalo wool, sheep's wool, and linen flax. Wool and flax fibers were often woven together to make a fabric called "linsey-woolsey." Settlers' clothes were frequently rough and scratchy and were sometimes soaked in warm water until the material became softer. Cloth was dyed with natural materials. Walnut hulls were used to turn cloth dark brown; ripe pokeberries turned it red; peach leaves turned cloth green; and smartweed was used for the color yellow. Buttons were made by wrapping flax thread and sewing the wrapped thread onto linen shirts, or by sewing a piece of cloth over a small piece of wood.

Settlers had few clothes. Women and girls might have two dresses; men and boys might have an extra shirt and pair of trousers. But as the pioneers became more prosperous, they were able to afford to make or buy dressy clothes for special occasions such as weddings and churchgoing.

It was important to the settlers not to waste anything, including clothing. Clothes were patched and mended and worn as long as possible. Children's clothes were handed down to younger members of the family.

## WHAT DID YOU DO FOR FUN?

Work to be done by a pioneer family was often shared by the community. The work brought people together, and such tasks as logrolling, wood chopping, cornhusking (shucking), apple paring, and barn raising became recreational get-togethers. The settlers worked, then ate, played fiddle music, and danced. Often, the task was turned into a competition. For example, at a cornhusking bee, two captains were chosen. Then each captain selected his team. The pile of corn was divided in half; then the team knelt down and, back to back, began to husk as the same moment. The huskers used husking pegs—sharpened pieces of wood held in the palm of the hand by a leather strap that fit over the fingers. The team who husked its pile of corn fastest won the competition. If a young man happened to husk a red ear of corn, the rules of the game stated that he could kiss the girl he liked.

Pioneer children played with homemade dolls, sleds, wagons, slingshots, and bows and arrows. They whittled whistles from willow tree branches, fished, swam in the creeks, and gathered hickory nuts, walnuts, and hazelnuts. During the long winter

nights, families popped corn, told stories, read books and magazines, sang, sewed, and held spelling bees.

## WHERE DID YOU GO TO SCHOOL?

Children were often taught by their parents until towns sprang up
on the frontier. One-room schoolhouses were built in these small
towns, and classes were taught by one teacher and attended by
children ranging in age from about six to the teen years. Teens,
usually girls, might go on to study to become teachers themselves.
Laura Ingalls Wilder, the author of the autobiographical *Little
House* books, described how, at the age of fifteen, after receiving
her teacher's certificate, she took charge of a school twelve miles
from her home.

Classes were frequently interrupted so that children could do
their farm chores, and winter blizzards sometimes made it impossible for students to attend school at all. School often had summer
sessions, so that most of the children in the town could go to class.

# CELEBRATIONS
## Wedding Customs

### BEST MAN

The tradition of a best man standing with the groom during the marriage ceremony is said to have originated around A.D. 200 in Europe. The Goths, a Germanic tribe, usually married within their own community. But if a suitable bride couldn't be found, a man would simply capture a woman from a nearby village. A male companion—the best man for the job—would accompany the groom to help him seize the unsuspecting bride-to-be. Since the woman's family might try to get their daughter back by force, the best man, alert and armed, stayed by the side of his friend throughout the wedding ceremony.

### WEDDING RINGS

Finger rings were first used in Egypt around 2800 B.C. To the Egyptians (and others) the circle symbolized eternity, because a circle had no beginning and no end. They thought of marriage as a union that should last forever—an eternity. Wealthy Egyptians and Romans favored rings of gold. A Roman wife would wear her gold ring in public, but at home she wore a more practical ring made of iron. Some Roman wedding rings had a tiny key welded to one side. The key symbolized an important aspect of the marriage contract: that a wife was legally entitled to half of her husband's wealth and could unlock his storehouse and help herself to whatever goods she needed.

### THE RING FINGER

The ancient Hebrews wore their wedding rings on the index finger. In India, rings were worn on the thumb. The Greeks of the third century B.C. believed that a "vein of love" ran from the third finger directly to the heart (the thumb wasn't considered the first finger of the hand). So the third finger seemed the logical one on which to wear a ring that symbolized the love between two people. In Christian wedding ceremonies, the groom would first place the ring on top of the bride's index finger, then the middle finger, and finally the third finger while naming the Trinity—the Father, Son, and Holy Spirit.

## THE WEDDING CAKE

Wheat, a symbol of prosperity and fertility, was associated with weddings in ancient times. Around 100 B.C., Roman bakers made smaller, sweet wheatcakes that were not only eaten, but often thrown at the bride. In a later ritual, the cakes were crumbled over the bride's head; then the newlyweds ate the crumbs together. The tradition of eating cake crumbs spread throughout Europe. In England, the crumbs were washed down with *bryd ealu,* "bride ale," from which we get the word "bridal."

During the Middle Ages, wheat or rice was again thrown at a bride. Guests baked their own biscuits or little cakes called scones, and brought them to the ceremony. Leftovers were given to the poor. The baked goods were piled into an enormous heap, and the newlyweds kissed each other over the mound. It was believed that the higher the heap, the greater prosperity was in store for the happy couple. Legend has it that a French chef, visiting London in the 1660s, saw a cake-piling ceremony. He hated the look of this messy mound, and he came up with the idea of baking a multilevel cake decorated with icing. This fancy wedding confection had caught on by the 1700s in England, and to this day, many consider it the traditional cake to feature at a wedding celebration.

## WEDDING DRESS AND VEIL

In ancient Rome, a bride was married in a yellow dress, and a flame-tinted yellow veil, called a *flammeum,* covered her face. Among Germanic tribes such as the Goths, only captured brides wore veils. The veil is said to be a male invention, intended to show that women had to be humble, dependent, and hidden from other men. During the Middle Ages, wedding dresses and veils could be of any color; what was important was the richness of the fabric and how fancily the dress was decorated. White, long a symbol of purity, became a popular color for wedding dresses in England and France in the 1500s. By the late 1700s, it was the traditional color. White was the fashionable color for formal gowns, and since weddings were formal affairs, brides wore white.

# Birthdays

## BIRTHDAY PARTIES

The first birthday celebrations took place in Egypt around 3000 B.C. They were held in honor of the pharaohs (kings) and were elaborate household feasts. As a symbol of royal generosity on such an important day, prisoners were often released to take part in the celebration.

The Greeks adopted the tradition of birthday celebrations and added the custom of a sweet birthday cake to make the occasion special. Each month, the Greeks celebrated the birthday of one of the gods, and the birthdays of the men of a Greek household were observed. But back then, women and children weren't considered important enough to be honored on their birthdays. The Roman senate decreed that the birthdays of important statesmen would be national holidays. In 44 B.C., Roman ruler Julius Caesar was assassinated, and his birthday was celebrated every year afterward. There was a public parade to mark the occasion, plus a circus performance, gladiatorial combats, an evening banquet, and a play.

## BIRTHDAYS IN THE CHRISTIAN ERA

Early Christians celebrated saints' "birthdays," called "feast days," which honored the day the saint was martyred, not the day he or she was born. But it was considered a "birthday" because it was the day a saint was "born" into heaven. (Earthly birthdays were also felt to be pagan traditions of the Egyptians and Greeks.) But in the fourth century A.D., after the Church settled on a birthdate for Jesus (the date had been debated for years), birthdays began to be celebrated widely. By the 1100s, parish churches in Europe were recording all birthdates and families were celebrating birthdays.

## BIRTHDAY CAKES TOPPED WITH CANDLES

Germans in the Middle Ages revived the Greek tradition of serving a cake at birthday celebrations. A party given for a child was called a *kinderfeste*. The birthday boy or girl was greeted at dawn by the arrival of a cake topped with lighted candles. The number of candles totaled one more than the *kind's* (child's) age; the extra candle represented the "light of life" (candles are longtime symbols of life). The candles were changed and kept lit throughout the day. The birthday child received gifts and was allowed to choose his or her favorite dishes for the family meal. Before the cake was eaten for dessert, the celebrant had to make a wish and blow out the candles with a single breath. But the wish had to remain a secret if it were to come true.

## "HAPPY BIRTHDAY TO YOU"—The Story Behind the Song

This ever-popular birthday tune started out as a classroom song entitled "Good Morning to All." It was written by sisters Mildred and Patty Hill (music and lyrics, respectively) as a welcome song to young students. Mildred was a school principal in Louisville, Kentucky and Patty was a teacher in the same school. The sisters copyrighted their song in 1893, but later it appeared without permission in a songbook edited by a Robert H. Coleman and was published by him in 1924. It was Coleman who added the birthday lyrics to the Hills' song. The revised song was published several times, and by 1933, it was shown as "Happy Birthday to You." In 1934, Mildred and Patty's sister, Jessica, learned that the song was belted out in a Broadway musical, *As Thousands Cheer*. Jessica decided to go to court to establish legal and financial rights to the melody of the song for her family. She won the case, and the Hills became entitled to royalties every time "Happy Birthday to You" was sung on stage and screen. But don't worry—it's pretty unlikely that anyone will take you to court if you happen to have a home video of your birthday party that includes a rousing rendition of "Happy Birthday to You!"

# HIGHLIGHTS IN THE HISTORY OF HOLIDAYS AND OTHER SPECIAL DAYS

**(The word "holiday" comes from the Middle English word *halidai*, meaning "holy day.")**

## New Year's Celebrations

### NEW YEAR'S DAY

For ancient people, the calendar year was the time between the sowing of seeds and the harvesting of crops. The earliest recorded New Year's celebration took place around 2000 B.C. in the city of Babylon, the capital of Babylonia (in present-day Iraq). A festival was held late in March, at the time of the vernal equinox, when spring begins. Two hours before dawn, a high priest washed in the sacred waters of the Euphrates River and offered a hymn to Marduk, the chief god of agriculture. The priest prayed for a bountiful new year of crops. Citizens consumed huge amounts of food and drink and a parade with music, dancing, and costumes was held. The parade began at the temple and ended at a special building called New Year House on the outskirts of the city.

New Year's day for the Romans was March 25, the first day of spring. But high-ranking officials constantly tampered with the calendar, lengthening months and years to keep themselves in office longer. Dates of public events kept changing until finally, in 153 B.C., the Roman senate decreed that the year would begin on the first day of the month named for Janus, the god of beginnings—January. However, that didn't stop Roman officials from continuing to meddle with the calendar and to mix everyone up. During the reign of Julius Caesar, the year 45 B.C. had 445 days and became known as the "year of Confusion." Caesar ordered a new calendar to be created, the Julian Calendar, which only had 365-¼ days and a leap year every four years.

For the early Christians, January 1 was a holy day, the Feast of Christ's circumcision (now observed as the Solemnity of the Blessed Virgin Mary). Celebrating New Year's was considered a pagan (non-Christian) tradition.

## NEW YEAR'S EVE

Early European farmers spent the evening before New Year's Day sounding horns and beating drums to banish the evil spirits who caused crops to become diseased. In China, people crashed cymbals and exploded firecrackers to encourage the forces of light, the *Yang,* to scatter the forces of darkness, the *Yin.*

The Iroquois Indians of North American linked the New Year with the all-important ripening of the corn crop. On New Year's Eve, the Iroquois gathered up clothes, furnishings, wooden household utensils, and uneaten corn and other grains, and tossed them into a huge bonfire. The burning of last year's possessions symbolized the start of a new year and a new life. Disguised men and women also "went from wigwam to wigwam smashing and throwing down whatever they came across," according to anthropologist Sir James Frazer. It was the one night of the year when people were supposedly not responsible for their actions.

The New Year's Eve festivities of the American colonists also got out of hand sometimes. Two months after a rowdy New Year's Eve in New York City in 1773, the legislature outlawed firecrackers, homemade bombs, and the firing of shotguns to welcome the New Year.

## NEW YEAR'S RESOLUTIONS

This tradition began with the ancient Babylonians. Their favorite resolutions were to pay off outstanding debts and to return all borrowed farming tools and household utensils.

# St. Valentine's Day

## WHO WAS ST. VALENTINE?

In Rome in the third century A.D., Emperor Claudius II abolished marriage, because he thought that married men made poor soldiers. Rome needed soldiers to keep the empire strong. Valentine, the bishop of Interamna, married young lovers in secret. When the emperor found out that Valentine was doing this, he had the "friend of lovers" brought to the palace. Claudius tried to convert Valentine to the Roman gods, but the bishop refused to renounce Christianity and was executed in A.D. 270.

In 496, Pope Gelasius outlawed a Roman festival called the Lupercalia. The Lupercalia featured a lottery which linked up eligible young men and women. The pope kept the lottery, but substituted the names of saints. Men and women were expected to live like the saints whose name they had drawn. The patron saint of this new lottery was St. Valentine.

## VALENTINE CARDS

For Roman women and men, mid-February was the traditional time for courting. After the Lupercalian lottery was abolished, men started the custom of writing affectionate letters to women they admired and wanted to get to know better. February 14 became the day to write such letters; St. Valentine, the "friend of lovers," became associated with them.

The earliest Valentine card existing today was sent by Charles of Orleans to his wife around 1415. Charles, a French duke, had been captured by the English at the Battle of Agincourt during the Hundred Years' War, and he sent the card while he was a prisoner in the Tower of London. The card shows Cupid, the son of Venus, goddess of love and beauty, shooting an arrow of love at the duke. The duchess stands nearby, holding out a bouquet of flowers to her husband.

Cupid, the chubby little winged child armed with arrows dipped in love potion, became a popular valentine image and was often seen on cards. By the 1600s, handmade valentine cards were large and fancily decorated.

## WHY XXXS SOMETIMES STAND IN FOR KISSES

Long ago, most people were not taught how to write. They signed documents with their "mark," an "X." They often kissed the "X" to show their sincere intention to abide by the agreement in the document. A series of XXXs to stand in for kisses became a popular addition to valentine cards and letters to loved ones. During World War II, soldiers were forbidden by the U.S. and British governments to include XXXs on their letters. It was feared that spies within the armed forces would use the XXXs as secret codes.

# St. Patrick's Day

## WHO WAS ST. PATRICK?

Details are sketchy about the life of Patrick, the patron saint of Ireland. He was born around A.D. 385, probably in Wales, and his given name may have been Maewyn or Succat. It's said that he was captured at the age of sixteen by Irish bandits and sold as a slave in Ireland. There, he worked as a sheepherder for six years. He escaped to Gaul and studied for the priesthood at a monastery. He adopted the Christian name, Patrick, and was eventually appointed bishop of Ireland. Patrick spent thirty years converting the Celts of Ireland to Christianity. He also founded monasteries, schools, and churches. Patrick died on March 17, c. 461, and is believed to have been buried in Downpatrick.

St. Patrick's Day is generally observed as a religious holiday in Ireland; in the U.S., it's usually a day for people of Irish background to celebrate their heritage.

# Easter

The name of this Christian religious holiday comes from the name of the Germanic pagan goddess of spring and offspring, Eastre. Missionaries in the second century A.D., trying to convert the Germanic tribes of Europe to Christianity, mixed aspects of the festival of Eastre with the Christian ceremony celebrating Christ's Resurrection. For decades, Easter was celebrated on a Friday, Saturday, or Sunday. But in A.D. 325, at the Council of Nicaea, the

Emperor Constantine decreed that Easter should be celebrated on the first Sunday after the first full moon on or after the vernal (spring) equinox. Since then, Easter has never fallen before March 22 or after April 25.

## THE EASTER BUNNY

A hare was the early symbol of the goddess Eastre. When German families came to America in the 1700s and 1800s, they brought the custom of the white Easter rabbit, a symbol of spring, with them.

## EASTER EGGS

For centuries, eggs have been a symbol of birth and rebirth. The Egyptians buried eggs in their tombs, the Greeks placed eggs on top of graves, and the Romans had a saying: "All life comes from an egg." Legend holds that Simon of Cyrene, who helped carry Jesus' cross, was an egg merchant.

Around the second century A.D., wealthy people would cover eggs with gold leaf and give them as gifts at Eastertime. Peasants often dyed their eggs, using dyes from flowers or other plants. During the 1880s in parts of Germany, Easter eggs were used as birth certificates. An egg was dyed a solid color; then a design, which included the person's name and date of birth, was etched onto the shell with a needle or a sharp tool. In a court of law, one of these Easter eggs could be used as proof of a person's identity and age.

# April Fool's Day

In France in the early 1500s, New Year's Day was observed on March 25, the beginning of spring. New Year's festivities lasted for a week, ending on April 1. In 1564, King Charles IX decreed that New Year's Day should be moved back to January 1. But many people either refused to abide by the new ruling, or simply forgot about it and continued to party and exchange gifts from March 25 to April 1. Pranksters who thought that these people were old-fashioned sent silly gifts to them, as well as phony invitations to parties that never took place. This practice turned out to be so much fun for the foolers that it became an April 1 tradition in France years after everyone had become comfortable with the new New Year's date. The custom reached England in the 1700s, and then came to America.

## Mother's Day

A West Virginia teacher, Anna Jarvis, came up with the idea of a special day to honor mothers after the death of her mother on May 9, 1905. Miss Jarvis (the title Ms. was unknown in those days) wrote letters to congressmen, governors, mayors, newspaper editors, ministers, and business leaders to generate public support for an annual Mother's Day. Her letter-writing campaign worked: the U.S. Senate approved legislation for the day, and on May 8, 1914, President Woodrow Wilson signed a proclamation designating the second Sunday in May as Mother's Day.

## Memorial Day

This holiday to honor those who died in wars was once known as Decoration Day. It was originally inaugurated in 1868 by General John A. Logan for the purpose of decorating the graves of both Confederate and Union soldiers.

## Father's Day

On Mother's Day, 1910, Mrs. Sonora Dodd sat in a Spokane, Washington, church listening to a sermon about mothers. As she sat, she thought about the fact that she and her five brothers had been raised by their father, a Civil War veteran and widower. Mrs. Dodd felt there should be a special day to honor fathers, and her idea gained support from Spokane's ministers, the local YMCA, and newspapers across the country. One of the first notable Americans to speak out in favor of a national Father's Day was the orator and political leader William Jennings Bryan, later to speak for the prosecution in the famous "Monkey Trial" of 1925 (see Chapter Six, "Three Famous Trials"). In 1916, President Woodrow Wilson and his family observed Father's Day, and in 1924, President Calvin Coolidge suggested that states should hold their own Father's Day celebrations. In 1957, Maine senator Margaret Chase Smith tried to convince Congress to give Father's Day national holiday status. Finally, in 1972, President Richard Nixon proclaimed that the third Sunday in June would officially be observed as Father's Day.

## Fourth of July

This holiday, also known as Independence Day, commemorates the adoption of the Declaration of Independence. Celebration of the Fourth of July began during the American Revolution, and it has been the most important and popular patriotic holiday in the U.S. ever since.

## Grandparent's Day

A sixty-five-year-old grandparent, Michael Goldgar, of Atlanta, Georgia, made seventeen trips to Washington, D.C., to lobby for legislation for a special day to honor grandparents. In 1978, seven years after Goldgar began his efforts, President Jimmy Carter signed legislation designating the Sunday after Labor Day as Grandparent's Day.

## Halloween

For the ancient Celts in Ireland in the fifth century B.C., October 31, "All Hallow's Eve," officially marked the end of summer. That night, Celtic families extinguished the fires on their hearths to make their homes cold and therefore undesirable for evil spirits. People gathered outside villages, where a Druid priest lit a huge bonfire to honor the sun god for the past summer's harvest and to frighten away spirits who might still be hanging around. The Celts also dressed up as demons, hobgoblins, and witches to frighten away the roving souls of people who had died the year before and were looking for people or animals whose bodies they would supposedly inhabit for the next twelve months before they could pass peacefully into the afterlife. Costumed Celtic families paraded noisily in and around their houses and towns to the bonfire. A villager who seemed to be "possessed" by a roving soul could be thrown into the fire to scare away other souls.

When Ireland became a Christian country, the custom of wearing costumes and the practice of noisy mischief-making on All Hallows Eve continued. Irish immigrants of the 1840s brought Halloween customs with them to the U.S. In New England, two favorite halloween pranks played by teens were overturning outhouses and unhinging front gates.

The custom of the jack-o'-lantern also arrived in the U.S. from Ireland. The ancient Celts had hollowed out large turnips, carved

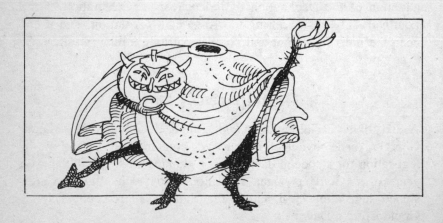

demon's faces on them, and placed a lighted candle inside. Pumpkins were more plentiful than turnips in the U.S. and became more popular as jack-o'-lanterns. In Irish folklore, Jack was a notorious ne'er-do-well who once tricked the devil into climbing up a tree. He made the trapped devil promise to stop tempting Jack into sinning. But when Jack died, he was refused entrance to heaven. Condemned to wander in frigid darkness, he was finally given a single hot coal by the devil. Jack placed the coal in a hollowed-out turnip and used the lighted turnip as his lantern.

**TRICK OR TREAT**
This custom of going from house to house to beg treats probably originated in the ninth century A.D. in Europe. On All Souls Day, November 2, Christians walked from village to village begging for "soul cakes"—square biscuits with raisins. In return, the beggars would pray for the souls of the dead relatives of the biscuit providers.

# Veteran's Day

This November 11 holiday to honor U.S. armed services men and women past and present was originally known as Armistice Day. It was created by President Woodrow Wilson to commemorate the signing of the Armistice that officially ended World War I. The Armistice was signed at the eleventh hour of the eleventh day of the eleventh month. An act of Congress on May 24, 1954, officially renamed the day Veteran's Day.

# Thanksgiving

Thanksgiving Day celebrations took place long before the Pilgrims of the *Mayflower* landed at Plymouth Rock in December, 1620, and enjoyed the first Thanksgiving in the New World in 1621. The ancient Greeks gave thanks to Demeter, the goddess of agriculture; the Romans honored Ceres, the goddess of corn. The Hebrews celebrated the eight-day Feast of Tabernacles to offer thanks for abundant harvests.

## THE PILGRIMS' THANKSGIVING

The Pilgrims had sailed to America with 102 people; by the fall of 1621, forty-six had died of scurvy (a vitamin-C deficiency disease) and pneumonia. The remaining Pilgrims had survived partly because of an English-speaking Pawtuxet Indian named Squanto, who helped them build houses and plant and cultivate crops of corn and barley. Squanto had been captured by explorers and sold into slavery in Spain. He escaped to England, where he spent several years working for a merchant, and returned to his village in America six months before the Pilgrims landed. Because of Squanto, the Pilgrim settlers were able to give thanks for a bountiful harvest in 1621. Governor William Bradford proclaimed a day of Thanksgiving in "Plimoth," and a celebration took place that lasted three days.

Among the guests invited to the feast were Chief Massasoit of the Wampanoags and ninety of his braves. Pilgrim soldiers led by Miles Standish blasted muskets and trumpeted bugles to make the celebration, and there were foot races, jumping contests, and displays of marksmanship. The Indians used bows and arrows; the settlers, their guns.

## WHAT DID THE PILGRIMS AND THEIR GUESTS EAT?

On the menu at the first Thanksgiving were ducks, geese, venison, lobsters, clams, bass, corn, watercress, leeks, wild plums, and dried berries. But even though Governor Bradford wrote that the men he sent off "fowling" came back with "a great store of Turkies," it's not certain that the birds the hungers bagged were really turkeys. To the people of the 1600s, a turkey could mean any large fowl with a featherless head, rounded body, and dark, speckled feathers. But wild turkeys did roam the Northeastern woods, so it's possible that turkey was one of the dishes eaten at the first Thanksgiving. The settlers had used up their stores of flour, but they made a kind of bread by boiling corn, kneading it into round cakes, and frying the cakes in venison fat. One modern Thanksgiving delicacy was enjoyed by the Pilgrims, however—cranberries, which were gathered by fifteen boys and then boiled and mashed into a sauce. And legend had it that Massasoit's brother, Quadequina, brought a delicious new treat to the feast in deerskin bags: popcorn.

## THANKSGIVING—The Holiday

Thanksgiving wasn't celebrated regularly after 1621. In October 1777, after the Americans won the Battle of Saratoga during the Revolutionary War, the Thirteen Colonies joined in a common Thanksgiving celebration. In 1789, President George Washington signed a Thanksgiving Proclamation, but many Americans, including Thomas Jefferson, felt that it wasn't important to have a national holiday commemorating the hardships of a few early settlers.

In 1827, magazine editor Sarah Josepha Hale, best known for penning the ever-popular nursery rhyme "Mary Had a Little Lamb," began a one-woman crusade to make Thanksgiving a national holiday. For nearly forty years, Mrs. Hale wrote editorials on the subject, as well as hundreds of letters to presidents, governors, ministers, and newspapers. Finally, on October 8, 1863, President Abraham Lincoln issued a proclamation designating the last Thursday in November as a national Thanksgiving Day.

# Christmas Traditions

Christmas, or "Christ's Mass," began to be celebrated regularly in the Western world in 337, after the Roman emperor Constantine was baptized and Christianity became the official state religion.

## CHRISTMAS TREES

Legend has it that in the early 700s, British monk and missionary St. Boniface was trying to convert a tribe of Germanic Druids to Christianity. To prove to them that the oak tree wasn't sacred (the Druids worshipped oaks), Boniface chopped one down. The mighty oak toppled down, crushing everything in its path, except for a small fir sapling. The converts were convinced this was a miracle, and later Christmases in Germany were celebrated by the planting of fir saplings. By the 1500s, fir trees indoors and outdoors were decorated for Christmas in Germany. Early decorations included roses cut from colored paper, apples, wafers, and sugar. Christmas tree lights are said to have been the invention of sixteenth-century Protestant reformer Martin Luther. One winter evening, as he was walking home, he marvelled at the beauty of the stars twinkling among the tall evergreens. When he got home, he set up a tree in the main room of the house and placed lighted candles on its branches.

In the 1700s, the German tradition of the Christmas tree spread to other parts of Europe. Christmas trees became popular in England in the 1840s after Albert, Duke of Saxe-Coburg–Gotha, arrived from Germany to marry Queen Victoria. Christmas trees and decorations were frowned upon by the Pilgrims and Puritans of America, who felt that Christmas should only be a sacred, not a festive, holiday. But by the 1800s, Americans were celebrating Christmas as a holy and festive day, with decorated trees, the singing of carols, and special Christmas feasts.

## SANTA CLAUS

The original Santa Claus was St. Nicholas, the bishop of Myra in Asia Minor, who died in the year 342. Nicholas was known for his generosity and love of children, for whom he became the patron saint. He was also the patron saint of sailors. Nicholas became associated with the giving of gifts at Christmas time. The early-European St. Nick of Christmas folklore wore red-and-white bishop's robes and a mitre (bishop's hat) and carried a shepherd's crook. He made his rounds on a lazy donkey and arrived on December 6, his feast day. St. Nick left such gifts by the family hearth as fruit, nuts, hard candies, and wood and clay figurines.

In Holland in the 1500s, children placed wooden shoes by the hearth the night of St. Nicholas's arrival. The shoes were filled with straw for his donkey. St. Nick left treats in the shoes. In Dutch, St. Nicholas's name was "Sint Nikolass," which became "Sinterklass" in America. When the British gained control of New Amsterdam from the Dutch, the area was renamed New York and "Sinterklass" became "Santa Claus."

The white-bearded, rosy-cheeked, plump Santa we know and love today was the creation of nineteenth-century magazine cartoonist Thomas Nast. His Christmas cartoons showed Santa making toys, reading childrens' requests for special gifts, and checking to see how well children had behaved throughout the year.

## CHRISTMAS CARDS

Before the 1840s, Christmas cards were handwritten and exchanged in person or by mail. The first card designed for sale was created in 1843 by illustrator John Horsley in London, England. Horsley had been commissioned by wealthy businessman Sir Henry Cole to design cards Cole could send to friends and business acquaintances. Horsley's card had three panels. The side panels showed a good deed—clothing and feeding the poor. The center panel featured a drawing of a family Christmas party. The printed message in the center panel of the card read, "Merry Christmas and a Happy New Year to you." Printed cards soon became popular, first in England, then in Germany, and finally, in the U.S.

"Merry Old Santa Claus," by Thomas Nast Published in Harper's Weekly, January 1, 1881

# Food, Glorious Food
## The Origins of Some Well-Known Foods

| FOOD/DRINK | YEAR/HISTORY |
|---|---|
| **Bread** | **2600 B.C.:** The Egyptians first roasted wheat and barley over open fires, then discovered that water gave the mixture a better texture and taste. They put layers of the water-grain mixture on hot stones to make flat bread. In 2600 B.C., Egyptian bakers discovered that if they let the grain and water mixture sit and ferment for a while, it leavened, or "rose." Result: the forerunner of the soft, doughy bread we know today. The Egyptians needed something in which to bake this new kind of bread, so they invented the oven. |
| **Breakfast cereal** | **1890s:** Michigan doctor John Kellogg first created a Granola cereal; in 1907, he packaged Corn Flakes. |
| **Candy** | **1000 B.C.:** Sugar wasn't used to make sweets until the Middle Ages, so the Egyptians mixed herbs, nuts, spices, and fruit juices with honey. Sugar cane was later cultivated in Persia and sugar was exported to Europe. Hard candies and taffy became popular "sweetmeats" in Europe. |
| **Candy bars:**<br>Hershey Bar | **1894:** Created by Milton Hershey, a Lancaster, Pennsylvania, confectioner. It was made of sugar, cocoa, chocolate, and milk. It sold for a few pennies and was an instant hit. |
| Tootsie Roll | **1896:** Candymaker Leonard Hirschfield came up with this popular candy, named after his daughter, Tootsie. |

| FOOD/DRINK | YEAR/HISTORY |
|---|---|
| Mounds and Almond Joy | **1921 and 1947:** In 1921, Peter Paul Halijian of New Haven, Connecticut, came up with Mounds, a nickel candy bar made of bittersweet chocolate and coconut. Almond Joy made its debut in 1947. |
| Baby Ruth | **1921:** This nickel fudge-peanut-caramel-chocolate candy bar was the inspiration of Otto Schnering who, it's said, named it in honor of President Grover Cleveland's daughter, Ruth. |
| The Mars Bars | **1920–1940s:** Minnesota confectioner Franklin Mars first dreamed up the Milky Way candy bar; then came Snickers and 3 Musketeers. The multicolored little candies that "melt in your mouth, not in your hand," M & M's, were created for World War II soldiers, who could pop them into their mouths any time, any place, when they felt like having a treat. |
| **Chewing gum** | **1860s:** After Mexican general Antonio Lopez de Santa Anna lost Texas to the U.S., he settled on Staten Island. He brought some taffylike *chicle* with him—the dried milky sap of the Mexican sapodilla tree, used for chewing. An acquaintance of Santa Anna's, photographer-inventor Thomas Adams, decided to market *chicle* balls for chewing at a penny apiece. Sold along the East Coast by one of Adams's sons, "Adams New York Gum—Snapping and Stretching," became a popular chew, even though it had no flavor. Before Adams marketed his gum, people had been chewing wads of paraffin wax. Flavored *chicle* made its debut in 1875 in Louisville, Kentucky, and was the |

| FOOD/DRINK | YEAR/HISTORY |
|---|---|
| | brainchild of druggist John Colgan. He used balsam of tolu, an ingredient in children's cough syrup, as a flavoring. Other flavored gums followed. In the 1890s, former soap salesman William Wrigley, Jr., became the best-known manufacturer of chewing gum, with his now-classic Wrigley's Spearmint and Juicy Fruit gums. |
| **Bubble gum and Chiclets** | **1928 and 1910s:** Brothers Frank and Henry Fleer dreamed up these popular gums. Frank wanted to create a gum that would blow bubbles. His first effort, Blibber-Blubber Gum, didn't work, but in 1928, he finally came up with a gum that did, Double Bubble. In 1910, Henry Fleer began to market a hard white candy with a pellet of chicle inside—Chiclets. |
| **Chocolate** | **1000 B.C.:** The Mayans, Toltecs, and Aztecs made a chocolate drink from the beans of the cocoa plant. Columbus later brought the cocoa drink back to Spain, where it was a big hit at the royal court of King Ferdinand and Queen Isabella. The word "chocolate" comes from the Aztec word *xocoatl* (pronounced sho-co-at), meaning "bitter water." In 1847, the English company of Fry and Sons mixed cocoa butter with a liqueur to produce the first solid |

| FOOD/DRINK | YEAR/HISTORY |
|---|---|

eating chocolate. In 1849, Daniel Peter of Switzerland added dry milk powder to chocolate and came up with the first milk chocolate.

**Coffee**

**Middle Ages:** Wild coffee plants, which look like evergreen bushes, were transported from Ethiopia to Arabia. The Arabs were the first to roast and brew coffee beans. Coffee was introduced into Europe in the 1500s, and coffee houses became popular in London around 1650. The custom of drinking coffee reached the American colonies in 1689, and coffee houses flourished in New York, Boston, and Philadelphia.

**Cookie**

**3rd century:** The first cookie was a dry, waferlike *bis coctum,* or "biscuit." The English of the Middle Ages called this biscuit *cracken,* which became the word "cracker." The moist, sweet cookie we know today probably originated sometime after the Middle Ages from the little Dutch wedding cake, the *koekje*.

**Chocolate chip cookies**

**Around 1930:** Apparently, the first chocolate chip cookies were created at the Toll House Inn outside Whitman, Massachusetts. The inn's owner, cook, and baker was Mrs. Ruth Wakefield. She chopped up chocolate pieces from a large Nestlé's semisweet chocolate bar and added the pieces to her basic butter cookie dough. The Nestlé Company was impressed with Mrs. Wakefield's creation and got her permission to print the recipe on the chocolate bar's wrapper. In return, Mrs. Wakefield

| FOOD/DRINK | YEAR/HISTORY |
|---|---|

received a lifetime supply of free chocolate. In 1939, Nestlé came out with Toll House Morsels, prechopped chocolate chips, which made the job of baking these delicious cookie treats easier.

**Doughnuts**

**1500s:** The Dutch doughnut didn't have a hole and was known as *olykoek* or "oil cake," because the batter was deep fried in oil. Doughnuts were brought to America by the Pilgrims, who had learned to make them during their stay in Holland in the early 1600s (they had left England because of religious persecution). Because the confections were small, about the size of a walnut, "oil cakes" became known in New England as "dough nuts." The Pennsylvania Dutch are said to have originated doughnuts with holes in the early 1800s. The doughnut "rings" fried up more evenly and there was no soggy center. But there's a bronze plaque in Rockport, Maine, dedicated to sailor Hanson Gregory, who is also said to have invented doughnuts with holes, in 1847, by poking holes in his mother's doughnuts.

**Hamburger**

**Middle Ages:** The Germans flavored shredded low-grade beef with spices and ate it cooked and raw. In the seaport of Hamburg, the beef dish became known as "Hamburg steak." In the 1880s, the Hamburg steak arrived in the U.S. with the German immigrants. Here, it was called "hamburger steak," or simply "hamburger." In 1900, Louis Lassen introduced the hamburger sandwich at his New Haven lunch wagon,

**FOOD/DRINK**

**YEAR/HISTORY**

and in 1904, a busy cook at the St. Louis World's Fair slapped broiled burger patties between buns and served the sandwich to the hungry crowd.

**Hot dog**

**1852:** The butchers' guild of Frankfurt introduced a curved sausage that was spiced, smoked, and packed in a thin casing. The butchers called their sausage "frankfurter," after their home town. It was also known as a "dachshund sausage" because its shape resembled that of a dachshund. By the 1890s and early 1900s, "franks" were popular in the U.S. In 1906, Chicago newspaper cartoonist Tad Dorgan was attending a baseball game in New York's Polo

| FOOD/DRINK | YEAR/HISTORY |
|---|---|
| | Grounds. He drew a sketch of frankfurters served there and made them look like dachshunds on buns. Beneath the cartoon he wrote "Hot Dogs." The name stuck. |
| Ice cream | **2000 B.C.:** At this time, the Chinese had just begun to milk farm animals, and milk was a precious commodity. Nobles enjoyed a soft iced paste made from overcooked rice, spices, and milk. The mixture was packed in snow to harden. The Chinese also developed fruit ices, made from fruit pulp mixed with either snow or milk ice. By the 1200s, a variety of iced desserts was sold from pushcarts on the streets of Peking. Explorer Marco Polo is said to have brought frozen desserts back from China to Italy in the 1200s, but Italian confectioner Bernardo Buontalenti is also credited with introducing them. Milk and fruit ices arrived in France with Venetian Catherine de Medicis, who married the French king Henry II in 1533. It was Catherine who introduced a semifrozen dessert made from thick sweetened cream. Ice cream arrived in the U.S. in the late 1700s with Thomas Jefferson, who had tasted it in France while he was the U.S. ambassador there. He brought a recipe back to Philadelphia, and the city soon became known as the "ice cream capital" because so much ice cream was made there. A popular flavor in the early 1800s was the "Philadelphia," a vanilla-and-egg ice cream. The city also became famous for its ice cream "houses" and for its introduction of the ice cream soda in 1874. |

| FOOD/DRINK | YEAR/HISTORY |
| --- | --- |
| Ice cream cone | **1904:** At the St. Louis World's Fair, two food vendors worked side by side—Syrian-American baker Ernest Hamwi and teenage ice cream salesman Arnold Fornachov. Fornachov ran out of paper ice cream dishes and rolled one of Hamwi's waffles into a cone, creating a new taste sensation. Another version has it that Hamwi gave Fornachov rolled zalabias—wafer-thin Persian pastries sprinkled with sugar—to use as ice cream cones. Whatever the true story, ice cream cones became a big hit at the World's Fair and emerged as one of the most popular ways to eat ice cream in the world. |
| Ice cream sundae | **c. 1890:** A customer at E. C. Berner's ice cream parlor suggested that he pour chocolate over a scoop of ice cream in a dish. This popular new taste treat was originally sold only on Sunday, hence the name. The sundae was more expensive than other ice cream dishes, so it was considered a once-a-week special Sunday treat by customers. |
| Popsicle | **1905:** One cold night, Frank Epperson accidentally left a mixing stick in a glass of lemonade on his windowsill. The next morning, Epperson found the lemonade frozen into the first known "ice lollipop." Epperson named his creation an "epsicle," after himself, but the frozen "lollipop" later became the "popsicle." |
| Ketchup | **1690:** The Chinese developed a tangy sauce for fish and poultry made of pickled fish, shellfish, and spices. They called it *ketsiap*. Its popularity spread to Maylasia, |

| FOOD/DRINK | YEAR/HISTORY |
| --- | --- |

where it was known as *kechap*. In the early 1700s, British seamen brought samples of the sauce back to England. But when English chefs made the sauce, they substituted mushrooms, walnuts, and cucumbers for the original Eastern spices. A misprint renamed the popular new sauce "ketchup." Tomatoes were first added to ketchup in New England around 1790. The first mass-produced bottled ketchup came out in 1876, from the factory of German-American chef and businessman Henry Heinz. By the 1890s, the ketchup was one of Heinz's "57 Varieties."

**Pasta**

**Before 1000 B.C.:** The Chinese prepared pasta noodles from rice and bean flour. When explorer Marco Polo and his father and uncle returned to Italy from China in the late 1200s, they brought recipes for the preparation of Chinese noodles with them. The Italians came up with their own names for the shapes of the noodles they made, such as *cannelloni* ("big pipes"), *ravioli* ("little turnips"), *spaghetti* ("little strings"), *vermicelli* ("little worms"), and *lasagna* ("baking pot"). They called the noodle dough "pasta," meaning "dough paste." Bottled spaghetti dinners and canned ravioli originated in the 1930s in the U.S. They were the creation of Italian-American chef Hector Boiardi, who thought that Americans weren't as familiar with Italian food as they should be. Boiardi successfully marketed his pasta dinners under an easy-to-pronounce spelling of his name—Boy-ar-dee.

| FOOD/DRINK | YEAR/HISTORY |
|---|---|
| **Peanut butter** | **1890s:** Peanut butter was the invention of a St. Louis, Missouri, doctor who was trying to improve the health of his patients. He spread mashed peanuts on bread and suggested that his patients eat his nutritional, high-protein "health food." |
| **Potato chips** | **1853:** In the summer of 1853, Native American George Crum was employed as a chef at elegant Moon Lake Lodge in Saratoga Springs, New York. On the restaurant's menu were French fries, prepared by Crum in the standard, thick-cut French style popular in France at that time and brought back to the U.S. by Thomas Jefferson in the 1790s. One customer found Crum's fries too thick and sent them back to the kitchen. Crum cut and fried a thinner batch, but these, too, were rejected. Then, in a fit of frustration, Crum prepared a batch of fries that were so thin and crisp they couldn't be stabbed with a fork. The customer loved Crum's thin crispy potatoes, which soon began to appear on the menu as Saratoga Chips. The chips were packaged and sold, first locally, then throughout New England. Crum eventually opened his own restaurant, featuring potato chips. |
| **Tea** | **c. 2737 B.C.:** Legend has it that the first tea drink was concocted by Chinese emperor Shen Nung, who was boiling water when leaves from a nearby bush floated down into the pot. Shen Nung drank the brew and though it delicious and refreshing. Tea arrived in Europe in the 1500s when trade routes to the Orient became regularly traveled by merchants. |

## 4 Famous Foods Named For People

**EGGS BENEDICT**
One morning in 1894, at the Waldorf-Astoria hotel, New Yorker Samuel Benedict ordered for breakfast a piece of buttered toast topped with a poached egg, bacon, and hollandaise sauce. The maitre d' hotel substituted an English muffin for the toast and ham for the bacon. This delicious new dish, soon popular, was partly the creation of the Waldorf-Astoria, but it was named for Benedict.

**MELBA TOAST**
This crispy cracker was named for Australian-born opera singer Nellie Melba (1861–1931). While staying at the Savoy Hotel in London, Melba was accidentally served burnt toast. To the chef's surprise, she liked the crisp slices of toast. Melba toast was added to the Waldorf's menu in her honor. A peach, raspberry, and ice-cream dessert was also named after Nellie Melba.

**SALISBURY STEAK**
In 1886, British physician James Salisbury prescribed a cure-all for a variety of diseases. He told his patients to eat well-done ground beef three times a day and to drink a glass of hot water after each meal. The so-called "Salisbury steak" was actually just a hamburger without a bun, but the name made it sound like a fancy dish, and many restaurants began to feature it on their menus.

**SANDWICH**
It's said that John Montagu, the fourth earl of Sandwich (1718–1792) was in the middle of a card game when he asked a servant to place

some cold roast beef between two slices of toast. The earl wanted to be able to eat with one hand and play cards with the other. However, some historians claim that the earl was writing or hunting when he ordered the first sandwich.

## At The Table—Useful Utensils and Manners That Mattered

### FORK

Romans and early Europeans ate with their fingers. But Roman patricians (aristocrats), who were considered people of breeding and refined manners, politely lifted their food with three fingers— taking care not to soil the ring finger or the small finger (pinkie). Plebeians (commoners) grabbed at their food with all five fingers.

The word "fork" comes from the Latin word *furca,* a farmer's pitchfork. Small forks for eating first appeared in western Italy in the eleventh century. Wealthy Italians had two-tined forks made for them in gold and silver, and it's said that in England, nobles at court used forks primarily for dueling. Until the eighteenth century, forks were thought of as silly novelties. French nobles in the 1700s began to use forks (with four tines) as a symbol of luxury, refinement, and status. People who ate with their fingers were looked down upon as ill bred and low class.

### KNIFE

Prehistoric people created the first stone knives for butchering prey. The word "knife" comes from the Anglo-Saxon *cnif;* the word probably came into use sometime between the fifth and eleventh centuries A.D. in England. For centuries, most men owned only one knife, which hung at the waist and might be used to spear a piece of cooked meat at the dinner table one day and to kill an enemy or an animal the next. Only nobles could afford to own separate knives for eating, hunting, and warfare.

The blunt-edged table knife we use today was created to put an end to an unmannerly custom. French noblemen often used the pointed ends of their knives to pick their teeth clean after meals. In the 1630s, Cardinal Richelieu, the power behind the throne of French king Louis XIII, forbade the practice at his own table, and he ordered the chief steward of his household to file the points off the knives in his house. These blunt-edged knives eventually became popular in households throughout France.

## SPOON

Spoons have been around for a long time. Archaeologists have found spoons in Asia that date back 20,000 years, to the Paleolithic Age. Spoons made of wood, stone, ivory, and gold have been found in the tombs of ancient Egyptians. Spoons were the first widely used utensil and the most practical for eating such foods as porridge and thick soups.

## CHOPSTICKS

These utensils originated in China centuries ago. The Chinese felt that it was impolite to expect dinner guests to spend the meal cutting up chunks of meat. They decided that food should be diced into small, bite-sized pieces in the kitchen, then served at the table. The Chinese created practical utensils made of wood, bone, and ivory for eating these bits of meat and called them *kwai-tsze*— "quick ones." When English-speaking people sounded out the word *kwai-tsze* it became "chopsticks."

## NAPKIN

In the days when people ate with their fingers, napkins were a practical necessity. The napkins used by the ancient Egyptians, Greeks, and Romans were the size of towels, and all three cultures used finger bowls filled with water scented by flowers and herbs. Napkins were also used as "doggie bags" in Rome in the sixth century B.C. Guests at banquets were expected to wrap up delicacies from the table in their napkins to take home. When people began to use forks instead of fingers, napkins became smaller.

The work "napkin" comes from the old French word *naperon,* meaning "little tablecloth." The English called it a *napron* and used the word to mean a large cloth tied around the waist to protect the front of the body and to wipe the hands on. The English shifted the pronunciation around, and *napron* became "an apron."

## TABLE MANNERS IN THE MIDDLE AGES

During the Crusades, when knighthood and its code of chivalry started to become popular, people began to take an interest in table manners. Etiquette books debuted in Europe in the thirteenth century and were eagerly consulted by those who were on their way up the social ladder. Below is some useful advice from several etiquette books of the Middle Ages on how *not* to behave at a Medieval banquet:

- Never gnaw a bone and then put it back in the dish.
- Do not sit over or on the table in the manner of hunters.
- When you blow your nose or cough, turn around so that nothing falls on the table. (In the days before handkerchiefs and tissues, people blew their noses into their fingers. This was acceptable behavior. However, it was considered bad manners to blow into a sleeve or tablecloth.)
- Always wash your hands before eating. (I hear that some eat unwashed," wrote one Mr. Manners of the Middle Ages, referring to diners who forgot to wash their hands before eating. "May their fingers be palsied!")

## Highlights in the History of Clothes

- People probably began to wear clothing more than 100,000 years ago. It's likely that they wore clothing for the same reasons we do today—for protection, to improve their appearance, and to tell other people something about themselves. For example, a prehistoric hunter might have worn the skin of a bear or a reindeer to keep warm, but also as a symbol of personal skill, bravery, and strength in hunting.
- The needle had been invented by the end of the old Stone Age—about 25,000 years ago. The needle enabled people to sew animal skins together into clothing. But our ancestors also learned to make yarn from the threadlike parts of some plants, or from the fur or hair of animals. They learned to weave yarn into cloth and began to raise plants and herd animals such as

sheep, so that they would have a steady supply of yarn and wool.

- There were no machines for making clothes until about 200 years ago. Most clothing was made by dressmakers or at home, usually by the women in the family. Some businesses paid groups of workers to make clothes, which the businesses then sold. People who were hired to make clothes usually worked at home.

- Clothing factories sprang up during the Industrial Revolution of the late 1700s and 1800s. Machines were invented to spin thread, weave cloth, and sew clothes. But many families, especially those who lived in rural areas, continued to have their clothes made at home. Tailors for men and designer-dressmakers for women often worked out of their own shops and were mainly used by well-to-do families, or for such special occasions as weddings.

- From 1890 to 1920 in the U.S., manufacturing methods for

making clothes improved and brought rapid growth to companies that made ready-to-wear clothing. Men and women began to wear clothes that had been mass-produced in factories and were sold in department stores.

# 6 Popular Styles of the Past That Will Probably *Never* Come Back into Fashion

**Beauty Patches**—Little black patches of fabric worn on the face by men and women to cover up blemishes and highlight the whiteness of the skin. Popular in the 1700s.

**Bustle**—A cushion that made the skirt stick out in back. Popular, off and on, from the 1600s to the late 1800s.

**Farthingale**—A device worn by women of the 1500s to support their long, wide skirts. One type of farthingale was an underskirt with a rigid frame made of whalebone, wire, or wood. The frame made the skirt stand out stiffly from the body. Another type was a long, thick pillow that a woman tied around her waist under her dress.

**Hobble Skirt**—A style popular around 1910. These ankle-length skirts were so tight at the bottom that a woman could barely walk in them.

**Periwigs**—Huge curled wigs worn by men of the late 1600s. Also called perukes.

**Upper Stocks**—Short, puffed men's knee pants sewn to tight stockings called netherstocks. Popular in the 1500s.

# How 5 Items of Clothing Were Named

**Bathing Suits** were so called because people of the mid-1800s were advised to "bathe" in lakes, streams, and the ocean for their health. Bathing meant wading, soaking, or paddling around in the water, not swimming. It would have been difficult for a woman to swim in those days. A woman bather of the 1800s wore a cumbersome outfit of flannel, alpaca, or serge, with a fitted bodice, high neck, elbow-length sleeves, and a knee-length skirt over bloomers (wide pants), black stockings, and low canvas shoes. One-piece, knee-length suits with sleeves and skirts for women became popular in the U.S. around 1915. Carl Jantzen, part owner of an Oregon knitting mill, came up with a rib-knit stretch suit that was advertised as "the suit that changed bathing to swimming."

**Blue Jeans** were named for "jeans," a twilled cotton cloth used for making sturdy work clothes. The cloth was made in Genoa, Italy, which French weavers called Genes. The cloth also came to be called "genes." In the 1850s, during the San Francisco gold rush, a seventeen-year-old tailor, Levi Strauss, made hard-wearing canvas overalls for prospectors. In the 1860s, Strauss replaced canvas with a softer fabric called *serge de Nimes* after the place it was made, Nimes, France. In the U.S., the fabric's name was pronounced "denim." Strauss made denim pants and dyed them blue so that stains wouldn't show up on them. Strauss's blue jeans became very popular, especially among cowboys of the old West. To achieve a snug fit, cowboys would don a pair of jeans that had been soaked in a horse-watering trough, then lie in the sun to let the material shrink.

**Cowboy Boots** were named for the American cowpunchers who began wearing them around 1850. The boots were designed with higher-than-average heels so that they would not slip through the stirrups of a saddle.

**Pants** were named after Pantaleone, a foolish and flirtatious character in Italian comedies of the 1500s. Pantaleone wore a pair of trousers that were baggy at the top and tight-fitting from knee to ankle. Troupes of actors traveled to France with these comedies, called *commedia dell' arte*, and there, Pantaleone and his trousers were called Pantalon. In England, the name became Pantaloon. In the 1700s, pantaloons were men's knee breeches (short trousers) and in America, the name was shortened to "pants."

**Sneakers** first appeared in the early 1900s. Vulcanized rubber soles were glued to canvas tops to produce athletic shoes. The shoes were called sneakers because a person who wore them could sneak around without being heard. Sneakers were originally brown with black soles.

# CHAPTER 8

# Arts and Entertainment

Featured in this chapter are highlights in the history of movies, TV, radio, theatre, advertising, and books, especially books for kids. There are great moments in music and ballet, facts on circuses, and the origins of popular sports, games, and toys. And for celebrity watchers, there's a list of young performers who won special Academy Awards.

# The Origins of Drama and Comedy

The first dramas were ancient Greek *diathyrambs,* choral songs and rowdy dances that featured a single speaker and were performed in honor of Dionysius, the god of the arts and wine. Dramas as we know them today were the creation of the Greek poet Thespis, from whom we get the word for actor or actress, *thespian.* Thespis wrote, directed, and starred in productions of literary works. These plays were tragedies that stressed human emotions like anger, desire, hurt, and sympathy. They featured dialogue and were accompanied by a flute and the dancing and singing of fifty men or boys. Greek drama reached its peak by the fifth century B.C. and contained three elements: the weakness of the main character (called a tragic flaw); his pursuit by the gods, who became angered by his actions; and his downfall, which often ruined his family and community as well as himself. The dramas of ancient Rome were similar to Greek dramas.

# Drama in the Middle Ages and Beyond

Medieval drama grew out of church teachings and consisted of several types. Morality Plays instructed audiences on the struggle between good and evil for human souls. They featured characters that represented virtues and vices. Mystery plays were based on Biblical events, and Miracle Plays dramatized the lives of the saints.

During the Renaissance, a period lasting from the end of the Middle Ages until about 1650, the arts, including drama, flourished. Dramatists of the Renaissance era used elements of Greek and Roman dramas in their plays. They did not focus on religion as did the playwrights of the Middle Ages. The greatest dramatist of the Renaissance was England's William Shakespeare (1564–1616). Shakespeare was an actor, poet, and playwright who wrote some of history's best-known tragedies, including *Hamlet*, *Romeo and Juliet*, *Julius Caesar*, and *Macbeth*. Shakespeare also managed London's Globe Theatre, where many of his plays were performed. Only men acted in plays then; they even played women's roles. Shakespeare's plays were very popular. Theatregoers loved to shout out comments to the actors during performances, and they booed and hissed characters they didn't like, or who were obviously up to no good. Adding to the chaos were foodsellers announcing the sale of snacks to the audience. In many ways, going to the theatre in Shakespeare's day was like attending a baseball game today!

The standard for playwrights of later centuries was set by the Greek and Roman dramatists and the playwrights of Shakespeare's time. Unlike the Medieval dramatists, who were only concerned with religious morality, they explored such important universal themes as guilt, envy, greed, love, hate, jealousy, revenge, despair, and fear.

# Laughing it Up—
# The Origins of Comedy

The first comedies were the miming plays of ancient Greece. An actor would portray, in an exaggerated, humorous manner, the problems and stupidities of everyday life. Mime was silent acting, but the actor sometimes made up words to heighten the comedy of his situation. Roman and Greek dramatists like Aristophanes wrote comic plays with dialogue. These plays were witty comedies that made fun of politics and issues of the day.

During the 1500s, a form of comedy called *commedia dell'arte* became popular in Italy. Actors and actresses wore masks and made up their own dialogue during each performance. The characters never changed, and they always became involved in zany situations. Audiences loved to watch the slapstick antics of such *commedia* stock characters as Harlequin, the acrobat; Columbine, his witty girlfriend; Panteleone, the silly flirt; and Brighella, the cowardly villain.

Shakespeare and other playwrights of England's Elizabethan Age (during the reign of Queen Elizabeth I) wrote comedies. They used elements of the *commedia,* such as slapstick, but developed their characters and situations more fully. Shakespeare's comedies include *A Midsummer Night's Dream, As You Like It, Twelfth Night,* and *The Comedy of Errors.* Many of Shakespeare's tragedies also feature comic characters and funny scenes.

As with drama, the standard for comedy in later centuries was set by the efforts of the Greeks, Romans, Italian *commedia* actors, and the Elizabethans.

# Highlights in the History of Advertising

## Ancient Times

- The first ads were vocal—street cries used by peddlers hawking their wares.
- A 3,000-year-old written ad from the ancient Egyptian city of Thebes called for the recovery of a runaway slave, stating, "For his return to the ship of Hapu the Weaver, where the best cloth is woven to your desires, a whole gold coin is offered."
- The Ancient Romans pasted up posters advertising circuses and gladiator matches.

## Middle Ages To The Late 1600s

- During the Middle Ages, handbills and tacked-up notices became popular. The goods of merchants were advertised on these posters, and the ads featured drawings as well as words, because few people could read. Street barkers were also posted outside shops to announce the merchants' wares to passersby.
- In 1665, an epidemic of the Black Death, or bubonic plague, hit London, England. Newspapers carried ads for such strange "preventatives and curers" as Incomparable Drink Against the Plague, The Only True Plague Water, and Infallible Preventive Pills Against the Plague.
- In the late 1600s, London was so full of large advertising signs that King Charles II proclaimed, "No signs shall be hung across the streets shutting out the air and light of the heavens."

## Colonial America

- The first issue of the first successful regular American newspaper, the *Boston News Letter* (1704), ran ads.
- Statesman, inventor, writer, editor, and publisher Benjamin Franklin was the father of American advertising. In 1729, he published the *Pennsylvania Gazette*, which carried ads for soap, books, and stationery and soon became the most widely read newspaper in the Colonies. Franklin wrote an ad for his newly invented stove which warned readers that if they used other, old-fashioned types of stoves, their teeth and jaws would go bad, their skin would shrivel, and their eyesight would fade!

## The 1800s

- American showman Phineas T. Barnam advertised his circus as "Barnum's Own Greatest Show on Earth" and used such tantalizing descriptions of its attractions as "most incredible," "amazing," "horrifying," and "death-defying" to draw crowds. Some of Barnum's sideshow "attractions" were fakes, like the Cardiff Giant, supposedly a huge fossilized man, and the Feejee Mermaid (put together from a stuffed monkey and a fish). Many customers complained, but Barnum wasn't worried about losing business because, in his words, "There's a sucker born every minute."

- The first celebrity to endorse a product was famous and beautiful actress Lily Langtry. She was hired by Pears Soap to appear in their ads.
- In 1882, the first electric sign was constructed and displayed by W. J. Hammer in London. Soon, New York City was alight with blinking electric signs.

## The Twentieth Century

- During World War I, advertising was often used in the U.S. and Britain to encourage patriotism. Posters asked young men to enlist in the services to fight the enemy, and ads for products were tied into the war effort. One ad for Cat's Paw Rubber Heels used the slogan "Stepping on to Victory."
- Radio became popular in the 1920s, and advertisers rushed to sell products on the new medium. Radio commercials often blended so well with the programs that it was sometimes hard for listeners to figure out whether they were hearing a show or an ad.
- After World War II, television sets began to appear in U.S. homes. Advertisers could now reach more consumers than ever before with TV commercials that gave viewers glimpses of the products manufacturers decided Americans needed to live happier lives. But the reality was that the happiest Americans turned out to be ad agencies and manufacturers who made a great deal of money when viewers took the TV commercials seriously and bought the often unnecessary products advertised.

## Highlights in the History of Radio

**1895**          Guglielmo Marconi, 21, and his brother Alfonso, transmitted radio signals across the hills behind their home in Bologna, Italy. The Italian government wasn't interested in

Guglielmo's invention, so he took it to England. The British Navy quickly realized the maritime potential of radio. By 1897, Marconi had established Marconi's Wireless Telegraph Company. For decades, the radio was referred to as the "wireless."

**Christmas Eve 1906**

The first U.S. radio program was broadcast from Brant Rock, Massachusetts. Reginald Aubrey Fessenden played the violin, gave a short speech, quoted the Bible, and played a phonograph recording. Fessenden broadcast a second program on New Year's Eve. Atmospheric conditions were so favorable that the Fessenden broadcast reached listeners as far away as the West Indies.

**November 1916**

Radio reporter Lee DeForest first broadcast presidential election returns. However, he incorrectly stated that Charles Evans Hughes had won the election over Woodrow Wilson.

**October 1921**

WJ2, Newark, broadcast the World Series for the first time, as the New York Giants beat the New York Yankees five games to three.

**November 1926**

NBC began broadcasting with a program from the Grand Ballroom at the Waldorf-Astoria Hotel in New York City. The first radio network, RCA, had been formed in 1919; CBS made its debut in 1928.

**1930s and 1940s**

Radio dramas, comedies, and variety and game shows became very popular. Listeners flocked around the radio to hear such soap operas as *The Romance of Helen Trent, Ma Perkins*, and *Our Gal Sunday* and situation comedies like *The Goldbergs* and *Fibber McGee and Molly*. Popular radio comedians

included George Burns and Gracie Allen,
Jack Benny, and ventriloquist Edgar Bergen
and his dummy, Charlie McCarthy. For kids
there was *Little Orphan Annie, The Lone
Ranger,* and *Jack Armstrong, the All-American
Boy.* Kids could send away for such program tie-ins as the Orphan Annie Secret
Decoder Ring. During each program, a secret message would be given, which only
the ring could decode. More often than not,
the decoded message advised kids to use the
product advertised on the show.

*Mortimer Snerd*

*Charlie McCarthy*

**Halloween Eve**
1938

Actor, director, and later filmmaker Orson
Welles caused a nationwide panic when his
Mercury Theatre broadcast a dramatization
of H. G. Wells's classic science-fiction story, *War of the Worlds.* The hour-long drama
presented the story of Martians invading the

U.S. as a "realistic" news bulletin with follow-up, "on-the-scene" reports, complete with horrifying descriptions of the aliens and the widespread destruction they were causing. Most listeners missed the station break, which clearly said that the "Martian landing" was part of a radio drama. By that time, huge numbers of people had left their homes to try to escape the Martians, convinced they were seeing spaceships in the night sky.

**World War II**

Radio journalist Edward R. Murrow, broadcasting from London, brought the sounds of the Blitz (German bombing of Great Britain) into American homes. On December 8, 1941, 79 percent of U.S. households were tuned in to President Franklin D. Roosevelt's speech to Congress concerning the bombing of Pearl Harbor, Hawaii. In 1944, news coverage of D Day, the Allied invasion of Europe, bumped all regular programming off the air.

**1950s to present**

In the 1950s, television was grabbing audiences away from radio. Said Robert Sarnoff, president of NBC, "Radio is dead." But he was wrong. Although many shows moved to TV, people continued to listen to new radio programs and to tune in to news, talk, and music stations. Those playing top 40 hits became especially popular, and local deejays became celebrities. Portable transistor radios and battery-powered "walkmen" made it possible for people to carry their favorite music around with them, or to listen to play-by-play coverage of baseball, basketball, and football games while on the go.

# Television Firsts

- The first images on a screen were created independently by John Logie Baird of England and C. F. Jenkins of the U.S. in 1925. These early, blurry images resembled silhouettes, but clearer pictures were eventually developed.

- The first TV star was cartoon character Felix the Cat. In 1930, Felix appeared in statue form on an NBC experimental program. The figure whirled on a turntable in front of a camera.

- In 1939, the first TV sportscast took place. It was a baseball game between Princeton and Columbia universities. Only one camera was used, and it was placed so close to the diamond that the camera operator spent most of the afternoon dodging balls.

- The first color broadcast in history was sent in 1940 from a CBS transmitter at the top of the Chrysler Building in New York City.

- The year 1947 marked the first TV broadcast of the World Series, and the Yankees beat the Brooklyn Dodgers in seven games. The longest-running news interview show to date, "Meet the Press," also debuted in 1947. And the first mega-popular TV show for kids began broadcasting that year. The show lasted through the 1950s and featured freckled-faced marionette Howdy Doody, human host Buffalo Bob Smith, Clarabell the Clown, and Indian princess Summerfallwinterspring.

- The first episode of "The Adventures of Superman" made its TV debut in 1950. The man of steel was played by actor George Reeves. Every show began with the words "It's a bird . . . it's a plane . . . it's Superman!"

- The Academy Awards were televised for the first time in 1954. When the show ran overtime, William Holden, the winner of the Best Actor Oscar, was cut off the air in the middle of his acceptance speech. Unhappy viewers had to learn from the next day's newspapers who had won the oscars for Best Actress and Best Movie.

- The first big-money quiz show, "The $64,000 Question," debuted on TV in 1954. The featured contestants, psychologist Dr. Joyce Brothers, shoemaker Gino Prato, and actor Vincent Price, were each placed in "an isolation booth" and asked questions about their special areas of knowledge. Brothers answered questions on prizefighting, Prato on opera, and Price on art.

- The largest daytime TV audience in history watched on May 5, 1961, as astronaut Alan Shepard became the first American to blast off into space.
- In 1965, TV's first black hero was played by Bill Cosby, who costarred with Robert Culp in the adventure series "I Spy." Cosby and Culp played CIA agents in the series.
- An estimated 600 million people worldwide watched the live 1969 telecast of astronaut Neil Armstrong taking the first step on the moon.
- Commercials for cigarettes were first banned on TV in 1971. Alcohol commercials followed soon afterward.
- "Roots," the first miniseries about the experiences of an African-American family from the nineteenth century to the twentieth century, was aired in 1977. Episodes of "Roots" remain among the all-time top-rated TV shows.
- In the 1980s, viewers began to hook up videocassette players to their TVs. For the first time in history, people could tape and watch shows and movies whenever they wanted.

# Movie Firsts

**1877**     Edward Muybridge of the U.S. made the first moving picture when he mounted still photographs of a galloping horse onto a revolving wheel and projected the photos with a strong light. The horse appeared to move as the wheel revolved. Muybridge had to use twelve cameras to photograph the complete galloping action of the horse.

**1882**     The first true motion pictures taken with a single camera appeared. Etienne-Jules Marey of France constructed a cylindrical photographic plate behind a lens that captured twelve images in one second as the plate made a full rotation. These were the first multiple exposures.

**1891**     William Dickson, an employee of inventor Thomas Edison, invented the first film strips. The film strips were designed to be viewed in a box called a kinetoscope by one person at a time. The first public showing of moving film took place at Edison's workshop in West Orange, New Jersey. Members of the National Federation of Women's Clubs watched a man bow, smile, wave, and tip his hat.

**1894**     Edison opened the first movie theater on April 14, on Broadway in New York City. For a nickel, a customer could look into a kinetoscope and watch moving film strips. Featured in Edison's films were bodybuilder Eugene Sandow, who lifted weights and did gymnastics, or former Wild West scout-turned-showman Buffalo Bill Cody, who mounted a horse and shot pistols. Nickel movie houses were later called nickelodeons.

**1895**     Brothers Louis and Auguste Lumiere of France patented a motion picture projector. The first film to be shown on a screen before a public audience was a short feature showing workers leaving the Lumiere factory.

**1902**     George Melies's *Voyage to the Moon* was the first sci-fi movie. Melies, a former magician, was the first to use special effects on film and the first to use the dissolve, double exposures, and fadeouts.

**1903**     The first Western feature film, *The Great Train Robbery,* was made. The movie lasted eleven minutes and was the first to use closeups.

**1908**     The first horror movie was made by Thomas Edison. It was a version of Mary Shelley's chilling novel *Frankenstein*.

**1909**     The first big movie stars were Florence Lawrence, known as the "Biograph Girl" because she worked for Biograph Studios, and Mary Pickford, who, because of her youthful appearance and corkscrew curls, usually played children or teens. She was known as "America's Sweetheart."

**1912–1913**   The first films were made in Hollywood, California. Movies had been shot in New York City studios, but independent producers headed west to take advantage of the good climate and the chance to film more movies outdoors on location.

**1917**   The first million-dollar Hollywood contract was signed by popular comic actor Charlie Chaplin, who agreed to star in eight movies.

**1927**   The first talking picture, *The Jazz Singer*, premiered. Produced by the Warner Brothers studio, it starred popular comedy actor/singer Al Jolson and was silent except for three songs sung by Jolson and one small scene. Other studios rushed to make the change from silents to "talkies." The first Academy Awards were handed out in 1927. The awards ceremony was attended by 200 people.

**1928**   The first all-talking movie was *Lights of New York*, a gangster drama. Walt Disney's Mickey Mouse also made his first screen appearance, in an animated film entitled *Steamboat Willie*. However, Mickey's original name was Mortimer Mouse.

**1935**   The first full-length movie shown in color was *Becky Sharp*, a version of William Thackery's famous novel *Vanity Fair*.

**1953**   *The Robe* became the first Cinemascope movie. Cinemascope used a type of camera that "squeezed" a wide picture onto a screen that is smaller than the picture. With this process, sweeping scenery and casts of thousands could be shown on screen. Other wide-screen processes were Panavision and Cinerama.

**1977** The hit sci-fi/fantasy movie *Star Wars* became the first to dazzle audiences with its high-tech special effects. *Star Wars* set the tone for many movies of the late 70s and 80s.

## 5 Kids Who Won Academy Awards

The young performers below were given special Oscars for their contributions to film:

**DEANNA DURBIN**
Born in 1921, Deanna sang and acted in movies of the 1930s and 1940s. She was awarded her Oscar in 1938 "for bringing to the screen the spirit and personification of youth."

**JUDY GARLAND**
The teenage singing star who played Dorothy in the classic movie *The Wizard of Oz* was born Frances Gumm in 1922. In 1939, seventeen-year-old Judy received a special Oscar "for her outstanding performance as a screen juvenile."

**MARGARET O'BRIEN**
Probably best known for her role as the bratty but funny Tootie in *Meet Me in St. Louis*, Margaret won her special Academy Award in 1944 at the age of seven.

**TATUM O'NEAL**
Ten-year-old Tatum, the daughter of actor Ryan O'Neal, was the first and only young person to have won a best supporting actress Oscar. She received the award for her role as Addie in the 1973 movie *Paper Moon*. The movie also starred her father.

**SHIRLEY TEMPLE**
A blonde curly-haired singing, dancing, and acting wonder, Shirley first appeared in films in 1931 at the age of three. She was the top

movie star of the 1930s and was awarded a special Oscar in 1934 "in grateful recognition of her outstanding contribution to screen entertainment." One of Shirley's best roles was that of Sara Crewe in the movie version of Frances Hodgson Burnett's classic children's book *A Little Princess*. Shirley grew up to become U.N. ambassador to Ghana and U.S. Chief of Protocol.

## Highlights in the History of Books

- The first books were ancient Babylonian and Assyrian clay tablets inscribed with cuneiform, a system of writing using wedge-shaped symbols to represent sounds within a word, objects, and concepts.
- Sometime before 2800 B.C., the Egyptians made paper out of papyrus, a reedy plant that grows by the Nile River. Egyptian

books were rolls of papyrus inscribed with hieroglyphics, the Egyptian system of picture writing. The Greeks developed leaflets of folded papyrus, which they bound together to make the first modern-looking book.

- In 300 B.C., Ptolemy I of Egypt founded a great library in Alexandria. The library was filled with scrolls of papyrus and stood for over 400 years. It was considered a cultural wonder of the world of its time.

- The world's first printed book was *The Diamond Sutra*. It was printed in China in A.D. 868 with individual wooden blocks. In 1450, German silversmith Johan Gutenberg invented the printing press. The first book printed on it was a Bible, in 1455.

- The first children's book printed in English was a book of rhymes entitled *A Book of Englyssh Metre of the Great Merchant Man Called Dives Pragmaticus*. It was printed by Alexander Lacy of England in 1563.

- The world's first magazine for children was *The Lilliputian*, published in 1751 by John Newbery of England. Newbery, a publisher and bookseller, established children's literature as an important branch of his publishing business. He published his books anonymously, but he probably plotted and wrote many of them himself. In 1922, the Newbery Medal was established to be awarded to the most outstanding American children's book of the year. The first winner was *The Story of Mankind* by Hendrik Van Loon. Other popular winners included *King of the Wind*, by Marguerite Henry (1949); *The Witch of Blackbird Pond*, by Elizabeth George Speare (1959); *A Wrinkle in Time*, by Madeleine L'Engle (1963); *Sounder* by William Armstrong (1970); and *Dicey's Song*, by Cynthia Voight (1983).

- The *Encyclopedia Britannica* appeared in England between 1768 and 1771. Three Scotsmen, Andrew Bell, Colin MacFarquhar, and William Smellie, compiled this distinguished book of information. The Britannica is the oldest continually published reference book in the English language.

- In 1828, Noah Webster published the first American dictionary, *An American Dictionary of the English Language*. Webster studied 26 languages to find the origin of the 70,000 words in his two-volume dictionary.

- The serialized novel started to become popular in England around 1840. Such authors as Charles Dickens wrote installments of three or four chapters, which appeared in a magazine. Readers would be left in suspense after the "cliffhanger" of the last chapter, and they waited eagerly for the next edition of the magazine to learn the fate of the hero or heroine.
- "Dime novels" appeared in the U.S. in 1860. The novels were popular American fiction published in a series and sold for a dime. The first series was "Beadle's Dime Novels." The novels were usually adventure and mystery stories.
- The Bobbsey Twins made their first appearance in 1904 in *Merry Days Indoors and Out*, by Laura Lee Hope. The twins are still going strong today.
- A Maryland librarian created the first bookmobile in 1905. The bookmobile was a horse-drawn wagon with shelves to hold 250 books. These traveling libraries took books to readers in remote rural areas.
- In 1926, the first book club was established in the U.S. It was the Book-of-the-Month Club, and it had 4,750 members.
- Franklin W. Dixon's fictional teen detectives, Frank and Joe Hardy, made their debut in 1927. The same publisher brought out the first Nancy Drew mystery, *The Secret in the Old Clock*, in 1930. Both the Hardy and Nancy mystery series are still popular today.

## 5 Real-Life People Who Inspired Characters in Famous Stories

**L. FRANK BAUM—The Wizard in the *Oz* books.**
It's said that Baum, the author of *The Wonderful Wizard of Oz* (1900) and several sequels, based the character of the Wizard on himself. Baum was a multitalented, imaginative man who often preferred fantasy to reality and who liked telling tall tales. He tried many different jobs during his lifetime, working as a salesman, journalist, editor, writer, and filmmaker. The Wizard had worked at a variety of jobs, too, before journeying to the land of Oz, where he managed to make people believe his tallest tale—that he was a great wizard.

## DR. JOSEPH BELL—The famous fictional detective Sherlock Holmes

Dr. Bell (1837–1911) was a surgeon and medical instructor at the Royal Infirmary in Edinburgh, Scotland. One of his students was author Arthur Conan Doyle, who was impressed by Bell's ability to simply look at a stranger and deduce much of his or her life and habits. Doyle used Bell as a model for his great detective Sherlock Holmes.

## WILLIAM BRODIE—Dr. Jekyll and Mr. Hyde

Brodie was an eighteenth-century cabinetmaker, union leader, and member of the Edinburgh town council. He was a respected businessman by day and the leader of a gang of robbers by night. He was finally caught and hanged. Author Robert Louis Stevenson was so fascinated by Brodie's double life that he used the man as a model for the character of Dr. Henry Jekyll in his 1886 horror novel *The Strange Case of Dr. Jekyll and Mr. Hyde*. By day, Dr. Jekyll is a kindly physician; at night, after drinking a potion of his own creation, he becomes crazed killer Mr. Hyde.

## JOSIAH HENSON—Uncle Tom in *Uncle Tom's Cabin*

Henson (1789–1883) was born into slavery on a Maryland farm. He became overseer of his master's estate and a Methodist preacher. After learning he was to be sold to a southern planter, Henson escaped to Canada with his wife and children. He made three trips to England, where he spoke out against slavery and was received by Queen Victoria. In Boston, Henson was interviewed by Harriet Beecher Stowe, who then used Henson as the model for the character of Uncle Tom in her 1852 best-seller about slavery in the U.S.

## ALICE LIDDELL—Alice in *Alice's Adventure in Wonderland*

Author Lewis Carroll (Charles Lutwidge Dodgson) named his famous title character after the ten-year-old daughter of his neighbors, the Liddells. The story started as a fantasy tale which Carroll told to Alice and her sisters. Carroll turned it into a book after Alice Liddell begged him to "write down Alice's adventures for me." The book was published in 1865, and in 1872, Carroll published another Alice adventure: *Through the Looking Glass*.

# 10 Historical Novels for Kids

*Caddie Woodlawn*, **Carol Ryrie Brink**—Lively Caddie and her family face many challenges, dangers, and delights living in the woods of western Wisconsin during the pioneer days of the 1800s.

*Dragonwings*, **Laurence Yep**—This novel portrays two Chinese immigrants, a father and son, who adjust to working in America, survive the 1906 San Francisco earthquake, and dream of reuniting their family.

*The Eternal Spring of Mr. Ito*, **Sheila Garrigue**—When Sara Warren is evacuated from England to stay with relatives in Canada during World War II, she befriends Japanese gardener Mr. Ito. After the Japanese bombing of Pearl Harbor in 1941, Mr. Ito and his family are taken to an internment camp far away. Sara must somehow find a way to bring the gardener his treasured 200-year-old bonsai tree.

*Johnny Tremain*, **Esther Forbes**—Johnny Tremain, a silversmith's apprentice during the American Revolution, becomes involved in events of the war, including the Boston Tea Party.

*The Little House* Books, **Laura Ingalls Wilder**—In this series of novels, Laura describes her own growing up in the 1800s in

Wisconsin, the Indian Territory of Kansas, Minnesota, and Dakota Territory. These books are full of rich detail about the everyday life of pioneers. The books in the series are:

*Little House in the Big Woods*
*Little House on the Prairie*
*On the Banks of Plum Creek*
*By the Shores of the Silver Lake*
*The Long Winter*
*Little Town on the Prairie*
*Farmer Boy*
*These Happy Golden Years*
*The First Four Years*

***My Brother Sam is Dead*, James Lincoln and Christopher Collier—** In 1775, impetuous and idealistic sixteen-year-old Sam defies his Tory father and joins the Continental Army to fight for American independence from England.

***Rifles for Watie*, Harold Keith—**The exciting story of a Union spy behind confederate lines during the Civil War.

***Roll of Thunder, Hear My Cry*, Mildred Taylor—**The story of a nine-year-old black girl in the South during the Great Depression of the 1930s.

***Summer of My German Soldier*, Bette Green—**This sensitive novel is set in a small Southern town during World War II. A Jewish teen helps a young German prisoner-of-war escape.

***The Witch of Blackbird Pond*, Elizabeth George Speare—**Independent, attractive sixteen-year-old Kit comes to live with her aunt and uncle in Puritan Connecticut. When Kit is branded a witch by superstitious townspeople, she is helped by a handsome young sailor and a small child.

## 10 Weird and Wonderful Words of the Past

**Bellibone** (1500s)—A pretty girl. This English word comes from the French phrase *belle et bonne,* meaning "beautiful and good."

**Bellytimber** (1600s to the 1800s)—Food, which is the "timber" you feed your body as wood is fed to a fire.

**Fellowfeel** (1600s to the 1800s)—To crawl into the skin of another person in order to feel what he or she is feeling.

**Flesh-Spades** (1700)—Fingernails, the "digging tools" that grow out of the flesh of the fingers.

**Keak** (1600s to the 1800s)—To cackle like a witch.

**Lip-Clap** (1600s)—A kiss.

**Merry-Go-Sorry** (1500s and 1600s)—A story that makes you feel both happy and sad.

**Prickmedainty** (1500s—A fancy dresser who always wears the latest fashion. Another old-fashioned word for this type of person is "dandy."

**Snirtle** (1700s and 1800s)—To snicker.

**Wurf** (900s to the 1200s)—A glance of the eye; a stone's throw away, meaning not too far.

## Great Moments in Music

- Early humans beat sticks together to scare away dangerous animals. Eventually, people used sticks to beat out a rhythm to accompany work songs in the fields. These "clappers" were also used in dance rituals to please the gods and thus bring about good harvests.

- Instruments used by early Mesopotamian civilizations such as the Sumerians, Babylonians, and Assyrians included ideophones, which resembled triangles; aerophones, tubular wind instruments that resonated a column of blown air; cordophones, stringed instruments; and membranophones, made of animal skins stretched over hollow objects.

- The lyre, a forerunner of the harp, originated in Mesopotamia around 4000 B.C. It became a popular instrument in Greece, Africa, and among the Celts of the British Isles and France. Today the lyre is still played in Ethiopia, the Sudan, and among the fishermen of the Persian Gulf.

- The lute, a stringed instrument from which the violin, viola, cello, and guitar developed, may have been used as far back as 2500 B.C. in Babylon. The ancient Romans spread the lute's popularity throughout the Roman Empire.

• Singing in harmony developed gradually during the Middle Ages. It may have come about when singers with different vocal ranges began singing at their most comfortable pitch levels, or when singers adopted the pitches used by organists, or when a melody was repeated and sung at the same time as the original line of the melody. (Rounds such as "Row, Row, Row Your Boat," "White Coral Bells," and "Down in the Valley" are examples of this last type of harmonizing.)

• Wandering minstrels became popular in the early Middle Ages. Men traveled from town to town playing and singing songs and performing acrobatics for money. The songs dealt with love, war, famine, and other issues of the day. Later French minstrels, called troubadours, wrote and sang their own poetry, which they performed at the courts of nobles. German minstrels of the fifteenth and sixteenth century were called *meistersingers* ("master singers").

• Opera, dramas performed entirely in song, originated in Italy in the sixteenth century. The first opera was *Dafne*, composed by singer-composer Jacopo Peri. Operettas—lighter-hearted dramas and comedies containing music and spoken dialogue—became popular in the 1800s. Operettas were the forerunners of the musical comedies of the twentieth century.

- The piano was invented in 1709 by Bartolommeo Cristofori of Italy. Cristofori modified early pianolike instruments, the harpsichord and clavichord, in which the strings inside are plucked (harpsichord) or struck by blades of metal (clavichord). He placed little hammers in his piano that hit the strings. Unlike the harpsichord and clavichord, the piano was capable of producing loud and soft notes, depending on how hard the player hit the keys.

- Modern forms of popular music such as jazz, blues, ragtime, and rock 'n' roll debuted in the twentieth century. Rock first emerged in the mid-1950s as a version of rhythm-and-blues, a blues style that often used amplified instruments to produce a heavy beat. The first national rock 'n' roll hit was "Rock Around the Clock," sung by Bill Haley and his Comets in 1955. The first rock superstar was Elvis Presley, who in the 1950s combined rhythm-and-blues with country and Western music to create his own special sound. The most popular rock groups of the 1960s were probably the Beatles and the Rolling Stones. The Beatles broke up in 1970, but the Stones remained popular throughout the 1970s and 1980s.

- The first MTV rock video was aired at midnight on August 1, 1981. It was "Video Killed the Radio Star," performed and sung by the Buggles.

## The Story Behind 4 Famous American Songs

**"Yankee Doodle"** was written in 1758 by British Army surgeon Dr. Richard Shuckburgh, during the French and Indian War. He wrote it to poke fun at the colonial troops, who dressed in an assortment of nonmilitary outfits and looked dowdy and ill-dressed next to the spiffy British troops in their spotless uniforms. When the Revolutionary War began, the colonists used the song, in turn, to poke fun at the dandyish British officers and their troops.

**"The Star-Spangled Banner"** was written by Francis Scott Key in September 1814, during the War of 1812. As Key watched the British bombardment of Fort McHenry from his ship in Baltimore Harbor, he wrote a stanza on the back of an envelope. The next day, he wrote out the poem and showed it to his brother-in-law, Judge J. H. Nicholson, who suggested that it be set to the tune of "Anacreon in Heaven." "The Star-Spangled Banner" was designated the U.S. National Anthem by Act of Congress on March 3, 1931.

**"America,"** also known as "My Country 'Tis of Thee," was first sung in public in July 1831, at a service in the Park Street Church, Boston, Massachusetts. The words were written by Reverend Samuel Francis Smith, a Baptist clergyman, who set them to a melody he found in a German songbook. Smith didn't know that he had chosen the same tune used for the British anthem "God Save the Queen/King."

**"America, the Beautiful"** was composed by Massachusetts educator and author Katherine Lee Bates in 1893. Bates was inspired to write the song after seeing the view from the top of Pike's Peak, a mountain in the Rocky Mountains of Colorado. The poem was set to the music of Samuel A. Ward's "Materna."

Over the years, it's been suggested that the U.S. change the National Anthem to "America" or "America the Beautiful." Both songs are easier to sing than the "Star-Spangled Banner," and many people feel that they contain more meaningful lyrics. But no one as yet has mounted a successful campaign to change the U.S. National Anthem.

# The Ages at Which 10 Famous Composers Began to Play Musical Instruments

**Johann Sebastian Bach** (1685–1750), the composer of some of the world's greatest instrumental and vocal music, first played the violin at the age of four.

**Wolfgang Amadeus Mozart** (1756–1791) was a true child prodigy. He could play melodies on the harpsichord at three and toured the European courts at four, playing the harpsichord, violin, and organ. He began composing soon after and in his lifetime wrote over 600 musical works, including 50 symphonies, more than 20 operas, nearly 30 piano concertos, 27 string quartets, and about 40 violin sonatas.

**Ludwig van Beethoven** (1770–1827), the composer of symphonies, sonatas, and other great works of music, took piano lessons at the age of three. Beethoven began to go deaf at thirty, and was completely deaf by his late forties. However, Beethoven's deafness did not interfere with his composing.

**Franz Schubert** (1797–1828) started taking music lessons at the age of seven, but studied piano on his own before that. Schubert went on to compose a number of great musical works, but is probably most famous for his over 600 *lieder* (songs).

**Frederic Chopin** (1810–1849), the great composer of classical piano music, played melodies on that instrument at five—before anyone had shown him how.

**Giuseppe Verdi** (1813–1901), composer of such famous operas as *Aida* and *Rigoletto*, started playing the piano at the age of seven.

**Johannes Brahms** (1833–1897) played the viola, violin, and piano at five and was already beginning to compose music.

**Peter Ilich Tchaikovsky** (1840–1893) was able to play the piano at the age of four, but he didn't begin to study music seriously until he was twenty-three. Among Tchaikovsky's most popular works are the ballets *The Nutcracker*, *Sleeping Beauty*, and *Swan Lake*.

**Stephen Foster** (1826–1864), the composer of such popular American songs as "Oh! Susannah" and "My Old Kentucky Home," was playing the guitar and organ and singing songs by the age of two.

**George Gershwin** (1898–1937) composed songs, concertos, musical comedies, and the first all-black opera, *Porgy and Bess*. Gershwin was able to play a song on the piano the first time he ever tried to play. He was ten years old.

# 6 Facts About Ballet

- Ballet, a form of theatrical dance that tells a story or expresses a theme, mood, or idea, originated in Italy in the 1500s as a feature of Italian court entertainments.

- Ballet was introduced into France in 1581 by Italian Catherine de Medici, who had married the French king Henry II. In 1661, King Louis XIV established the first ballet school. Its ballet master, Pierre Beauchamp, created the five basic foot positions.

- Early eighteenth-century ballet was part of opera. Dancers wore heavy costumes that hampered their movements. By the mid-1700s, pantomime ballet had evolved, in which all the meaning of a story was expressed by movement. French choreographer Jean-George Noverre made ballet an independent art that combined plot, set design, music, and movement.

- Ballet in the 1800s stressed the lightness and grace of the dancers. Dancing *sur les pointes* (on the tips of the toes) appeared, as did the filmy, calf-length ballet skirt, and the short skirt called the tutu. Russia became the world center of ballet, and the famous Tchaikovsky ballets *The Nutcracker, Sleeping Beauty*, and *Swan Lake*, debuted there.

- In the early 1900s, ballet became popular in France again because of the Ballets Russes (Russian Ballets) of manager Sergei Diaghilev. Some of the greatest dancers in ballet history danced and toured with the Ballets Russes, including Anna Pavlova, Vaslav Nijinsky, and Leonide Massine.

- Ballet was established in the U.S. by Russian-born choreographer George Balanchine. His New York City Ballet, founded in 1948, combined the formal movements of classical ballet with the looser, less delicate movements of modern dance.

## 5 Dances of the Past

**Minuet**—French dance in which partners danced with delicate, measured glides and steps. The minuet first became popular in 1650, at the French court of Louis XIV. It remained popular through the eighteenth century.

**Waltz**—Romantic gliding and twirling dance, which originated from the ländler, a German folk dance, and became popular in the 1700s. In the 1800s, Austrian composers Johann Strauss and his son, Johann the Younger, wrote famous waltzes known as Viennese Waltzes.

**Charleston**—Popular U.S. dance of the 1920s. The Charleston was danced to jazz music and featured outward heel kicks and elaborate arm movements. It was first performed in Charleston, South Carolina, around 1903 and had made its way to Harlem, New York, stage shows by 1913.

**Jitterbug**—A jazz dance of the 1930s and 1940s. Partners swung, twirled, and lifted each other in time to the music.

**Twist**—Dance craze of the early 1960s. Partners stayed in one place moved their shoulders, arms, and hips back and forth to such Twist hits as "Let's Twist Again" by Chubby Checker and "Twist and Shout" by the Isley Brothers.

## 5 Facts About Circuses

● The first circus was the Circus Maximus in first-century A.D. Rome. Staged in amphitheatres like the huge Roman Colosseum, the circus featured such sporting events as horse races and chariot races. Less pleasant, but definitely popular, events included gladiator fights, wild animal vs. gladiator fights, wild animals fights, and Christians and slaves fed to starving lions. These inhumane "entertainments" finally ended in 563 A.D.

● The circus as we know it today was the brainchild of English equestrian Philip Astley. In 1768, Astley performed tricks on horseback for an audience. His stage was a horse ring covered with sawdust. He and a troupe of riders took their show to France, thus beginning the tradition of the traveling circus.

During his lifetime, Astley established eighteen circuses in Europe.

- Soon after Astley's circus debuted, other circuses sprang up in England. Country fairs were declining in popularity, and fair performers like acrobats, jugglers, tightrope walkers, gymnasts, and strong men rushed to join the circuses.

- The circus made its first appearance in the U.S. in 1793. It was directed by John Ricketts and was seen in New York and Philadelphia. Imitators formed traveling shows, performing under an enormous tent called the "Big Top."

- In 1871, American showman Phineas T. Barnum opened his famous circus, "The Greatest Show on Earth." Among his attractions were Siamese twins Chang and Eng Bunker, midget General Tom Thumb, Swedish singer Jenny Lind, and Jumbo, the 6½-ton African elephant. In 1881, Barnum merged with his competitor James A. Bailey, and the circus became the Barnum and Bailey Circus. The five Ringling brothers bought out Barnum and Bailey in 1907, and the combined circus became the largest in the world by 1930.

# The Origins of 8 Popular Sports

## BASEBALL

The American pastime developed from an English sport called rounders, in which players used bats and balls and rounded bases. The founder of modern U.S. baseball was surveyor Alexander J. Cartwright, who sketched out the first diamond, laid out the first rules, and formed the first team. The first baseball game on record took place on June 19, 1846, in Hoboken, New Jersey. The "New York Nine" defeated Cartwright's Knickerbockers 23 to 1 in four innings. The umpire, who happened to be Cartwright, fined a Knickerbocker player six cents for swearing at him during the game.

## BASKETBALL

The Aztecs of Mexico played a game in which a rubber ball was put through a ring placed high on one side of a stadium. The captain of the losing team was often executed. Modern basketball was invented by Canadian-born Dr. James Naismith, a physical education teacher at the Training School of the International YMCA College at Springfield, Massachusetts, in December 1891. Dr. Naismith's original game used seven men on each side and two peach baskets. By 1906, the modern hoop was in use. The first public basketball game was played on March 11, 1892.

## FOOTBALL

American football developed from an English kicking and tackling ball game called rugby. In 1869, Harvard University in the U.S. established the "Boston game," which allowed running with the football, as well as kicking and tackling. The first game played under Harvard Rules took place in Cambridge, Massachusetts, in May 1874. In August 1895, the first professional football game was played between two teams from Latrobe, Pennsylvania, and Jeannette, Pennsylvania.

## ICE HOCKEY

An early version of ice hockey was played on the frozen canals of the Netherlands in the 1600s. The modern sport probably originated in Canada in the 1850s and 1860s, when British soldiers stationed there adapted field hockey to a game played on frozen lakes near their bases. The first recorded use of a puck instead of a ball was probably at Kingston, Ontario, in 1860.

## SKIING

Skis discovered in bogs in Sweden and Finland are believed to be between 4,000 and 5,000 years old. A rock carving found in a Norwegian cave shows two men on skis and dates back to about 2000 B.C. When the Scandinavian Vikings invaded Europe in the tenth and eleventh centuries, they brought the idea of snow skiing as a form of transportation with them.

Until the mid-1800s, skiers were attached to their skis by tow straps. In 1860, Sondre Nordheim of Norway introduced stable bindings that fastened boots to skis. The new bindings enabled skiers to control their skis better. Nordheim also invented skis with sides that curved inward. Skiers could now change direction and stop more easily.

The first downhill race took place at Montana, Switzerland, in 1911. But it wasn't until the first Winter Olympics in 1924 that skiing was recognized as a major competitive sport.

## SOCCER

During the third and fourth centuries B.C., the Chinese played a ball-kicking game called *tsu-chu*. An Italian version of soccer was played in Florence around 1630 and featured 26 players on a team. In 1580, an Italian manual entitled *Discorsa Calcio* outlined the rules of the game. Soccer became a standardized sport in 1863, after the formation of England's Football Association (the English call soccer football). In 1870, the rule stipulating eleven members to a side went into effect. The first World Cup was held in Montevideo, Uruguay, in 1930. Uruguay was the winner.

## TENNIS

Tennis developed from an indoor racquet game called *jeu de paume* ("palm game"), popular with French and English royalty starting in the late 1400s. In the late 1700s, an outdoor version of the game was known as field tennis, lawn racquets, and pelota. Lawn tennis, similar to today's sport, was invented in 1873 by Major Walter Wingfield of Wales.

Tennis became popular in the U.S. around 1874, after New Yorker Mary Outerbridge watched British soldiers play the game on Bermuda. She returned home with a net, two racquets, and a

set of balls, and, with her brother, set up a tennis court on Staten Island. Another court was built in Nahant, Massachusetts, and the sport soon spread throughout the country. The first national tennis championship for men was held at Newport, Rhode Island, in 1881; in 1887, the first women's championship was held at Newport.

## TRACK AND FIELD

The Ancient Egyptians held track and field events, as did the early Irish around 1829 B.C. The Ancient Greeks featured track and field at their Olympic Games, which began in 776 B.C. and were banned by the Roman emperor Theodosius in 393 A.D. The first and only Olympic event is said to have been a 200-yard foot race near the small city of Olympia. Men competed in the Olympics, women in the Heraea Games. One popular contest in the Heraea Games was the 165-yard dash.

The first college track meet took place in England in 1864 between Oxford and Cambridge Universities. The first collegiate track meet in the U.S. was held in 1876. Track and field events were featured at the first modern Summer Olympics held in Athens, Greece, in 1896.

# How 10 Popular Toys and Games Were Invented

- **Silly Putty** was the invention of engineer James Wright of the General Electric Company in the 1940s. The substance was invented as a substitute for rubber, but was found to have no industrial uses, so it was marketed as a toy instead.
- **Slinky** was invented by marine engineer Richard James in the 1940s. James was trying to develop a special kind of spring for ships, but came up with Slinky instead. James's wife thought her husband's invention would make a great toy. In 1946, Richard and Betty James founded the company that makes these popular toys.
- **Checkers** began in Egypt around 2000 B.C. as a form of wartime strategizing. Called *alquerque*, the game featured "enemy" pieces, "hostile" moves, and "captures." Alquerque was played by two people who moved as many as a dozen pieces across a checkerboard.
- **Monopoly** was the 1933 invention of Charles B. Darrow, an unemployed engineer. Out of work and poor because of the Great Depression, Darrow spent his time developing a high-stakes, buying-and-selling real estate game. After Parker Brothers bought the rights to Monopoly in 1935, royalties from the sale of the popular game made Darrow a millionaire.
- Another victim of the Depression was Albert Butts, the inventor of **Scrabble**. In 1931, Butts created a crossword game using 100 lettered wooden tiles to make words. Each letter had a point value. Butts named his game Criss Cross, but changed the name to Scrabble at the urging of a friend.
- **Frisbees** were named after the lightweight pie plates manufactured by the Frisbee Pie Company of Connecticut. In the 1870s, a popular pastime of Yale college students was throwing the pie plates to each other. The Frisbee game was still going strong in the 1950s when the toy flying disk called "Flyin' Saucer" was invented in California by Walter Frederick Morrison and marketed by the Wham-O Company. When Wham-O's president, Richard

Knerr, saw Yale students flinging Frisbee pie plates, he decided to change the name of the Wham-O toy to "Frisbee."

- The **yo-yo** originated as a weapon used by Philippine Islands warriors in the 1500s. These yo-yos were four-pound spheres, each with a twenty-foot cord. The first toy version was developed by toy manufacturer Louis Marx and appeared in 1929.

- The first **Barbie Doll** was produced by the Mattel Toy company in 1958. In 1964, she was made with knee joints that enabled her legs to bend, and eyelids that could open and shut. In 1967, Barbie could bend at the waist. By 1980, her clothes were designed by a top New York fashion designer.

- **Jigsaw puzzles** began as a game for teaching kids geography. In 1760, British teacher John Spilsbury glued a map of England onto a piece of wood. He then cut the map into pieces along the boundary lines of counties. His students were asked to put the pieces together again correctly.

- The first **video game** was developed in 1962 by college students at the Massachusetts Institute of Technology. It was called "Space War."

# CHAPTER 9

# Predictions of the Future

. . . . . . . . . . . . . . . . . . . . . . . . . . . . .

This book has featured facts about the past. But scientists and other experts have always thought about the future. As you'll see, some of their predictions were way off base. As for the year 2000 and beyond, well, we'll find out soon enough if the predictions in this chapter are accurate or not!

# 10 Predictions
# That Didn't Come True

- "Man won't fly for a thousand years," predicted Wilbur Wright to his brother Orville in 1901.
- The former executive secretary of NASA, Edward Welsh, predicted that there would be one or more permanent bases on the moon by 1982.
- In 1970, *Life* magazine predicted that families would soon own helicopters instead of cars.
- In 1969, Harold and June Shane, professors of education, predicted that kids would soon start school at the age of two.
- "Radio has no future," said engineer and physicist Lord Kelvin in 1904.
- In 1964, the Reverend Billy Graham said, "The Beatles are just a passing phase."
- The *Literary Digest* predicted in 1889 that the automobile, then called the "horseless carriage," would never be as widely used as the bicycle.
- In 1926, U.S. inventor and radio pioneer Lee De Forest predicted that television would be a commercial and financial failure.
- *Science Digest* said in 1948 that it would take science 200 years to put a person on the moon.
- And in 1970, U.S. fashion designer Rudi Gernreich predicted that men would wear skirts.

# Predictions for the Year
# 2000 and Beyond

- In the year 2000, a paperback book will cost $12.50; a magazine, $15.00; a movie ticket, $17.50; a candy bar, $1.50; a pack of gum, $1.25; and a 12-oz can of soda, $2.25.
- Sometime after the year 2000, over 2,000 people will be living and working on the moon. Back on earth, predicts the United Nations, over 600 million people will be living in poverty.

- Reference books, such as *The World Almanac* and *The Kids' World Almanacs*, will be too expensive to produce. People will get information from their computers or videodisc systems.
- By 2010, humans will be able to control the weather, thus enhancing global food production.
- Rock 'n' Roll music will still be around in the year 2000, but most of it will be generated by synthesizers and other computerized methods.
- The first "test tube dog" will be created by genetic engineers by 2020.
- Americans born in the year 2019 will live for 120 years.
- Sometime after the year 2000, the family will spend its leisure time in a "video environment" rather than a family room. At the touch of a button on a computerized entertainment system, a family will be able to surround itself with a simulation of a tropical rain forest or the landscape of another planet. People will also be able to watch movies on a 360-degree screen.
- By 2020, cavities will be a thing of the past for 95% of the population.
- By 2010, antiaging drugs will be available on prescription.
- Sometime after 2000, scientists may begin the process of "terraforming," by which outer-space environments are made fit for human occupation. This could lead to a colony of humans living on Mars. Terraforming will probably become a reality between 2010 and 2020.
- People will wear thin, durable clothing made from synthetic material. By pressing a button on a special power belt, a person will be able to control the warmth of his or her outfit.
- By 2050, over 7,500 people will be living in outer space.
- Some of those people may be former Californians, since it's predicted that a devastating earthquake will have nearly destroyed that state. However, scientists have been predicting the "big one" for California for decades.
- The number of cars on the road will double, but they'll be smaller and more fuel-efficient than those we drive now. As a result, there will be a decrease in air pollution.
- By 2010, satellites high above the earth will collect sunlight,

convert it to microwaves, and beam the power to earth.

- By 2030, after years of searching, we will still have received no messages from extraterrestrial beings.
- By 2020, robots will be sent into space to mine the moon and asteroids.
- By 2010, the world population will be seven billion.
- By the year 2000, computer printout terminals in every neighborhood will publish and bind any book you request right before your eyes.

# Index